Author
Kerry Moran has lived in Nepal since 1985, working as a freelance writer and sometime trek leader. She has published three other books: *Hong Kong Handbook* (Moon Publications, 1995); *Nepal Handbook* (Moon Publications, 1995, 1991) - winner of the Lowell Thomas Journalism Award for Best Guidebook; and *Kailas: On Pilgrimage to the Sacred Mountain of Tibet*.

Photographer
Born in Finland, Helka Ahokas has lived in Hong Kong for the past twelve years. Since becoming established as a freelance photographer, she has traveled extensively around Asia, particularly the Himalayan region. She has photographed for several travel magazines as well as for the *Odyssey Illustrated Guide to Berlin*.

NEPAL

Kerry Moran
Photography by Helka Ahokas

PASSPORT BOOKS
a division of *NTC Publishing Group*
Lincolnwood, Illinois USA

Published by Passport Books in conjunction with
The Guidebook Company Ltd

This edition first published in 1995 by Passport Books, a division of NTC Publishing
Group, 4255 W Touhy Avenue, Lincolnwood (Chicago), Illinois 60646-1975, USA,
originally published by The Guidebook Company Ltd © The Guidebook Company Ltd.
All rights reserved.

ISBN: 0-8442-9984-7
Library of Congress Catalog Card Number: 94-80162

Grateful acknowledgment is made to the following authors and publishers for permissions
granted:

Viking Penguin, a division of Penguin Books USA, Inc., and Donadio & Ashworth Inc. for
The Snow Leopard by Peter Matthiessen © 1978
J Bayard Morris © W W Norton & Co Inc

John Murray (Publishers) Ltd. for
The Sherpas of Nepal by Christoph von Fürer-Haimendorf © 1964

Hodder & Stoughton Publishers Ltd., and AP Watt (permission applied) for
Shopping for Buddhas by Jeff Greenwald © 1990

Alfred A Knopf Inc. for
Video Night in Kathmandu by Pico Iyer © 1988

University of Hawaii Press for
In Praise of Panavati from *Songs of Nepal: An Anthology of Newar Folksongs and Hymns*,
translated by Siegfried Lienhard © 1984

Himal Books, Lalitpur, for
Mustang Bhot in Fragments by Manjushree Thapa © 1992

University of California Press for
Thus a Nation Pretends to Live by Min Bahadur Bista, from *Himalayan Voices: An
Introduction to Modern Nepali Literature* by Michael Hunt © 1991 The Regents of the
University of California

Aurum Press, London, for
Travels in Nepal by Charlie Pye-Smith © 1988

Sahayogi Press, Kathmandu, for
Jang Bahadur in Europe translated by John Whelpton © 1983

Diadem Books Ltd (permission applied) for
Nepal Himalaya by H.W. Tilman © 1952

Photography: Helka Ahokas
Additional Photographs: Nigel Hicks (12–13, 172–173, 214–215); Earl Kowall (44, 75);
Bill Wassman (76)

Archival Material from Gulmohur Press, New Delhi
Design: Gulmohur Press, New Delhi
Maps: Tom Le Bas & Bai Yiliang
Produced by Twin Age Limited, Hong Kong
Printed in Hong Kong

Contents

Excerpts

Offerings, Tengboche Gompa

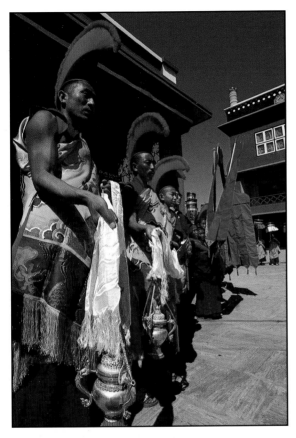

Losar celebration, Boudhanath

INTRODUCTION

There are many Nepals, as many as there are valleys in this folded, corrugated land. Nepal is a blend of diverse landscapes, peoples, customs, cultures and languages, a mixing rather than a melting pot. It is impossible to reduce the country to a single image. The crowded narrow streets of old Kathmandu contrast with the wide open spaces of the mountains, where the only sound is the distant roar of a glacier-fed stream. There are elegant marble-floored hotel lobbies, sprawling stucco palaces...and the mud-walled houses which shelter the vast majority of the population. Tourist districts awash with knicknacks and souvenirs clash with the basic reality of a land with an average per capita income of US$180 a year. Kathmandu is a city of supermarkets and computer offices, buffalo herders and Jyapu peasants carrying great swinging baskets of radishes suspended from shoulder poles. Over the entire contradictory patchwork, calm all-seeing painted eyes gaze from the great stupas of Swayambhunath and Boudhanath, alone able to reconcile all the various parts of this whole.

Few other countries on earth encompass such diversity, beginning with sheer altitudinal variation. Nepal stretches from the near-sea-level Terai, a flat and steamy strip along the southern border, to the summit of Sagarmatha/Everest, the world's highest mountain. To the north is a towering array of Himalayan peaks, including eight of the world's ten highest mountains. In between is the Hills, a rugged region of deep valleys and terraced ridges. Nepal's area totals 147,181 square kilometres (56,811 square miles), approximately the size of Austria or the state of Georgia, yet the undulating landscape, if it could somehow be detached from the rugged terrain and stretched flat, would approximately equal the area of the United States.

The heart of Nepal is the Hills; slopes so incredibly steep that it is impossible to imagine that there could be people clinging to the sides, yet there they are, working on tiered fields stacked up towards the sky. This landscape is the legacy of centuries of dogged perseverance with the rudest of tools. Nepal's inspiring scenery serves merely as a backdrop to daily life. Nature is not seen as a pristine preserve, but by turns as a friend and an adversary. The Nepali farmer is on intimate terms with his land, and is not inclined to romanticize it, though people retain a deep attachment to their own region and new arrivals to the city will longingly recall the pure air, the space and silence, and guardian mountains.

Rural Nepal is the reality for 90 percent of the population. To see it you must walk into the hills and mountains, regions too rugged to ever be penetrated by roads. Aeroplanes fly over it, but the views from above are deceptive, presenting an unreal perspective. Only when you have measured the ascent to the lowest of passes with your footsteps, can you comprehend the immensity of this rough country. Traversing the endless ridges is sweaty, dusty toil: climb up one, and the view rewards with the sight of countless more steep climbs and descents. It never stops. The land is relentless in its ruggedness.

There are many Nepals, as many as there are people. With dozens of ethnic groups and hundreds of languages, Nepal is many countries combined into one. Even religion is a multiple here: the official boast is that Nepal is 'the world's only Hindu Kingdom', but interwoven with the predominant religion are strands of Buddhism, animism and tantra, which mellow the predominant religion, making it more tolerant and open than the Hinduism practised in India. After the unrelenting intensity of India it is a palpable relief to cross the border into relaxed Nepal.

There is a Nepal of pilgrims, of traders, of refugees, of artists, kings and farmers, and of tourists too. Each is a different place: as different as a Thamel guest-house, an old Rana palace, and a thatched-roof village hut. Nepal encompasses these multiple realities and more. They are overlapping and contradictory, but each is undeniably true, and you must discover your version and define it.

Planning Your Trip

Sixty percent of the visitors to Nepal come during the main tourist seasons: autumn (October–November) and spring (late March–April). Autumn is particularly pleasant, with mild temperatures and superb mountain views, but it is possible to visit and even trek at any time of the year.

Most visitors make the Kathmandu Valley the focal point of their trip. Wonderful as it is, it is an anomaly: sophisticated and relatively rich, an outpost of modern civilization in the midst of a thoroughly rural country. Compared to Kathmandu, every other town in Nepal is a village. Destinations equipped to handle tourists are limited, and transport is relatively undeveloped.

Ideally you should allot nearly a week for the Kathmandu Valley, possibly adding another three days each for visits to Pokhara and Chitwan National Park. If you're at all inclined to walking among mountains, go trekking. Lovely short treks can be done in as little as five days, though two weeks is better, and three or even four weeks guarantees a thoroughly fulfilling experience.

Glimpses of Nepal

Dawn in Kathmandu, *looking out over a sea of rooftops growing ever higher. The city never really sleeps, especially in the warm summer months. All night long, sounds drift through the open window: men coming home from a night of drinking, a group of Newari women assembling at 4 am to visit Swayambhu, water tossed out of the window with an abrupt splat—the gods help anyone beneath it. Dogs bark, and roosters begin crowing hours before dawn. Kathmandu is still little more than a large village—this is its charm and its torment.*

The smell of damp air, burnt milk, the cooing of pigeons. The sky lightens to violet, then deep blue, as the clouds wrap the surrounding hills in mist. Swayambhu's lights twinkle in the distance. A woman shuffles out onto the rooftop, yawning, to water clay pots of yellow flowers and pick the blossoms for her morning puja. She tosses rice in offering, and pigeons immediately swoop down upon the grains. Next door a man wrapped in a lungi *held up with one hand steps out, blinking into the dim light, and recites his prayers with folded hands, head bowed towards Swayambhu. He goes inside and on a neighbouring roof another comes out, like cuckoo clock figures emerging to greet the dawn. The sound of bells, followed by the first taxi horn, morning throat-clearing, distant laughter, the insistent cooing of pigeons. At precisely 6 am hundreds of radios snap on, broadcasting Radio Nepal's morning hymn to Sita and Ram, the reveille of Nepali life.*

The September full moon blazes over temple roofs *upon the milling crowds gathered in the old town for Indra Jatra, Kathmandu's greatest festival. 'Hangsey, hosey', shout the men straining at the ropes of the heavy chariots of the Kumari and her child attendants, Ganesh and Bhairab. The chariots rumble past, each bearing a tiny, regal figure laden with gold jewellery. Masked dancers glide past like ghosts in the darkness, dressed in flowing skirts and heavy bracelets, brawny farmers transformed for an evening into deities. Bells strapped to their calves jingle as they float on to another temple, following a route centuries old.*

Magic is most definitely afoot for the eight nights of Indra Jatra, and people pour into the streets to enjoy it. Families crowd in front of the fierce blue-and-silver mask of Akash Bhairab, the Bhairab fallen from the sky. The sweet perfume of jasmine fills the air, as adoring hands pile on garlands of flowers, tossing up red powder, coins and grains of rice, snatching a blossom as a blessing. A man on a motorcycle pulls up in front of the image, folds his hands in prayer, then roars away sanctified by the brief encounter. On a platform across the way, old men sing bhajans *for hours, swaying back and forth to the music, impelled by devotion and the rhythmic vibration of tabla and harmonium, and perhaps fortified by* ganja.

Late at night the two small boy–gods are carried home in the arms of their barefoot attendants. Their wide kohl-rimmed eyes gaze calmly at the people who come up to touch their foreheads to their feet or the hem of their ornate brocade robes. Adorned with jewels and gold, they float slowly across the square in the arms of their bearers, a fanbearer fluttering solicitously at their side. Behind them, the great chariots are already being disassembled and packed away until the next year.

The same full-moon day in the hills west of Kathmandu, *three Tamang shamans bound and leap in a ritual dance, their peacock-feather headdresses bobbing, white robes flaring out in a circle about their stamping feet. Bell-bedecked harnesses strapped across their chests jingle, as they beat their ritual drums and sing with heads thrown back and eyes closed in utterly unselfconscious abandon. An ever-growing crowd of ragged boys and barefoot peasant women follows the mad pied pipers across the hillside.*

At Boudhanath, everything is circles, *from the great dome of the stupa and the people constantly circumambulating it to the squeaky whirling prayer wheels and the tiny round butter lamps lit in offering. The stupa's imperturbable painted eyes miss nothing taking place under their steady gaze. Tibetans from the plateau sell* tsampa, *butter and brick tea along with comic books, Thermos flasks and prayer beads. As the sun burns away the winter fog, the crowd encircling the stupa grows. There are Dolpo women in striped woollen blankets and Chinese sneakers, maroon-clad monks in yellow ski jackets, bent old grandmothers with rosaries, a man* with his beloved Lhasa Apso slung over his shoulder like a furry shawl. A goat nuzzles in an old nun's metal bowl, overriding her feeble protests. Leaning from the top of a ladder, a man touches up the stupa's giant painted eyes. Dogs and ragged beggars slumber in the sun, racing boys roll hoops, and toddlers waddle in padded winter clothes as their mothers sit on shop steps to gossip and watch the ever-turning scene.

The monsoon rains fall steadily and soothingly, rolling in from the south at dusk with a wall of rushing sound. You can hear it coming a long way off. People rush out to bring in laundry and tethered goats as an invisible breeze ripples the shoots of rice. A wild freshness touches the still air, and suddenly it's here, a wall of silvery water cleansing the air, linking sky and earth. The monsoon moisture stains everything in deep hues: bruised red-brick, deep moss-green. Everywhere, life bursts out of its seed casings. Grass sprouts on tile roofs and foliage erupts from tiny cracks, transforming crumbling chaitya into giant flowerpots. There is a feeling of abundance in the humid air, underscored by the long drawn-out songs of the mud-stained rice planters.

Walking through Kathmandu's old bazaar is a dance of constant movement through the jostling crowd. Between the tall buildings, an endless river of people flows down the narrow streets, past shops spilling their colourful contents into the sunlight: stacks of brass pots, bolts of gaily coloured cotton, gold-embroidered saris and porcelain cups, Thermos flasks, dried beans, flower garlands and soap. Bicycle bells shrill, mingling with the solemn clang of temple bells, the silvery tinkle of puja bells, the ugly croak of a rickshaw's horn. A cart carrying oil drums pushed by straining coolies creaks down the street, followed by a man with twin baskets of radishes suspended from a shoulder pole, and a taxi, its trunk stuffed with squawking chickens. The crowd eddies and swirls around the

Children, Terai

little golden island of a temple, its bright brass banners fluttering stiffly in an imaginary breeze. Light and shadow, rich brilliant colours, bells and horns, incense and garbage blend into an all-encompassing experience that leaves a newcomer overwhelmed. The stuff of a short walk could fill lifetimes.

A few blocks north, in the tourist district of Thamel, signboards spew forth a non-stop barrage of urgent messages: 'Good News! Inquire here for trekking, bus to Pokhara, river rafting, jungle safari'. 'Nepalese Jewellery'. 'We serve Mousaka, French Onion Soup, Croissant'. As if the visual bombardment were not enough, skulking young men in doorways hiss furtive messages: 'Hashhhhh?... Change money? good rate, better than bank....Massage, madam?' To stroll through here is to run the gauntlet. The eyes richochet between carpets, bookshops, pieshops and displays of prayer wheels, dodging hustlers all the while. No wonder everyone takes refuge in restaurants, where a sybaritic existence can be purchased for 35 rupees: cappucino, eggs and toast in a sunny garden where a loop of Kitaro plays over and over.

Dasain in Kathmandu, and every vehicle is garlanded with marigolds and tinsel, the front fender daubed with blood from a sacrificial chicken or goat to ensure its safety in the coming year. Families parade the streets in new clothes, denim ruffles for the girls and new jeans on every boy; women in purple silk saris with iridescent green beads, and their government-employed husbands in crisp black and white, rows of medals jingling on their chests. Everyone wears a sticky fresh tika, and every temple, stone and god is daubed with crimson powder and decked with golden blossoms. Bells clang, as worshippers touch their foreheads in reverence and circle in and out and around the temples. Shops shuttered and traffic gone, Kathmandu regains its soul as people take over the streets, moving at a leisurely pace, everyone smiling.

The plane swoops over a rock-strewn ridge, its shadow like a gull on the snow below. The pilot flies among the mountains, not over them, and you sense the vulnerability of this fragile metal-skinned craft drifting on currents of air. The landscape overwhelms, even when you float above it. The windshield frames an apparent piece of heaven, mountains blazing white in the sun. The pilot skilfully weaves in and out among them, tilting to avoid clipping the wing-tips on bare rock. Suddenly the ground is near and drawing

rises to meet the plane uncomfortably fast. We tumble out of the tiny compartment into the dazzling light, space and silence of the mountains, the air tinged with the crisp scent of snow.

On the trail the days melt into one another in an unbroken flow of walk, rest, walk, eat, and walk again. The time of day, the day of the week become irrelevant. More important is the name of the next stop, hunger, the position of the sun in the sky. The body aches at the unaccustomed activity, but soon adapts itself. To walk easily, to rest and stretch lazily, eat hungrily, sleep peacefully, laugh and talk in brief once-in-a-lifetime encounters with people met on the trail…life is distilled to its essence by these hard hills. After a while, it seems that the trekking is the real life, and the other part is just waiting.

The autumn months bring a special crystal clarity to the air. Perhaps this is why the greatest festivals occur now, when the air and light alone are cause for celebration. Simple farmhouses of ochre-coloured mud suddenly look idyllic, garlanded with squash vines scrambling over the thatched roofs, the eaves strung with necklaces of drying corn. Towering groves of green bamboo arch gracefully overhead, shading the trail. Women in saris of glowing shades of red, pink and orange work in fields of yellow mustard. Outside the village, children are scampering towards a ping, a holiday swing fashioned of long bamboo poles bound together at the top. The scene has the texture and vibrance of a promised land: clean, well-kept villages, chubby children and smiling faces everywhere.

Up in the mountains, there is nothing but clean wind and space, and the dazzling light reflected off towering snow-covered peaks. Avalanches give off a distant roar: first the snow plume rises, and only then comes the sound, a muffled thunderous whooooomp as the powder drifts up, then gently settles. Bands of rock pigeons soar into the air downslope, creating a giddy sense of height. With the thin air and immense spaces, I feel like I'm flying too. There is the sweet distant clanging of yak bells, the pungent smoke of a yak dung fire, the scent of fragrant juniper incense.

BACKGROUND

History

The history of Nepal is essentially the history of the Kathmandu Valley, the political, emotional and spiritual centre of the country. This flat stage ringed by rugged mountains has seen political scheming and bloody intrigue of the highest magnitude, as well as the quiet drama of centuries. History remains a living process embedded in ancient practices that are alive and well today, like the Machhendranath processions, the *guthi*, the sacred cow, and the intricate caste system.

Early History

Once upon a time, say the ancient chronicles, the Valley was a vast lake rimmed by mountains (and indeed this is confirmed by geology). It was called Nag Hrad, 'Tank of Serpents', and magical snake-beings called *nagas* guarded treasure lying at the bottom. Into the placid depths of this lake a Buddha tossed a seed, which blossomed into a thousand-petalled lotus of blazing light. Aeons passed; then the Bodhisattva Manjushri came from the north, and with a single stroke from his Sword of Wisdom, cut a gorge in the mountain wall ringing the lake. The waters rushed out, leaving the flat and fertile bowl that remains today.

Early histories continue in this mythical vein, relating tales of gods who roamed the Valley as humans, and of kings as powerful as gods, a single one of whom might reign 1,000 years. It was a magical realm, where kings endowed temples with images of deities which sweated, spoke, bled and communicated their desires. Murky legend focuses into historical fact with the advent of the Licchavi dynasty (AD 300–879). Perhaps related to Indian rulers of the same name, these kings were tolerant, non-sectarian rulers, supporting both Buddhist and Hindu temples and endowing the Valley with many fine sculptures and delicately carved *chaitya*.

By this time the Valley was an important Himalayan trading centre. The wealth amassed from trade and farming nurtured a rich culture, fertilized by diverse influences from across Asia. Standing on the border between the great cultures of the Indian subcontinent and Central Asia, the Valley has historically served as a bridge, channelling and transforming influences and adding its own unique contributions. It has woven diverse cultural and religious strands—Indian, Himalayan, Tibetan, a hint of Chinese; Hindu, Buddhist, animist, Tantric—into a rich tapestry all its own.

The Valley also became an important centre of Buddhist study. In the *bahals* of Patan, Indian, Tibetan, Nepali and Chinese scholars and monks met and exchanged knowledge. After the Muslim invasion of the late 12th century wiped out Indian Buddhism in its homeland, the Valley served as a refuge for fleeing Buddhists and a safe haven for ancient texts and traditions. Later Muslim raids on India drove successive waves of Hindu refugees into western Nepal. Intermarrying with local women, they moved slowly eastwards, playing an increasingly important role in politics and culture.

The Malla Era

The cultured kings of the **Malla Dynasty** (1201-1768) sponsored much of the splendid art and architecture that remains today, and also instituted many current customs and festivals. The dynasty began with Jayasthithi Malla (1365-95), a wise and powerful king who arranged the Newari people into 64 castes with multiple subdivisions. By 1382 he had consolidated his rule over the separate kingdoms of the Valley. His grandson, Yaksha Malla, was another paragon of virtue and wisdom, but on his deathbed in 1482 he divided the Valley among his sons, sowing the seeds for future discord.

For the next three centuries, three dangerously jealous dynasties squabbled over control of the Valley. Most often the arguments revolved around the lucrative trade route to Tibet. Political rivalry flared into occasional fighting, but it also spurred the three kingdoms into productive competition in art and architecture. Each sought to sponsor a more lavish Taleju temple, a more exquisitely carved stone bath, more and better and higher shrines. Efforts focused on the Durbar Squares across from the three principal palaces, where veritable forests of temples and shrines sprouted in stone, brick and wood, embellished with vast quantities of precious metals.

The Malla kings also supported popular culture, sponsoring public dance performances and instituting the great chariot festivals of the three cities which continue to this day. They prided themselves on their culture, studying music, literature and tantric mysteries, composing poems and religious dance-dramas for public performance. Famed for their religious tolerance, they renovated Buddhist shrines and built Hindu temples beside them. In the 18th century, Christian missionaries were briefly allowed to proselytize, becoming the first Westerners to visit the Valley.

Royal excesses sometimes reached ridiculous levels of extravagance. One king ordered the Pashupatinath *linga* to be bathed with water poured from golden vessels for a fortnight; another submerged it beneath an offering of oranges. Kings gave away their weight in gold and jewels, and donated 1,000 cows at a time to Brahmans, all for the sake of acquiring religious merit. Such actions had their practical side, too, in the water taps (*dhara*) and rest-houses (*sattal* and *pati*) and shady resting places for porters (*chautara*) sponsored by individuals hoping to gain religious merit, and maintained by their families as a contribution to society. The tradition of social giving was a fundamental component of a well-integrated and stable society that endured unchanged for centuries.

Life could be brutal too: epidemics of cholera and smallpox swept the crowded cities, and earthquakes regularly shook the Valley, bringing the tall brick houses crashing down. The gods were propitiated by massive offerings and, occasionally, human sacrifice. The Hindu custom of *sati*, the burning of a widow on her husband's funeral pyre, was practised among the upper classes until 1926; slavery, although limited, also existed. Religious tolerance was not always widespread, and periodic persecutions of Hindus or Buddhists took place, depending on who had the upper hand at the time

Conquest of the Valley

From Chandragiri's top I asked, 'Which is Nepal?' They showed me, saying 'That is Bhadgaon [Bhaktapur], that is Patan, and there lies Kathmandu.' The thought came to my heart that if I might be king of these three cities, why, let it be so.

[Prithvi Narayan Shah, Dibya Upadesh, 1774]

The future of the Valley lay in the hands of **Prithvi Narayan Shah**, ruler of the small kingdom of Gorkha in Central Nepal. An exceptionally talented and persuasive leader, he had desired the Valley from the moment he first set eyes upon it, and singlemindedly turned his considerable intelligence and energy to achieving this goal. It took 26 years of battles and sieges, and cost countless lives, but in September 1767, during the great festival of Indra Jatra, Prithvi Narayan Shah entered Kathmandu virtually unopposed by the inebriated Newari defenders. Patan fell shortly after, and the following year Gorkha soldiers broke into the Bhaktapur palace and found the three Newar rulers huddled together in defeat. The Three Kingdoms were united under a dynasty that continues to rule the country to this day.

The Anglo–Nepal Wars

With the Valley united under the Shah Dynasty, the other small kingdoms of Central Nepal rapidly followed. Prithvi Narayan Shah lived only seven years after his conquest of the Valley, and none of his descendents proved quite as able, but the war machine he had created remained largely unopposed. The Gorkha kingdom expanded to take in Kumaon, Garhwal, Sikkim and large tracts of the plains to the south. Exasperated with this continual nibbling away at territory they considered their own, the British declared war in 1814. Nepal lost, after some hard fighting that impressed Britain with the quality of Gurkha soldiers. The Treaty of Segouli signed in 1816 demarcated the country's current eastern and western boundaries.

Another consequence of the treaty was the admission of a British Resident to Kathmandu. The Nepalese government did so only reluctantly, grudgingly assigning the poor man a fetid, malarial tract of land north of the city, and then resolutely ignored him, except for a mandatory annual meeting.

The treaty also required that Nepal's contact with other Western nations be only through British intermediation. In a sense Nepal was a political dependent of the Raj, but the British exerted no direct influence over it.

The Rana Era

While Nepal is proud of never having been colonized by a foreign power, for 104 years the country was ruled by a dynasty more despotic than the British Empire ever was: the Rana family, founded by the bloodthirsty, dashing **Jung Bahadur Rana** (née Kunwar). The Nepalese court was far from being a gentle place before his rise to power, but Jung Bahadur took murderous ambition to new heights. After assassinating his uncle, the prime minister, he engineered the infamous Kot Massacre of 1846, in which over a hundred members of the court were slaughtered.

Jung Bahadur then deposed the weak Shah king and placed the young and malleable crown prince on the throne as a figurehead. Proclaiming himself prime minister, he made the post the hereditary property of the Kunwar family. Lastly, he adopted the name Rana, based on a dubious claim to descent from Indian Rajput royalty. Having improved his caste, he proceeded to intermarry his numerous offspring with the royal Shahs, a practice which continues to this day (the present Queen of Nepal is a Rana). As Jung Bahadur fathered over 100 children, there were extensive possibilities for increasing connections.

For the next century the Shah kings became powerless, pampered figureheads, indulged and kept out of politics. The Prime Minister and his

family ruled the country absolutely, treating it as their private estate.
National revenues went to support their sumptuous lifestyles, while the
people remained in poverty. Progress was viewed, and rightly so, as a threat
to their personal security: there was no public education, no medical care,
no transportation beyond porters and foot-tracks. Nepal had one hospital
and one college, and these were the personal gifts of its rulers. The national
literacy rate in 1951 was 2 percent. Closed to outsiders, Nepal remained an
essentially medieval state, its borders jealously guarded.

The Ranas close relationship with the British helped them stay in
power. Jung Bahadur sent Nepalese troops to aid in the Indian Mutiny
campaign of 1857–8, and as a reward the grateful British returned portions
of the Terai that had been seceded under the Treaty of Segouli. From their
first encounters the British had been impressed with the tough Nepali
fighters, who they called Gurkhas after Gorkha, Prithvi Narayan Shah's
home town. They found them far more efficient than Indian soldiers, who
took three hours to satisfy ritual requirements when preparing meals. The
Gurkhas managed to eat in half an hour, and in addition were incredibly
brave and, tempered and toughened by a rugged environment, remarkably
sturdy. The British and the Ranas developed an unofficial understanding: a

The Rana Maharaja with royal guests, surrounded by his courtiers

steady supply of high-performance mercenaries in exchange for non-interference in Nepal's affairs. This can be criticized as exploitative, as it indeed was, but it helped Nepal remain an independent state.

Modern Nepal: Restoration, Revolution and Democracy

The end of World War II and the advent of Indian independence heralded dramatic changes for neighbouring Nepal. In November 1950 **King Tribhuvan** escaped his gilded cage, taking refuge in the Indian Embassy and later fleeing to New Delhi, as Nepali Congress forces mounted an armed attack on Terai towns. Deprived of their greatest ally, the British, the Rana government needed only the slightest push to crumble. Tribhuvan returned in February 1951 as ruler of his country, presiding over a coalition government.

Tumultuous politics continued through the 1950s, with the death of Tribhuvan in 1955 and the coronation of his eldest son Mahendra. The country's first free elections, held in 1957, put a Congress Party government in office. But in December 1959 Mahendra declared a state of emergency, dissolving the elected government and arresting leading politicians. Political parties were outlawed, as Mahendra assumed responsibility for government under a new Constitution.

This arrangement, the *panchayat* system, continued for the next 30 years. Named after traditional assemblies of village elders (the term literally means 'council of five'), it allowed limited input from the populace through indirect elections. Political abuses, corruption and heavy-handed suppression of dissent all served to fuel growing opposition over the next few decades.

In 1990, Nepal's largest outlawed political parties declared a joint campaign to restore the multi-party system. Agitation grew through the spring, reaching a crescendo with police firings on demonstrators and bystanders, which incited even the normally apolitical. On 6 April a huge crowd rallied in Kathmandu and marched towards the Royal Palace, shouting 'Death to the Panchayat System!' and 'Long Live Democracy!'. Police on Durbar Marg tried to stop them with tear-gas, and when the wind blew it back into their faces they resorted to bullets. Several hundred demonstrators were killed, and a shoot-at-sight curfew was clamped on the city. Several tense days later, **King Birendra** acquiesced to popular demand and lifted the ban on political parties. The following month he dissolved the *panchayat* system.

Lifestyles of the Rich and Famous

The decadent lifestyle of the Ranas, the absolute rulers of Nepal for more than a century, has simultaneously fascinated and repelled generations of observers. Rulers of a land of poor peasants, they led lives of ostentatious luxury, treating the country as their own personal estate. This was of course the way things were done in traditional societies, though the Ranas continued this exploitation longer than most.

The dynasty and its luxurious tastes began with **Jung Bahadur** who, for a tyrant, was personally quite progressive. In 1850 he defied the strictures of Hindu caste to sail to England and visit the sovereign of the cow-eaters, Queen Victoria. He returned with a new definition of grandeur, and set to work constructing a palace in Thapathali (destroyed in the 1934 earthquake) that would replicate the glory of Europe. The palace's public rooms displayed jumbled curiosities from England, India and Nepal—everything from baby clothes to a reflecting telescope. There was a 30-foot crystal chandelier from London, a roomful of distorting mirrors, dozens of hunting trophies annually replenished by hunting expeditions, and an elephant stable.

Jung Bahadur's visit had far-reaching impact on the urban landscape of Kathmandu. The resulting Rana infatuation with European baroque inspired elaborate palaces painstakingly fashioned from clay, brick, and plaster made from mud and cow dung. Behind the colonnaded white stucco porticoes were Carrera marble pillars, chandeliers of Belgian crystal, gigantic gilded mirrors and furniture from Harrod's, all ordered from Europe and carried over the mountains by teams of sweating porters.

Even the Ranas' motor-cars were carried into Nepal. S. Dillon Ripley, an American ornithologist who visited Nepal in 1948, reported the technique: the car was driven onto a framework of bamboo poles, the wheels were removed, a dustcloth was placed over it, and 'sixty men simply bent down, picked up the frame-work, and walked off, chanting and stepping in time. For the largest vehicles 120 men were used. It seemed simple but unbelievable, especially over the passes.'

The greatest of all these palaces was **Singha Durbar**, once the largest in Southeast Asia, with 17 interlocking courtyards

containing 1,700 rooms, up to 500 of these occupied by concubines. It was built on the order of Prime Minister Chandra
Shamsher in 1901 to accommodate his extensive family, but his
sons soon wanted palaces of their own. So he sold Singha Durbar
to the State as the prime minister's official residence–an easy
move, since the prime minister *was* the State–and with the
proceeds built palaces for all his sons.

The Italian scholar Giuseppe Tucci described Singha Durbar
under Chandra Shamsher:

> You passed through hall after hall, every one of them as big as
> a parade-ground, glittering with marble and crystal and showy
> furniture which made anyone with good taste feel quite
> seasick, and everywhere there were civilians and military and
> uniforms. Soldiers sprang to attention and clicked their heels
> as the visitor went past, and voices were hushed, as if in a
> hospital waiting room. Then the Maharaja himself, in ceremo-
> nial dress, as solemn as a god on the altar.

Another aspect of Rana rule was their prolificacy. Jung Bahadur
was one of seven brothers, and he alone sired over 100 children.
It soon became necessary to classify descendents according to the
caste and status of their mothers. 'A–Class' Ranas, born of senior
wives, received the most privileges and the right to rule the
country. 'B–Class' family members, the sons of second wives
whose marriage was legitimized after birth, were highly privileged
but cut out of the line of succession. Most numerous were the
'C–Class' Ranas, the illegitimate offspring of concubines, who
were limited to lower positions in the military or civil service.

As a summation of their personal splendour, 'A–Class' Ranas
wore jewel-encrusted helmets topped with plumes, which they
carried carefully about in hatboxes lest the feathers be crushed by
the roofs of their motor-cars. The prime minister's was the most
magnificent, encased in pearls, set with large flattened diamonds
and hung with pear-shaped emeralds, with a great cluster of
emeralds like grapes to one side and enormous plumes from the
New Guinea Bird of Paradise sprouting from the crown. Today
this dazzling headgear is worn only by the king on ceremonial
occasions.

Old family photographs of the Ranas reveal moustached men
with chestfuls of medals and a haughty demeanour, and plump

women wrapped in gold-encrusted brocade and dripping with jewels. Occasionally a slim dark-eyed beauty gazes back at the camera, but most appear overfed and discontented. Life in enforced luxury must have been stupefyingly boring. Tended by legions of servants (Singha Durbar had a staff of 1,500), with the upper class's disdain of work and no need to earn a living, the Ranas had little to do but idle the days away polishing their medals and jewels. Elaborate household protocol dictated that family members use only the royal *hajur* form in speaking to one another, and that children touch their parent's feet with their forehead when entering a room. Tutors were hired to provide what little education boys received; girls were married off at the age of eight or nine. A 19th-century observer reported seeing Rana children carried virtually everywhere on the backs of their servants.

A favourite pastime was hunting in the private game preserve of Chitwan. Perhaps as an escape from the gilded cage, the Ranas applied themselves to the sport of shikar, bagging incredible numbers of endangered species. Over the course of seven seasons, Prime Minister Juddha Shamsher shot 433 tigers, 53 rhinos and 93 leopards.

The Rana era ended with King Tribhuvan's re-establishment of Shah dynasty rule in 1951. Facing hard times, family members sold off their old palaces. Some now house government offices or hotels (a few examples: the Hotel Shanker, and wings of the Yak & Yeti, the Kathmandu Guest House, and Hotel Shakti). Others, like Singha Durbar, were demolished, or devastated by fire. Several dozen remain hidden away in residential Kathmandu, transformed into private residences, garment factories and orphanages. Not that the Ranas have entirely lost their influence: many remain active in the military, and the present king and queen are both descendents of Jung Bahadur Rana.

Mohan Shumsher and J.B. Rana

Jung Bahadur Visits England

The Prime Minister took aim with bow and arrow and with a rifle in the areas set aside for this, and everyone was amazed at his constant success. Whatever amusement he went to see, the crowd kept pressing round him.

People were full of praises, commenting on the Prime Minister's handsome appearance, his elegant dress, his skill at rifle-shooting and archery, the great intelligence displayed in his conversation and the presence of mind with which God had endowed him, and also on the nation which could produce such a man. Wearing the most splendid gems, worth hundreds of thousands of rupees, exceedingly beautiful women, the wives and daughters of lords and dukes, came up to touch and look at the Prime Minister's costume. They fetched interpreters and then talked and joked with him and kissed his hand. They talked on and on, their faces assumed flirtatious expressions, blushes came to their cheeks, perspiration stood out on their foreheads, their bosoms swelled and they were altogether consumed with passion. When the Prime Minister started to move off, saying that it was late and time for him to go home, they quickly seized his hands and urged him to stay a little longer.

They treated him with great respect. They asked him when he was returning to Nepal, and when he said he would leave soon, they asked him why and begged him to stay for good if possible, or failing that for ten years or at least for one year. Their faces fell and they said it was hardly worth having come at all for such a little time and that when they heard him say he was going, they felt as if arrows were piercing their hearts. They asked whether, if he had to go, he would at least leave a portrait with them so they could look at it and always be reminded of him. They said they would be glad if, when he got home, he would write to them to say he had arrived, and as they were speaking their eyes filled with tears and their hearts became so heavy that they were finally unable to say any more. Such was the honour shown him by the really fine people there. Even with a thousand tongues it would be impossible to describe those people adequately.

From an account of the Prime Minister's 1850 visit to England written by a member of the party.

Translated by John Whelpton in Jung Bahadur in Europe, 1983.

Post-Revolution: The Present

A new Constitution was drafted, defining Nepal as a 'multilingual, multi-ethnic, democratic, independent, indivisible, sovereign, Hindu, and constitutional Monarchical Kingdom'. The king remains as a symbol of national unity and constitutional monarch. Elections held in April 1991 installed a 205-member House of Representatives. Voters gave a majority to the Nepal Congress Party, with a healthy opposition in the Nepal Communist Party–UML (United Marxist-Leninist) and a half-dozen or so smaller fringe parties.

Heavy political infighting marked the first years of the Congress Party's five-year mandate. The party's majority collapsed in mid-1994, triggering a mid-term poll in November 1994. Disgusted with governmental inaction and corruption, voters gave the Communists a bare majority of 88 parliamentary seats, making Nepal the World's first Communist-ruled Hindu monarchy. Politics continues to be strife-ridden. Government corruption is endemic—a 1994 audit found three billion rupees in government funds unaccounted for—but even more serious is the lack of political will. With politicians engulfed in petty power struggles, little is being done to address the pressing needs of Nepalis.

Peasant women along the trail to the Annapurna Sanctuary

The Economy

Economic experts rushing into a newly opened Nepal in the early 1950s pronounced the economy 'pre-feudal'. Economically speaking, Nepal was starting from scratch, and it still has a long way to go. Statistically it ranks around the world's tenth-poorest country (figures vary annually), with a per capita GNP of US$180 a year, though most people earn much less than that. Much of the economy—perhaps 70 percent of production—remains unmonetized, operating on barter systems such as the ancient trans-Himalayan trade of Tibetan salt in exchange for lowland grain.

Most Nepalis are subsistence farmers, coaxing enough from their tiny plots to feed their families and buy the few necessities they cannot produce themselves: cloth, sugar, tea, salt, pots and pans. Only about 18 percent of land is arable to begin with, but the situation is worsened by inequitable distribution: the bottom 50 percent of the population owns less than 7 percent of land. A family of six survives on an average plot of half a hectare.

Life is simple and there is little to spare, but starvation is avoided because the annual monsoon ensures that crops will grow. With industry producing less than 14 percent of GNP—one of the world's lowest rates…there are few alternatives to farming apart from portering loads over mountain trails, the most extensive non-farming activity in the country.

Nepal possesses few natural resources, and even fewer means of processing and transporting those that exist. Hydropower is a tremendous potential asset, but only a small fraction has been tapped and most of the country remains without electricity. Landlocked Nepal must rely on its giant neighbour India for imports and exports, including vital petroleum products. Major exports are carpets (51 percent of total), and garments (22 percent). Tourism brought in US$61 million in 1991–2, second only to carpets, though much of this flowed back out to pay for foreign goods consumed by tourists. Over 255,000 foreign tourists, plus 75,000 Indian tourists, visit annually, and estimates indicate that this number will increase to 800,000 in the next decade.

Nepal *has* struck gold in its geopolitical location: wedged between China and India, it has benefited from numerous foreign donors over the last 40 years. King Mahendra was particularly skilled at playing off one country against another, reaping aid from China, the USSR and the US. Foreign aid totalled US$320 million in 1991–2, with the World Bank, the Asian Development Bank, Germany and Japan the leading donors.

Development projects support everything from irrigation projects in the Terai to bridges in Kathmandu Valley, but after 40 years the process has not yet taken root. Corruption and inefficiency are major problems, as is the chronic inability to utilize the funds allocated.

The government is making efforts to liberalize the economy, privatize public companies, open areas up to competition and encourage private investment. Following India's lead, it is moving towards full convertibility of the Nepalese rupee over a period of several years.

The People

Nepal is among the most diverse and complex of Asian countries, with a huge range of cultures united only by recent nationalism and the resulting common language. Traditionally Nepal was a collection of loosely federated kingdoms and tribes. Not until the mid-18th century was it unified into a country, and not until the 1950s has a national identity transcending ethnic differences been promoted.

Gurung woman

Sherpa couple

The term 'Nepali' encompasses a tremendous range of people. Nobody is *just a Nepali*: ethnic group and caste play even more important roles in defining an individual. A Bhotiya yak herder, a Newar rice farmer and a Tharu tribesman in many ways have less in common with each other than a Frenchman, a German and an Italian.

The diverse human mosaic can be roughly sorted into two categories: lowland and highland, rice-eaters and barley-eaters—the Hindu Indo-Aryans from the south, who predominate in the Terai and the lower hills, and the Buddhist Mongolian peoples from the Tibetan Plateau, who flourish in the high mountains. The ethnic tribes inhabiting the rugged hill zone in between are varying blends of these two basic themes, becoming more Tibetan and more Buddhist the higher you go.

The Brahmin-Chetri Hindu castes constitute a relatively small portion of the population, but together with the Newars they dominate the government and the economy. More importantly, their Hindu values have become the mainstream norm, overriding local customs and practices. Though ethnic groups are increasingly adopting Hindu values, this process is a two-way street: Nepal's caste Hindus are mellowed by contact with the *matwali* (alcohol-drinking) ethnic groups, and are much more relaxed about caste restrictions than their Indian brethren. Overshadowing both these processes is modernization, which is changing traditions and values of all groups faster than anyone would ever have believed.

Caste and Ethnic Groups

Hindu caste is an important element in Nepali society, though there are gaps in the traditional system. At the top of the heap are the **Bahun** or Brahmans, who may be peasant farmers, government employees or land-owners; then the more numerous **Chetri**, who traditionally served as soldiers. The traditional homeland of both these groups is the hills of Western Nepal, but they have spread throughout the country. The middle caste slots are filled by the ethnic groups described below. At the bottom of the Hindu strata are the low status occupational castes such as the **Kami** (blacksmiths) and **Damai** (tailors), and even lower down the scale, butchers and sweepers.

Nepal's patchwork of ethnic groups has resulted from centuries of interaction between various hill and mountain peoples. Their languages belong to the Tibeto-Burman family, and they traditionally practiced animistic folk religions leavened with Buddhism, though more recently many have become Hindu. The **Newars** of the Kathmandu Valley are a particularly interesting example. Equally skilled in trade, farming and art, their society is divided into 64 occupational castes, paralleling the Hindu system. They remain a tightly knit society practising a number of unique customs. The **Tamangs** of the hills surrounding the Valley tend more towards Buddhism, mixed with animistic beliefs. They constitute one of the largest ethnic groups—5 percent of the national population—but remain relatively poor. Many work as porters, farmers and craftsmen.

The homeland of the **Gurung** people is the foothills north of Pokhara, though they can be found in many mid-hill regions. Originally nomadic, they have settled in neat villages with houses built of stone, and enjoy a relatively high standard of living. Together with the **Magars**, who farm slightly lower slopes in the same areas, they form the mainstay of Gurkha regiments. Eastern Nepal is the home of the independent-minded **Rai** and **Limbu** tribes, easily distinguished by their distinctive high cheekbones and almond-shaped eyes. They both have their own related language, but share a mixture of animistic, Buddhist and Hindu beliefs.

The higher Himalayan regions are home to Tibetan-related peoples, loosely and sometimes derogatorily termed **Bhotiya** or **Bhotey**. Their largely caste-free society is a totally different culture from midland Nepal's, centred around Buddhism, barley and yaks. Best-known are the **Manangis** of the Manang Valley in Central Nepal, renowned traders and smugglers, and the famous **Sherpas** of Solu–Khumbu who have made a handsome living in trekking and mountaineering.

Languages

Reflecting its ethnic diversity, Nepal's people speak a hodgepodge of languages and dialects, anywhere from 25 to well over 100, depending on which source you consult. Like the people, languages can be divided into two groups: Sanskrit-based Terai tongues like Maithili and Bhojpuri, and the Tibeto–Burman languages of the hill tribes, which often appear in regional sub-dialects.

The *lingua franca* and national language is Nepali, an Indo–Aryan tongue related to Sanskrit and similar to Hindi. It is derived from the ancient language of the Khas hill tribe of northwest Nepal. Probably 60 percent of the people speak it as their mother tongue, and another 30 percent are fluent in it. As public schools teach only in Nepali, it is increasingly replacing tribal languages and the cultures they represent.

Like Sanskrit and Hindi, Nepali is written in the Devanagri script. Most of the tribal languages are unwritten. A special case is Newari, a linguistically unique language vaguely related to the Tibeto-Burman group and spoken by many residents of the Kathmandu Valley.

While Nepali is a rewarding and relatively easy language to learn, the casual traveller will find plenty of eager English speakers in tourist destinations and along the main trekking routes. Indeed, it's hard to pick up much Nepali in Kathmandu, as everyone seems bent on practising their English.

Religion

Nepali religious beliefs form a complex tapestry, interweaving Hinduism and Buddhism against a backdrop of more ancient animistic cults. These elements have interacted over the centuries, creating a unique religious synthesis epitomized in the Newars of the Kathmandu Valley, a formerly Buddhist people who since the 14th century have lived under a Hindu-influenced caste system. Most modern Newars are Hindu, but their popular pantheon incorporates Hindu, Buddhist and local deities. Kathmandu's ancient Nara Devi temple is a good example: an ancient animistic goddess worshipped with blood sacrifice in a Hindu Tantric temple tended by Newari Buddhists. Another example is the institution, unique to the Valley, of the Kumari: a young Newar Buddhist girl worshipped as the incarnation of the Hindu goddess Durga.

Mahavaishnavi, Bhaktapur

Among the Newars, at least, it is virtually impossible to identify someone as purely Hindu or Buddhist. People are not as interested in ideology as in efficacy. Religion is seen as a way of improving one's prospects in this life and the next, through the process of accumulating merit from worship and virtuous actions.

Nationwide, if the census is to be believed, 86 percent of the population is Hindu and only seven percent is Buddhist. In reality people practise a mixture of both, with a healthy dose of ancient folk beliefs tossed in for good measure. Hinduism is the dominant religion, and many convert to it in an effort to improve their social status, but conversion doesn't mean they throw the old ways completely overboard.

Religion is not at all a Sunday morning affair: it appears everywhere at all times, exploding with greatest intensity in the numerous festivals. Deities dwell everywhere, in temples, homes, images, atop mountain summits and high passes, in sacred ponds, rocks and trees. Religious ritual structures daily life. Offerings are made early each morning to important neighbourhood gods, usually by women and their daughters. In Kathmandu, the most common gift is the 'five-fold offering' of red *sindhur* powder, uncooked rice, flower blossoms, oil lamps and incense. Devotees paste a bit of *sindhur* onto an image, then take a fragment back as blessing (*prasad*). Bells are rung, circumambulations performed and prayers muttered imploring the deity for favours: wealth, luck, health, harmonious relations, and the avoidance of all obstacles and troubles. Buddhists and Hindus have their preferred temples, but each will visit the others' on occasion, sometimes honouring the deity inside as one of their own.

Add to this already elaborate system, ancient folk beliefs like the mother goddess cult, the rain-bringing **naga** or protective serpents twined about temple doorways, the invisible malevolent forces propitiated by crossroad offerings, and the local **deuta** presiding over each village or neighbourhood. The world is full of invisible beings, most of them hostile to man. To deal with

Losar procession, Boudhanath

unfriendly forces beyond their control, Nepalis turn to *jhankri*, shamanistic healers who mediate between villagers and the spirit world, acting as oracles and diagnosing illnesses. Treatment might include animal sacrifice, herbal medicine or physical manipulation.

Complicating things still further is tantra, a mystic technique developed in sixth-century India that influences both Hinduism and Buddhism. Tantra aims at harnessing physical energies to attain spiritual enlightenment, using a repetoire of tools like *yantra* (geometric diagrams), *mudra* (symbolic gestures) and *mantra* (magical syllables). The point is not ritual for its own sake (though it often becomes that), but the state of consciousness evoked.

Hinduism

Hinduism's 5,000 years of continuous development is rivalled only by the culture of China. It is a vast and complex collection of cults and philosophies, encompassing mother goddesses, powerful deities, cultural heroes, sacred trees, plants, stones, animals—even monotheism.

Hinduism results from the blending of various cultures, primarily the Aryan-speaking settlers from the Caucasian steppes who arrived in India around 1700 BC to mingle with indigenous Dravidian and Indus Valley civilizations. The Aryans introduced a Vedic religion emphasizing social structure and priestly rites. Their economy was cattle-based, resulting in the veneration of the cow which subsists to this day. The indigenous cultures contributed the phallic symbolism still found in the Shiva cult, and the devotional emphasis which pervades Hindu worship. Added onto this blend is a veneration of elemental forces and a reverence for natural powers as expressed in deities of places. Within this framework, much latitude is left for individual worship, centred around the offerings or puja which forms an important and colourful part of daily life in Kathmandu.

Beneath its vast pantheon, Hinduism has a stable core of philosophical beliefs. The ultimate end of ethical and religious disciplines is *moksha*, liberation from limited individual ego-consciousness and the realization of one's fundamental unity with the ultimate Reality beyond distinctions, called Brahman. Hindus work towards this goal in a series of lives, their circumstances determined by karma, which rather than impersonal fate is simply the result of past actions. The doctrine of karma has been criticized as fatalistic, but it is a two-way street: if past actions are responsible for present suffering, present actions are determining future conditions here and now.

HINDU DEITIES

Hinduism embraces an enormous pantheon of diverse gods and goddesses, each capable of appearing in many different manifestations. All are essentially expressions or aspects of the same formless Absolute, the ultimate reality called Brahman. Ordinary people don't spend much time pondering such esoteric issues; they simply worship their preferred deities, hoping thereby to improve their prospects in this life and future ones.

The dizzying profusion of deities is supported by a rich symbolism which infuses Nepali art. Multiple limbs and heads express their limitless power; the fiercer ones are depicted trampling on a helpless corpse, representing ignorance. Major deities are easily identified by their emblems, symbols and gestures. The simplest indicator is a deity's particular *vahana* or animal mount, usually crouched in a subservient pose opposite the main temple entrance. Shiva is attended by the white bull **Nandi**, Vishnu the winged bird-man **Garuda**; Durga rides a lion, and portly Ganesh a **rat**.

The Hindu triad (*Trimurti*) of Brahma-Vishnu-Shiva was in place by the fifth century BC. **Brahma**, the Creator, is largely ignored in both Nepal and India—some say because his work is already completed—but Shiva and Vishnu are worshipped everywhere.

Shiva is the Destroyer and more importantly the Transformer, epitomizing the forces of vitality, change and fierce energy. He is manifested in 108 principal forms, often as the majestic **Mahesvara**, the Great Lord, with his beautiful consort Parvati on his knee. As **Yogesvara** he is a dreadlocked, ash-smeared ascetic seated in meditation atop Mt Kailas in Tibet; as **Nataraja**, Lord of the Dance, he whirls as a multi-limbed embodiment of universal energy.

Nepal's special patron, **Pashupati**, the benevolent 'Lord of the Beasts', is a remnant of an early cult worshipping Shiva as a guardian deity of cattle, who by extension became the protector of all creation. Shiva is also the terrifying fanged **Bhairab**, who embodies the principal of movement, and is placated with offerings of blood and alcohol. His universal symbol, the **linga**, is rendered as a stone cylinder, abstract or graphically phallic. This ancient emblem adopted from a Dravidian cult, serves as a symbol of generative power. Shaivite devotees paint their foreheads with three vertical lines representing the trident, another token of his power.

Vishnu the Preserver is a gentler, more humanized deity concerned with the benefit of mankind. As **Narayan** he is the epitome of goodness and mercy, depicted as a handsome standing man holding a conch shell, discus, club and lotus. Vishnu is said to have been manifested in ten principal incarnations (*das avatara*), rendering him capable of absorbing elements of various ancient popular cults. Flirtatious flute-playing **Krishna**, for example, was adopted from a more ancient Dravidian cult, while **Rama** is the stalwart hero of the epic Ramayana. Even the historical **Buddha** was embraced as an incarnation, though in this case it was essentially theoretical. Vishnu also appeared as various creatures who saved the world in one legend or another, including a **fish, tortoise, boar, man-lion,** and **dwarf**. Since the 13th century Nepal's kings have proclaimed themselves Vishnu avatar, in a tradition still respected today by many Nepalis. Devotees of Vishnu paint three horizontal lines on their foreheads and offer no blood sacrifices: Vishnu's cult is based on the practice of *bhakti* or devotion.

The most popular of all Hindu deities is the pot-bellied, elephant-headed **Ganesh**, the bringer of luck and remover of obstacles. Loyal, strong and benevolent, the apparently jovial Ganesh is not beyond mischief or even malevolence if not properly propitiated. Thus he is worshipped so that he does not create obstacles and indeed removes them. He is invoked at the start of activities and journeys by both Buddhists and Hindus, and is always worshipped before any other deity so that the ensuing devotions will be successful. Other names for him are **Lambodara**, Big Belly, and **Ekadanta**, One Tusk. He is usually shown wielding a rosary, axe and radish, with a bowl of *ladoo* (milk sweets) raised to his trunk. He may wear a girdle of serpents and dancer's bells on his stumpy legs. Ganesh appears everywhere, in shrines of fierce as well as placid deities. He is worshipped with tantric rites, offered blood sacrifices, sesame, radishes, boiled eggs and, of course, *ladoo*.

Hindu goddesses take on one of two aspects: compassionate and motherly, or fierce and cruel. Their ultimate source is **Shakti**, the embodiment of cosmic energy in female form which activates all that the male evokes. Tamely beneficent goddesses include Shiva's spouse **Parvati**; Brahma's consort **Saraswati**, the goddess of speech and learning; and **Lakshmi**, the consort of Vishnu and the goddess of wealth and abundance, who is worshipped in the festival of Tihar.

Nepalis are most impressed by the fierce female manifestations like **Durga**, the slayer of the buffalo demon, who is celebrated in the great festival of Dasain. **Bhagwati** is a generic name for all sorts of goddesses of this type. Black-faced **Kali** evokes devotion despite her terrifyingly ugly appearance, while **Chamunda** represents the power of death. **Sitala**, the dreaded smallpox goddess, has become unemployed with the worldwide eradication of the disease, but she is still worshipped as a protector of children. There are also collective manifestations of feminine power, like the **Ashta Matrika** or Eight Mothers, emanations of Durga, worshipped with blood sacrifice. Local Newari divinities like the *mai* and *ajima*, or terrible grandmother goddesses, are often embodied in unadorned rocks, reminders of their ancient origins as nature deities.

Shiva-Parvati images from the Navadurga temple, Kathmandu Durbar Square

Buddhism

Buddhism evolved in part as a reaction to Hinduism's overemphasis on form and ritual. It worships not a god but the principle of enlightenment, as exemplified by the historical Buddha, Siddhartha Gautama. Unlike other major religious leaders, Siddhartha never proclaimed himself a divinely inspired prophet or special being. The state of being he embodied can, at least in theory, be realized by every human being.

Gods exist in Buddhism, but like human beings they are subject to karma and the forces of death and rebirth. Only human beings can obtain enlightenment or release from *samsara*, the cycle of delusory existence. The Buddha's teachings were simple and direct, relentlessly turning the listener's mind back to his or her own experience, but this austere approach proved unappealing to ordinary people. Gradually more and more ritual was adopted from Hinduism, and the Buddhist pantheon was expanded to include worshippable Buddhas and bodhisattvas—technically not deities, but in practice little different from them.

By the second century AD Buddhism had split into two schools: the more austere Theravada of Southeast Asia, and the Mahayana which predominated in India and Nepal, and formed a base for the tantric Vajrayana which developed in India and spread to Tibet.

Newari Buddhism

The unique form of Buddhism practised in the Kathmandu Valley is the last surviving link with the long-vanished Buddhism of India. Over the centuries it has become distinctly Hinduized, incorporating Buddhist imagery into basically Hindu rituals. One oddity is its structuring around *barey*, a hereditary caste of priests who conduct life-cycle rituals and elaborate offerings for their clients. The rituals remain popular and the big annual festivals still draw crowds, but few *barey* understand the symbolism of the ceremonies they perform or the ancient texts they read, and Newari Buddhism is in danger of dying of obscurity.

Buddhist temples and art seldom depict the historical Buddha, but turn instead to a legion of bodhisattvas, compassionate semi-divinities who help suffering beings. Favourites among the Newars are **Manjushri**, who cleaved the Valley with his sword of wisdom, and the graceful lotus-holding **Lokesvara**. The five Buddhas (**Pancha Buddha**) painted over the doorways of Newar houses are protective images, each representing a different divine wisdom. In addition there is an array of local folk deities associated with Buddhism, most prominently the Valley's patron, **Machhendranath**, who comes in red and white forms. Such gods are not worshipped for enlightenment but for practical things: rain, health, wealth, children. They influence present life, the Buddha the future life—a very rational division of labour for both deities and worshippers.

Tibetan Buddhism

The people of northern Nepal generally follow Vajrayana Buddhism, the tantric-influenced 'Diamond Vehicle' of Tibet, as evidenced by the *mani* walls of carved stones and the fluttering prayer flags that dot the Himalayan landscape. Practises range from simple offerings of butter lamps, pure water and fragrant juniper smoke to highly sophisticated meditation and visualization. In Kathmandu, the Tibetan Buddhist scene focuses on Boudhanath and to a lesser extent Swayambhunath, where refugee leaders of different sects have built magnificent monasteries (*gompa*).

The historical Buddha plays only a small part in the vast pantheon of deities which includes the female bodhisattva **Dolma** (**Tara** in Sanskrit), the 1,000-armed- and -eyed **Chenresi** (**Avalokitesvara**), and a whole range of ferociously fanged and clawed protective embodiments of fierce energy who, despite their appearance, are said to be inspired by compassion. Spiritual progress is dependent on one's relation with a spiritual teacher or lama, who may or may not be a monk. High-level lamas, called *tulkus*, are considered emanations of enlightened principles incarnated in human form to help sentient beings.

Wheel of Dharma

FESTIVALS

The Nepali calendar is crammed with festivals, anywhere from 50 to 120 holidays, plus countless minor holy days. Inspired by religion, they are infused with an exuberant sense of joy and release. Festivals may be serious but they are never solemn. They provide a splash of vivid excitement in ordinary life, serving as an escape valve for tensions and pressures as well as a living link to history. There are festivals to celebrate gods and goddesses, placate demons, ogres and spirits, and honour dogs, frogs, snakes and cows.

For visitors they are an unrivalled access point to diverse aspects of Nepali culture. They also provide superb opportunities for photographs, both of the colourful events and the equally colourful crowds of bystanders.

Festivals fall according to the Nepali calendar, which consists of twelve lunar months of 28 to 32 days. This means their dates according to the Gregorian calendar can shift by several weeks. Complicating matters further, there are four different calendars in use: the official Nepali year, which begins in April; the Newari year, which starts in November; the Tibetan year, commencing in February; and the Western Gregorian calendar. This makes it difficult to pin down what occurs when each year. Check upon arrival to see if your visit coincides with any major celebrations.

The Nepali New Year begins in mid-April, celebrated in Bhaktapur with the rowdy **Bisket Jatra**, when the god Bhairab and his spouse Bhadrakala are hauled in massive wooden chariots down the steep cobbled streets. A month or so later it is Patan's turn for a chariot festival: the great procession of **Raato Machhendranath**, whose progress is slower and more stately. It can take up to three months for the god to make his tour of town, culminating with the **Bhoto Jatra**, the public display showing off his tiny sacred vest to a huge crowd—usually in mid-June.

Buddha Jayanti on the May full moon marks the triple anniversary of Buddha's birth, enlightenment and death. Temples and stupas are spruced up and elaborate pujas held at Swayambhunath and Boudhanath. Newari Buddhists mark the rainy month of **Gunla** (July–August) with intensive early-morning puja at Swayambhunath, special exhibitions of normally hidden temple treasures at various *bahals*, and processions of the devout.

The festival season begins in earnest in August. **Janai Purnima** (usually the August full moon) is celebrated at the Kumbeswar Mahadev temple in Patan, with the exhibition of a sacred silver linga in the middle of the temple water tank. Meanwhile, hill people flock to the great *mela* held at the sacred lake of Gosainkund, three day's walk north of Kathmandu. A few days later is **Gai Jatra**, a sort of Nepali masquerade with costumed processions featuring small boys banging sticks, mincing men dressed in their sisters' saris, and satirical vignettes poking fun at politicians. The real purpose, however, is to commemorate the souls of those who died in the past year, with towering paper effigies borne on shoulder litters. Bhaktapur's processions are the most imaginative, but Kathmandu Durbar Square is not far behind in pomp and colour.

Soon after comes **Krishna Jayanti**, honouring the much-loved Lord Krishna with processions and elaborate puja. The focal point is Krishna Mandir in Patan's Durbar Square. **Teej** (September) is an exclusively women's festival, commemorating the austerities Parvati performed to attract Shiva. Women feast, fast and bathe in the sacred Bagmati at Pashupatinath or Teku. Then, dressed in their finest red and gold saris, they spend the afternoon singing and dancing: the only time such a spectacle by married women is condoned.

The finest festival of all is **Indra Jatra** (September), when the old town of Kathmandu comes alive for eight nights with a string of processions, masked dances, costume dramas, religious hymns (*bhajan*) and displays of ancient artefacts. The huge painted masks of Seto and Akash Bhairab are displayed, and the Kumari makes several appearances, drawn about town in a chariot.

Life, or at least business, slows to a crawl in October with **Dasain**, the most important of all Nepali festivals, involving ten days of feasting, visiting and gifts. Dasain is family-oriented and there's not much to see for visitors. Offices close for the last four or five days, traffic vanishes, and the streets fill with happy families dressed in new clothes going to visit relatives and friends. Massive public sacrifices of buffalo are performed in honour of the goddess Durga, as well as smaller sacrifices meant to protect motor vehicles from accidents in the coming year.

Two weeks later is **Tihar**, a series of special ceremonies culminating with Lakshmi Puja. Homes are cleaned and tiny oil lamps lit to invite the goddess of wealth for the coming year. The glowing buildings make a pretty sight, though the growing popularity of firecrackers makes a stroll through the old town a hazardous experience. Groups of children and young men go from house to house singing and begging for sweets and money, and men gamble day and night.

Things slow down after this festive spree. The next celebration of note is **Losar** or the Tibetan New Year, generally falling in February. Most events occur inside the home, but on the morning of the fourth day everyone congregates at the Boudhanath stupa for prayers, climaxing with the jubilant tossing of *tsampa*. This season is also a good time to observe masked dances at monasteries.

Shortly after comes **Shiva Ratri**, the great Night of Shiva. Indian and Nepali pilgrims and groups of dreadlocked sadhus throng to Pashupatinath for a splendid example of a medieval temple fair. The full moon of March is celebrated with **Holi**, a licentious festival involving the tossing of coloured water and powder.

Losar celebrations, Boudhanath

Average Monthly Temperatures
(in degrees Centigrade)

	Meghauli (Terai)		Kathmandu (Hills)		Namche (Mountains)	
	Max.	Min.	Max.	Min.	Max.	Min.
Jan.	23	8	17	2	6	-6
Feb.	28	11	21	3	6	-4
March	33	17	25	9	8	-1
April	37	19	27	11	11	1
May	37	22	28	16	14	3
June	34	23	28	19	15	7
July	33	25	28	20	16	8
August	32	24	27	20	16	8
Sept.	32	24	26	19	15	7
Oct.	31	19	25	12	11	1
Nov.	27	14	21	8	8	-3
Dec.	24	8	19	3	7	-4

50

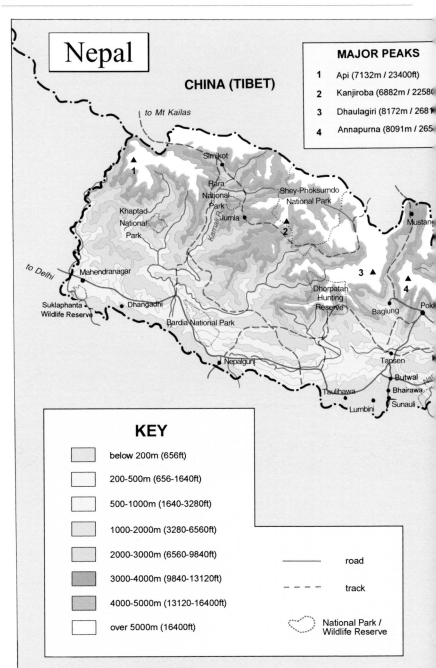

Nepal

CHINA (TIBET)

to Mt Kailas

MAJOR PEAKS

1	Api (7132m / 23400ft)	
2	Kanjiroba (6882m / 22580
3	Dhaulagiri (8172m / 2681
4	Annapurna (8091m / 265

Simikot
1

Rara
National
Park

Shey-Phoksumdo
National Park

Khaptad
National
Park

Jumla
2

Mustan

to Delhi

Mahendranagar

3

4

Dhorpatan
Hunting
Reserve

Baglung

Pok

Suklaphanta
Wildlife Reserve

Dhangadhi

Bardia National Park

Nepalgunj

Tapsen

Butwal

Taulihawa

Bhairawa

Lumbini

Sunauli

KEY

below 200m (656ft)

200-500m (656-1640ft)

500-1000m (1640-3280ft)

1000-2000m (3280-6560ft)

2000-3000m (6560-9840ft)

3000-4000m (9840-13120ft)

4000-5000m (13120-16400ft)

over 5000m (16400ft)

road

track

National Park /
Wildlife Reserve

The borders shown on this map are neither authentic nor correct

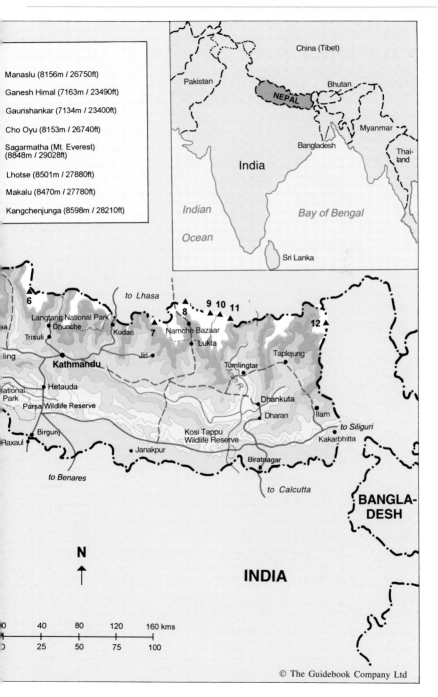

Manaslu (8156m / 26750ft)

Ganesh Himal (7163m / 23490ft)

Gaurishankar (7134m / 23400ft)

Cho Oyu (8153m / 26740ft)

Sagarmatha (Mt. Everest)
(8848m / 29028ft)

Lhotse (8501m / 27880ft)

Makalu (8470m / 27780ft)

Kangchenjunga (8598m / 28210ft)

China (Tibet)

Pakistan

Bhutan

NEPAL

Myanmar

Bangladesh

Thai-
land

India

Indian

Bay of Bengal

Ocean

Sri Lanka

to Lhasa

6

Langtang National Park

Dhunche

Trisuli

Kodari

7

Namche Bazaar

Lukla

8

9 10 11

12

ling

Kathmandu

Jiri

Taplejung

Tumlingtar

ational
Park

Hetauda

Dhankuta

Parsa Wildlife Reserve

Dharan

Ilam

Birgunj

Kosi Tappu
Wildlife Reserve

to Siliguri

Raxaul

Kakarbhitta

Janakpur

Biratnagar

to Benares

to Calcutta

BANGLA-
DESH

N

↑

INDIA

0   40   80   120   160 kms

0   25   50   75   100

© The Guidebook Company Ltd

FACTS FOR THE TRAVELLER

Getting There

Kathmandu is connected by direct flight to Dhaka, Bangkok, Singapore, Osaka, Shanghai, Hong Kong, Lhasa, Rangoon, Moscow and Karachi, as well as Delhi, Varanasi, Calcutta, Patna and Bombay in India. Flights to Paris, Frankfurt and London go via Dubai. Most travellers arrive after an overnight stop in Bangkok or Delhi. Assuming roughly equal distances, Bangkok is the pleasanter alternative, just as Thai Airlines is pleasanter than Air India.

Tribhuvan International Airport, four kilometres east of Kathmandu, was built on pastureland dedicated to the sacred cows of the nearby Pashupatinath Temple. A desk in the airport lobby arranges taxi service to hotels. Freelance taxi drivers outside the door expect at least Rs100 into town. A very inexpensive bus shuttle operates between the airport and popular tourist areas like Thamel and Durbar Marg. Trekking companies and major hotels meet guests just outside the terminal doors, along with the usual array of hotel touts.

Overland routes to Nepal run from India or Tibet. Delhi–Kathmandu involves a train ride with two changes, followed by a gruelling bus trip from Gorakhpur. The three-day Lhasa–Kathmandu road is even rougher—cold, dusty and bumpy—but the transition from the high-altitude Tibetan Plateau down to Nepal's rolling hills is among the most spectacular rides in the world. Travellers from Tibet arrive by Land Rover or public bus; there are also direct flights from Lhasa.

Leaving Nepal

Travel agencies on Durbar Marg will help you find the cheapest onward airfare. It pays to shop around. Flights out of Kathmandu are heavily booked in November, around Christmas and in April, but it's usually possible to find a seat. Save enough rupees to cover the Rs700 airport tax levied on departing international passengers.

For **India**-bound travellers, small private companies around Thamel and Freak Street offer bus≈train packages to various destinations. This saves the trouble of buying the tickets on the spot, but more often than not the sleeper reservations will have disappeared on your arrival and you'll end up buying them again.

A trip to Nepal is easily combined with visits to Tibet or Bhutan. Local companies run budget trips to Tibet from roughly April–October, either overland or via the Kathmandu–Lhasa flight. As of winter 1993, the Chinese embassy in Kathmandu refused to issue visas to independent travellers, but it's a different matter if you arrive with a Chinese visa already in your passport. Bhutan is more restrictive: the government limits tourism to groups (any size) at rates averaging US$150 per person per day.

What to Take

Pack light, as suitcases invariably swell with souvenirs, and wardrobes can be easily expanded in Kathmandu. Simple cotton shirts and dresses, and woollen sweaters are especially good buys. Trekkers can rent down jackets, sleeping bags and camping equipment from shops in Thamel and Pokhara, though selection may be limited in the autumn season.

Clothing should be comfortable and easy to wash and dry. Hotels offer laundry service, but trekkers will probably end up washing clothes at the village water tap. Dress casually but modestly; women especially should avoid sleeveless, tight or short garments. Bare legs above the knee are frowned upon for men and are *verboten* for women, although many young travellers disregard this. For April–September bring light, loosely cut cottons and rainwear. Winter visitors (November–February) will need a warm pile jacket at night, and warm sleeping clothes as most hotels are unheated. The daytime sun warms things up considerably.

Trekkers need warmer clothes, but expensive, high-tech outdoor gear is not necessary. Think in layers: a wool sweater, some sweatshirts, warm trousers and a good down jacket should be sufficient. A poncho and umbrella provide enough protection from the rain for the normally dry autumn and spring. Lightweight, lug-soled hiking boots (and lots of socks) are the foundation of your trek. Field-test and break them in before departure, and don't count on finding them in your size in Kathmandu.

Other useful items for trekkers and non-trekkers alike are a brimmed hat, sunscreen and good sunglasses (the sun is strong even in Kathmandu, and at altitude it can become fierce); a small flashlight, a sturdy water bottle and a water-treatment method (discussed in **Health**). Photographs of your home and family or picture postcards of sights from your country are useful for breaking the ice. Most toiletry and grocery items are available in Kathmandu, though not in the range you find at home.

Everything But Nepali

Nepal, of course, had long been famous for adapting to Western tastes and fashions with unparalleled swiftness and skill. In the forties, before the country was even linked to the outside world by road, Kathmandu was said to be the place in the Himalayas for cinemas and cars. The king at that time, Tribhubana (he of plucked eyebrows and scented breath), was a celebrated connoisseur of mail-order catalogues who sent porters across the mountains to bring back lounge suits and gadgets for the royal palace. In that respect, at least, little seemed to have changed. When I stepped into a local store in the ten-hut village of Tandi Bazaar in the malarial lowlands of Nepal, I found, on the counter, an issue of The New York Review of Books, nine months old, open to an article entitled 'The Melancholy of Montaigne'. And whenever Westerners staying in India felt homesick, a Nepali who lived in Benares informed me, they simply hurried off to Kathmandu.

'We Solve you all Travel Problems,' promised Pawan Travels, 'and make you Journey Easy and Funny'.

Nepal's prodigious versatility was most apparent, however, in the smorgasbord of its menus, which could easily have put the United Nations cafeteria to shame. Every one of them, so it seemed, offered everything from borscht to quiche and sukiyaki to soyburgers. The Jamaly restaurant served up 'Mecxican food,' Italian, American Chop Suey, Moussaka, Curry and 'Viena Schnitzel'. Shiva's Sky, in the Continental section of its menu, provided 'Mexican Takos,' Vegetarian Chop Suey and Chow Mein. The Nor-Ling posted outside a twenty-six-line billboard listing its offerings, and beginning: 'We offer delicious Tibetan, Italian, Indian, Nepal, Chinese dishes, minestrone soup, Fr. onion soup spagetti, lasagne, mousake a 'La'Greece' Everything of every nationality was available here—except things Nepalese. When I asked a man in a candy store for Nepalese chocolate, he looked distinctly put out. 'We have Indian chocolate, English, American, German. You can have Thai chocolate. You can have Chinese marshmallow. But Nepalese, no. Here only international chocolate.' And when I asked another local what he served in his Kathmandu restaurant, he answered crisply, 'Indian, Chinese, Continental, German, American, Mexican.' And Nepalese? 'No. Nepalese, very difficult.'

Pico Iyer, Video Night in Kathmandu, 1988

Photography

Casual photographers will be best served by a light auto-focusing subcompact. Serious photographers will want a wide-angle lens (24 or 28 mm) for architecture and shots of crowded city streets, a standard 50 mm, and a telephoto or zoom for closeups of mountain peaks and discreet portraits of people.

People who pose for you will usually ask for a copy of the photograph. Frequently they expect it to materialize on the spot. If you have a Polaroid, prepare to be mobbed. If not, copies of prints can be quickly made in Kathmandu.

Print, slide and black-and-white film are sold in Kathmandu and Pokhara, as are small LCD and flashlight batteries. A number of shops offer same-day developing service for prints. Slides tend to get scratched so it is best to develop them outside Nepal.

Trekkers should bring plenty of film as it is seldom available on the trail, together with several extra sets of camera batteries, which tend to die quickly in cold weather. At high altitudes you may end up warming your camera in your sleeping bag in order to capture sunrise over the mountains. Automatic light meters often can't cope with the dazzling intensity of snow-covered mountains. Set the exposure by reading a medium-toned object in similar light—a sweatshirt, a wall, the ground—and bracket your shots.

Visas and Customs

Valid passports and visas are required for all nationalities except Indian. One-month tourist visas can be obtained for US$25 from any Nepalese embassy or consulate or at the airport on arrival; 15-day visas are US$15. Visas can be extended up to 120 days, 150 days in special circumstances. Extension fees are minimal, US$1 per day.

Customs inspection on entry is fairly cursory, as officials are mainly concerned with gold and drug smugglers. The standard allowance is 200 cigarettes and a bottle of liquor (Johnny Walker Red and 555 cigarettes are the locally preferred brands and make good gifts). Tourists can bring in items like mountain bikes, video cameras, and tape recorders for personal use, though officials may write these in your passport and ask you to produce them at departure.

Departure from Nepal

The major restriction is on the export of antiques, defined as any item over 100 years old. Very few objects meet that criteria, but if you anticipate difficulty with a major item like a statue or *thangka*, ask the merchant to help you obtain an export certificate from the Department of Archaeology, south of Singha Durbar.

Money

The Nepali rupee (written Rs) is linked to, but different from the Indian rupee. It comes in denominations of Rs1, Rs2, 5, 10, 20, 50, 100, 500 and 1,000. Notes are easy to distinguish as they have different colours and images (usually engravings of wildlife or holy sites) on the reverse side, where the amount is written in English. A rupee consists of 100 paisa: it's difficult to distinguish between the 50, 25, 10 and 5 paisa aluminium coins, but their value is negligible.

The official exchange rate in early 1995 was Rs49 to the US dollar. The black market, highly touted by street hustlers in tourist neighbourhoods like Thamel, yields three or four rupees more and is hardly worth the trouble considering its illegality. It's important not to be left with extra money since the rupee is a non-convertible currency. On departure, the bank at the airport will convert 15 percent of the amount shown on your bank exchange receipts into foreign currency.

Carry money in travellers' cheques; a few large-denomination notes in US dollars might facilitate bargaining. Major credit cards are seldom accepted outside larger hotels and travel agencies. Try not to run out of money. Funds can be transferred from a correspondent bank abroad (ask local banks for a list), but local banks often float the money for a week or two (or three), reaping the interest while stonewalling your enquiries. Travellers' cheques can also be obtained with a major credit card, the best reason to bring one.

Travellers can change money at banks and hotels around Kathmandu, as well as at Central Immigration and the airport. Service and general ambience is best at modern banks like Grindleys, Nabil or Indo-Suez; rates are set by the government and day-to-day fluctuations are slight. Banking hours are Sunday–Thursday, 10 am–3 pm; Friday, 10 am–noon.

Changing money outside the main towns is sometimes difficult. When trekking, bring as many rupees as you think you need plus a 50 percent cushion and possibly a few travellers' cheques for an emergency flight out. Independent trekkers should stock up on notes of smaller denomination as Rs1,000 notes can be difficult to change on the trail. Group trekkers need little cash.

Tipping is on the increase in Kathmandu, but be wary of handing out lavish tips indiscriminately. Porters at the airport get Rs5–10 per bag. Tipping is not mandatory in restaurants, but five percent might be given for good service. Taxi drivers should not be tipped except, perhaps, for a full day's service; tour guides deserve a small gratuity.

Trekking staff rely on tips to boost their meagre salaries. Companies provide guidelines, but a good rule of thumb is US$1–2 per trekking day per group member, to be divided among the trekking staff, with the *sirdar* and cook at the top of the list. Porters are tipped on the last day of the trek, perhaps one day's extra salary per week of the trek.

A visit to Nepal can be remarkably cheap; on the other hand, you could spend almost any amount if you put your mind to it. US$30 per day allows a simple but comfortable stay in Kathmandu, while luxury hotels and their restaurants can increase the cost to over US$200 per day. Restaurants in particular are amazingly cheap: the food bill rarely tops Rs500 per person, and enormous meals can be had in Thamel for Rs100.

Communications

Both receiving and sending mail is a gamble in Nepal, as letters often disappear or arrive months late. Service to and from Europe takes around a week; ten days to the US. The General Post Office at Sundhara is open from 10 am≈5 pm daily except on Saturday, closing earlier in the winter and on Fridays. Queues are often long and chaotic, and it's a haven for pickpockets. You can also buy stamps at your hotel, bookstores, or telecommunications centres. Outside Kathmandu and Pokhara, mail becomes even less reliable.

The poste restante service is chaotic but functioning. American Express provides free mail service for card and cheque-holders (PO Box 76, Kathmandu, Nepal); others must pay US$1 per enquiry. Some embassies, including the US, French and British, will accept letters for citizens; or have your mail sent c/o your hotel or trekking company. Faxing is quick and reliable if more expensive; try the major hotels or telecommunications offices.

International phone calls are expensive (Rs105–120 a minute for most countries) but easy. If your hotel does not have an international line, visit one of the 'Communications Centres' around town advertising ISTD dialling. The Central Telegraph Office, south of the Post Office, is open 24 hours and is slightly cheaper. Collect calls are allowed only to Canada, Japan and the UK, but your respondent can call you back on the spot.

The local telephone service is less efficient, and what with the constant tea breaks and flexible office hours it is difficult to conduct business by phone. Public phones located in shops charge Rs1 or Rs2 per call; others allow the use of their private phone for a slightly higher fee. There are few telephone directories. Directory assistance is 197.

Time

Nepal is in its own special time zone, 15 minutes ahead of India and five hours 45 minutes ahead of Greenwich Mean Time. Noon in Kathmandu is 6:15 am in London, 1:15 am in New York, 10:15 the preceding evening in Los Angeles.

Government offices are open from 10 am to 5 pm, Sunday through Friday; most close at 4 pm in winter and around 3 pm on Fridays. Most shops and offices close on Saturday, and while Sunday is not an official holiday, the pace is more leisurely. Shops open around 10 am and close around 8 or 9 pm, earlier in winter. Many offices close for an hour around noon for lunch, and tea breaks are a common phenomenon. It seems that 11 am and 3 pm are the best times to find someone in the office.

Information

The main English language paper is the government-owned *The Rising Nepal*, a source of amusingly edited and headlined stories, principally on national subjects. *The International Herald Tribune*, *Time* and *Newsweek* are available in hotels and bookstores. Pick up a copy of the locally published *Himal*, a provocative bimonthly magazine covering development and environmental issues.

Radio Nepal broadcasts English news at 8 am and 8 pm, while the Nepal Television Corp. airs a brief English broadcast at 9:40 pm. Major hotels offer satellite TV, including CNN and Star TV for BBC service. Plenty of bookstores in Kathmandu sell new and secondhand English books; the selection is particularly good for Himalayan subjects, including Tibet, Buddhism and mountaineering. Locally published and Indian editions of popular paperbacks are inexpensive. Good bookstores include Mandala Bookpoint on Kanti Path, Pilgrim's Bookhouse in Thamel and Himalayan Booksellers.

The government-sponsored tourist information offices in major cities have pathetically little information and are seldom worth visiting.

Good maps are hard to find, but check out the exquisitely detailed, if outdated, Schneider series for maps of Kathmandu, Patan and the Kathmandu Valley, and trekking areas in Eastern Nepal. Locally produced dyeline maps (the Mandala series) cover popular trekking routes; they're inaccurate but provide a vague idea of what's down the trail.

Trekkers should make it a point to visit the Himalayan Rescue Association office (tel 418 755) in the Hotel Tilicho building in Thamel, right next to Central Immigration. HRA hosts daily talks on altitude sickness for trekkers, and distributes information and answers questions. Its logbooks on popular trekking routes are a fascinating compendium of information from recently returned trekkers. One block further is the office of the **Kathmandu Environmental Education Project** (KEEP), which sponsors slide shows and lectures on how trekkers can minimize their negative environmental and cultural impacts. The centre's coffee shop is a good place to meet people, and a bulletin board advertises trekking partners. Both offices are open from 10 am to 5 pm daily except Saturdays.

Notice-boards at the Kathmandu Guest House and Pumpernickel Bakery are also good places to check for trekking partners. The best source of up-to-date information on the trek routes and travel to Tibet is the traveller's circuit in Thamel.

Getting Around

Air
The national airline, Royal Nepal or RNAC, offers domestic and international flights. The main RNAC office on New Road sells tickets for Lukla and Pokhara; more remote destinations are available at the Domestic Service Office in Thapathali. Go in person and be prepared to wait. It's easiest to buy tickets through a travel agent.

Private airlines like Everest Air, Nepal Airways and Necon Air fly to popular destinations like Lukla, Jomosom and Pokhara. Airfare is identical to RNAC's, but service (or at least office organization) is better. Whatever the airline, the plane is likely to be small, light and often unpressurized. Landing strips in the Hills are little more than grassy fields carved out of steep mountains, and flights are often cancelled due to weather conditions, creating bottlenecks in the tourist season. Avoid scheduling tight connections following a mountain flight.

Bus

Long-distance bus travel in Nepal is a gruelling endurance test. The excruciatingly slow buses experience frequent breakdowns and are crowded with passengers, including goats, chickens and motion-sick villagers. But they are the most inexpensive way to get to many destinations, and the *only* way to reach many trekking trailheads, apart from renting a taxi. Despite their drawbacks, buses immerse you forcibly in the gritty reality of Nepal. If you can tame your impatience and accept the grindingly slow pace, they can be perversely enjoyable.

The long-distance bus park is at Gongabu, north of Kathmandu on the Ring Road, a 20-minute walk from Thamel along a noisy, dusty road. Buy tickets at least a day in advance to guarantee a seat, though once out of town you may well end up sitting on the roof perched on the luggage, which offers a better view and greater leg room. Fares are cheap, usually under Rs100. Long-distance rides are broken by quick stops for tea and *dal bhat*; it's not wise to venture out of sight of the bus for long. Tourist buses to popular destinations like Pokhara are still reasonably priced but less crowded and more efficient. Book tickets through reservation offices in Thamel.

Rentals

Hertz and Avis are represented by American Express on Durbar Marg (tel 226 172). Car rentals cost US$48 per day, which includes a driver and 50 km of travel within the Valley. Taxis can be hired by the half-day or day, and drivers will even go to Pokhara, Chitwan, and other long-distance destinations. Ask hotel staff for assistance in arranging a taxi, or start asking drivers on the street. Figure around Rs800≈900 for a half day of travel in the Valley, Rs2,000 for a full day of travel outside.

Motorcycles can be rented from shops on New Road and Thamel; a Nepali or International Driver's License is required and cost averages Rs500 per day.

Transport In Kathmandu

Taxis are plentiful, at least in the daytime, and relatively inexpensive. Look for a car with black licence plates (private vehicles have red) and a meter— and insist the driver use it. Be prepared, however, for a surcharge (currently 60 percent), as the meters are seldom up to date. After dusk the fare is negotiable and depends on destination. One and a half times the meter fare is reasonable; double the meter fare is likely. For night taxi service, call 224 374.

Tempos, noisy little three-wheeled covered scooters, are a slightly cheaper and far more uncomfortable alternative, but they are more common than taxis, and drivers complain less about out-of-the-way destinations. Try however to avoid them on unpaved roads.

Brightly painted cycle rickshaws negotiate the crowded backstreets of the old town. Rates should be less than tempos, but won't be unless you bargain hard. Always negotiate the fare in advance: a few blocks should be Rs20.

Bus

Blue city buses and box-like minibuses cover most of the city and Valley, but they are slow, crowded and not recommended unless there is no alternative. (The exception is the Chinese trolley bus from Kathmandu to Bhaktapur.) Six-seater tempos and noisy, smoke-belching blue 'Bikram' run set routes along main roads; simply flag one down, hop in, and pay the driver when alighting.

Bicycle

Cycles are a wonderful way of getting around Kathmandu, though city traffic and air pollution can be intimidating. For in-city travel opt for the simplest styles which run less risk of theft than the mountain variety. Basic Indian cycles are rented in Thamel, Freak Street and Bhotahiti for negotiable rates. Look for bicycles made in China, slightly more expensive but better constructed and more comfortable.

Mountain bikes are ideal for exploring the Valley, but you must be wary of theft, especially in the city. Thamel shops rent them for Rs 70–200 per day, depending on the cycle, the season, and your bargaining skills.

On Foot

Your own two feet are the best way of exploring the old city. Nothing else moves sufficiently slowly and unobtrusively to take in all the densely

On the way home, Annapurna region

packed details. Day walks, in judicious combination with motorized transport, are the ideal way of exploring the rural sections of the Valley. And the outlying hills and mountains, untouched by roads, can only be explored on foot, a process for some reason known by the old Boer term 'trekking'.

Health

No immunizations are required to enter Nepal, but many are recommended, including a tetanus–diphtheria update within the last ten years, a polio update and a gamma gobulin injection or Hepatitis A vaccine. Trekkers should consider adding typhoid, meningococcal A and C, and pre-exposure rabies vaccinations. Malaria prophylaxis is advised for extensive travel in the Terai, though for a few days in Chitwan, mosquito repellent and a net over the bed should suffice.

Gastrointestinal illness is a common result of Nepal's abysmal sanitation and strikes nearly everyone sooner or later. The local version of

Delhi Belly, dubbed Kathmandu Quickstep, is simply a typical tourist's ailment. More insidious are giardia, dysentery (amoebic and bacterial), and a mysterious new disease informally termed 'blue–green algae'. Typhoid and hepatitis are also transmitted through contaminated water. Stool tests are available in Kathmandu and Pokhara. Pharmacies sell all sorts of medicines, generally Indian-made, inexpensively and without prescription.

Prevention is easier than any treatment: avoid untreated water (including ice cubes), raw vegetables and unpeeled fruit. Water needs to be filtered, then boiled to get the bugs out; it's doubtful whether hotels and restaurants take such precautions, so keep to bottled water and soda (though there is no guarantee of bottled water's purity). To purify water, add five or six drops of Lugol's Solution (an iodine solution available in Kathmandu) per litre/quart of water, and let stand 20 minutes before drinking. Avoid food that has been left standing out and unboiled milk.

Be cautious, but not overly so. Paranoia can ruin a trip, and some gastric distress is almost inevitable. When diarrhoea strikes, treat with lots of liquid (no caffeine or alcohol) and a reduced diet of mild foods (rice, bananas, dry toast). If symptoms are severe or the condition does not improve after a few days, consult a doctor.

Respiratory ailments are a close second in common complaints, aggravated by Kathmandu's dust and pollution, and the cold, dry air of the mountains. 'Trekker's hack' has kept many up at night—and not just the sufferer.

For medical care visit the American-run CIWEC Clinic off the road to the Yak & Yeti (tel 228 531) or the Nepal International Clinic across from the Royal Palace (tel 412 842). Both provide 24-hour emergency service. Kathmandu's hospitals are crowded and basic. Patan Hospital in Lagankhel (tel 522 278) and the Teaching Hospital in Maharajganj (tel 412 303) are the best of the lot, which isn't saying much. Medical facilities in the countryside are even poorer, though Khumbu and Manang have Trekker's Aid health posts run by the Himalayan Rescue Association and staffed by foreign doctors in season. Trekkers must be prepared to doctor themselves. In emergencies you can hope for a helicopter rescue—at US$600 an hour, a good reason to arrange for comprehensive trip insurance before departure.

Altitude sickness, more specifically Acute Mountain Sickness or AMS, is the bane of trekkers. It can strike as low as 2,500 metres (7,500 feet) and is quite common above 3,000 metres (9,000 feet). Perhaps 75 percent of all trekkers experience mild symptoms of AMS: headache, restless sleep, swelling of the face and extremities, breathing irregularities, loss of appetite and drowsiness. In 2 percent of cases these develop into something more serious, generally pulmonary or cerebral oedema, which can end in death if ignored. Age and physical condition are no predictor of altitude sickness: Olympic athletes have died of it, while 75-year-old grandmothers have waltzed over the Thorung La.

Gradual ascent is necessary to guard against AMS; no more than 300 metres (900 feet) a day is a good rule, with strategic rest days built into the schedule. If symptoms persist, stay put for a day or two; if they worsen, the only treatment is immediate descent. Drink plenty of liquids to counteract the dehydration which occurs at high altitude and rest often. Avoid alcohol and sedatives. Acetazolamide (Diamox) is sometimes prescribed for altitude but should be taken with caution as it may simply mask the warning signs of AMS.

Conduct and Customs

—Improper dressing is probably the most significant and visible *faux pas* committed by visitors. Modesty applies to men as well as women, but women should be especially careful to cover the upper arms and legs and avoid tight or revealing clothing.
—When entering homes, shoes are usually left at the door. The same applies to temples and monasteries, especially if the shoes are leather ones. Watch what others do.
—Children can become veritable pests in their desire to pose for photographs, but it's polite to seek permission before photographing an adult: by smile and gesture, if not verbally.
—Don't sit or stand on statues, *chortens*, *chaityas*, prayer walls or any vaguely religious object.
—You may be subjected to a rapid barrage of questions on personal subjects: Are you married? How many children? Why not? What do you do? How much money do you make? (Sometimes this concludes with 'Will you help me go to your country?') This is not considered rude, but if you feel it is you can change the subject, or start questioning the questioner.
—Among the Hindu castes, cooked food is a primary vehicle for ritual contamination. Any food or utensil that touches the lips is *juto*, ritually impure, and should not be given to anyone else. Empty glasses and dishes should be placed on the ground, away from cooked food.

—The left hand, traditionally used to clean after defecation, is also ritually impure. Present objects or money with your right hand, or as a special mark of respect, with both hands.

—Drinking *chang* or butter tea in a Sherpa home is a ritual in which a guest's glass is refilled (or at least topped up) at least three times in the course of the first few minutes. Pace yourself and allow the server to do his or her duty.

—Body language can be confusing. Bobbing the head from side to side signals agreement, not 'no'; and when a Nepali waves 'come' it looks as if he's saying 'go'. Pointing with the finger is impolite; villagers use their chins to point.

—Physical contact between the sexes, even hand-holding, is frowned upon in public, but it's perfectly all right between members of the same sex.

—Nepalis are an intensely social people, and interactions are fed by a desire to avoid confrontation and to please. Phrases like 'So, the tickets will be ready tomorrow' or 'Is the village near?' will invariably evoke a 'yes'. Anticipate this when formulating questions and try not to build in a ready-made answer.

—As in most of Asia, time is a malleable concept, and promptness is a relative thing. *Bholi*—tomorrow—is the Nepalese equivalent of *mañana*, conveying the time when something will be completed. This charmingly, relaxed approach can be infuriating if you are waiting for something urgent. Keep cool, maintain steady but polite pressure, and check frequently.

—Confrontation and aggression are avoided at all costs, and people will go to great lengths to save face and not push an issue or a person to the wall. Polite persistence may clarify a situation, but aggression will not.

—Kathmandu's numerous and hardworking street hustlers are a challenge to deal with. If you're too polite they won't ever go away. Try to minimize interaction, and calmly make it clear you're not interested in the object they're shoving in your face.

—It's good to donate a few rupees to genuine beggars: religious mendicants, wandering minstrels (*gainey*), or the blind, crippled, or ill. Beggars who harass are a different category, as are begging children. Many of them are quite well off, and play 'one rupee, one pen, one chocolate' as a game. The popular trekking trails have become a steady stream of importuning kids created by previous trekkers: don't add to the problem. There are plenty of ways of interacting without handouts.

Theft and Safety

Common sense is all that is necessary: be discreet with money, and keep valuables, including passport and airline tickets, out of sight and in a safe place (larger hotels have safes). Minimize the money you carry with you, or carry it in a money-belt next to your body (inside clothing) and have change handy for minor purchases to avoid displaying the entire bank. Pickpockets are a problem, especially in crowded places like buses, bazaars and festivals. Never carry money in your back pocket or in an open bag. The Interpol Unit at the Hanuman Dhoka Police Station deals with thefts from tourists.

Women travellers can feel quite safe, though verbal harassment and the occasional grope is increasing in Kathmandu. Trekking alone is not recommended for either men or women for several reasons: first is the potential for problems which accompany any walk through mountains; a distant second is the possibility of robbery. Trekkers should register with their embassy before departure and provide details about their route and anticipated date of return. They should also report back to their embassy on their return.

Food and Drink

The national dish is *dal bhat*, boiled rice (*bhat*) topped with a sauce of lentils (*dal*) and served with curried vegetables (*tarkari* or *subji*), seasoned with a dab of spicy pickled vegetable (*achar*). This meal is eaten morning and evening with monotonous regularity by all who can afford it. Rice is expensive in the unirrigated higher hills, where the staple is *dhiro*, a pasty boiled mush of millet or corn. Up in the mountains, cuisine turns Tibetan and *tsampa* holds sway. This roasted barley flour can be mixed with tea and eaten without further cooking, convenient in a fuel-scarce region. The Sherpas of Khumbu live on exceptionally tasty high-altitude potatoes. Trekkers here should sample *rigi koor*, crisp potato pancakes served with yak butter, chillies and deliciously creamy yak-milk yoghurt.

The two main meals are taken around 10 am and just after sunset. Gaps are filled in by snacks: unleavened bread, ranging from the fried rice-flour rings of *sel roti* to flat Indian *chapati*; rice in a multiplicity of forms, small dishes of curried vegetables and fried meat, and crisp roasted corn or soyabeans. City shops purvey intensely sugary Indian sweetmeats, most based on boiled milk, some decorated with fine edible paper of pure hammered silver. All is washed down with *chiya*, an invigorating potion of low-grade dust tea brewed with milk and sugar that serves as the national motivator.

Though simple, Nepali food is tasty and functional, especially when trekking has worked up a gargantuan appetite. Cooks season their food with garlic, onions, fresh ginger and an array of spices, including cumin, turmeric, mustard seed, coriander and chilli. Food is hot but not fiery, but tourist restaurants know by now to leave the chilli out, so specify whether you want the real thing.

Tibetan dishes are a subset of Nepali cuisine. Most popular are *momos*, small steamed dumplings stuffed with minced meat. Fried *momo* (*kothey*) are even tastier. *Thukpa* or noodle soup is another favourite, though the traditional version has been supplanted by packaged instant noodles.

Home-brewed liquor is available everywhere, and although sanitation is dubious, home-made *rakshi* or grain alcohol is preferable to commercial bottled liquor from the point of view of flavour, as well as the purity of the ensuing hangover. Bars at major hotels serve imported spirits, and Kathmandu boasts five brands of locally produced beer, the best being Tuborg and San Miguel. Traditional beer, a refreshing brew made from rice, millet or barley, is called *jand* in Nepali, *chang* in Tibetan. A variation on this theme is *tongba*, fermented mash mixed with hot water in a wooden container and sipped with a bamboo straw.

Pitcher of plenty

In Upper Langtang

Having done the honours of the gompa, Nima Lama asked us to his house where his wife made us welcome with fresh buckwheat cakes and a relish of pounded chilies and salt. Tea, of course, was provided for all, but Nima and I devoted our attention to a wooden bottle of undeniable five-star arak *conveniently placed between us. The tea, made in Tibetan fashion with butter, came fresh from the churn, a three-foot long piece of bamboo of nine-inch bore which the operator held upright on the floor by means of a thong attached at the base in which she put her foot. The salty relish provoked a thirst which, thanks to Providence and Nima's foresight, we had the means of assuaging. Presently a second bottle replaced the first and the flood of miscellaneous information offered by Nima Lama and interpreted by the lieutenant, who wisely drank tea, seemed to be getting a little turbid; or perhaps the lama was lucid enough but my attention, distracted by the buckwheat cakes, did not strictly correlate the miscellaneous facts—the butter, saints, salt, red pheasants, straying yaks, ancient passes, Abominable Snowmen, bears, and the price of umbrellas in Kathmandu. I managed to grasp his fairly lucid exposition of the trade cycle which began by sending butter to Kyirong where it was exchanged pound for pound with salt; the salt then being carried over the Ganja La to Helmu to be exchanged for rice, which rice was taken to Kyirong*

during the winter, when butter was scarce. But then, I recall Nima began to relate an anecdote of how he had been the last man to cross the traditional pass in 1854 just before it was closed, accompanied by the now canonized Guru Rumbruche, then a very old man, carrying a load of salted rice done up in butter which they were going to exchange for twenty-five umbrellas at Kyirong. On the pass they met an Abominable Snowman riding the missing yak, which thereupon turned into a red pheasant which Guru Rumbruche shot with a catapult, thus incurring a fine of Rs100—and if I cared to pay the fine I could have the pheasant, the very bird I had just been admiring in the gompa.

At this point Mrs Nima Lama removed the arak bottle and reminded her huband that he was due to start for a minor celebration in honour of one Gombu at a sacred rock a day's march up the valley. Preparations for this had been in active progress for a little time; that is to say six long baskets, built for back-packing, were being loaded with a few pitiful parcels of atta and some immense wooden jorums of beer—one half-pennyworth of bread, in fact, to an intolerable deal of sack. In turn the bearers of this precious freight bowed low to present a plateful of grain and a pat of butter to the Rev. Nima Lama, who sat with immense but slightly swaying dignity, and gave each a perfunctory blessing by clapping on their bowed heads three small pieces of butter. Greatly affected by this solemn scene the lieutenant and I bowed too, and withdrew swiftly with unbuttered heads.

H.W. Tilman, Nepal Himalaya, 1952

Shopping

Nepal offers an abundance of unique goods. The sheer quantity of prayer wheels, statues, *thangkas*, ornate *khukris* and jewellery is overwhelming. Don't be fooled by claims of antiquity: most of it is mass-produced in tiny workshops around Kathmandu. Which is not to say don't buy it—that silver-inlaid goat skull will look wonderful when you get it home; just don't pay antique prices. Shop in the Kathmandu Valley: there is little of note elsewhere, and prices increase with altitude along popular trekking routes.

Thamel shops are bursting with Indian goods: Kashmiri papier mâché, gilded filagree statues, sandalwood carvings, silk paintings, embroidered hangings. Kathmandu is a good place to buy Tibetan and Bhutanese goods as access to these remote Himalayan areas is restricted, and products tend to be genuine rather than mass-produced souvenirs. Beware of Nepal-made 'Tibetan' souvenirs: bracelets inscribed with OM MANI PADME HUM in Nepali script, and blocks of wood carved with crypto-Tibetan gibberish.

Restrain early purchases until you've had a chance to differentiate between the unique and the commonplace, and get a feel for prices. The asking price for identical items can vary by 300 percent, making it pay to shop around. Bargaining is essential when buying tourist-oriented goods. It is a social interaction structured by subtle rules, a leisurely process meant to be a friendly yet strategic game. Often merchants will ask *you* to state the price, hoping you'll offer some incredible amount. Decide in advance the maximum you're willing to pay for an object, then make an offer several increments below it. Work up slowly, and once you get to the last price, stick to it. If the deal founders, try a smile, shrug and a slow stroll out the door. If you're close, the seller will call you back; if not, you can always return.

Oil lamp

Carpets

Rs20,000–30,000 is not unusual for an old Tibetan carpet in good condition; an exceptionally fine 3' × 6' can fetch US$2,500. The best places to shop are Boudhanath, Jawalakhel, and Durbar Marg, which has stacks of exquisite (and expensive) old carpets.

New carpets are very reasonably priced. When shopping for new rugs, examine the wool, dye and number of knots per square inch. Handspun Tibetan wool is the best, but most carpets blend Tibetan wool with cheaper New Zealand wool. Look for as high a percentage of Tibetan wool as possible. Natural vegetable dyes and quality chemical dyes are both acceptable. The average rug has 40–60 knots per square inch, up to 100 for top-quality carpets.

The best place to look for new carpets is in the shops clustered around the old Tibetan refugee camp in Jawalakhel. Prices are determined by size, and vary according to quality and the number of knots per square inch. To see weavers at work, step into the cavernous hall of the Tibetan Refugee Handicraft Centre, where singing women seated before huge upright looms swiftly knot the yarn around a gauge rod and tamp it down with wooden mallets.

Statues

Metal images of Buddhist and, to a lesser extent, Hindu deities have been produced by the craftsmen of Patan for over one thousand years, using the ancient technique of *cire perdue* or 'lost wax' casting once practised across the Indian subcontinent. The molten metal, either brass or bronze, is poured into a clay mould and left to cool. The rough metal image that emerges is then filed, polished, engraved, and perhaps plated with a thin coat of gold or set with semi-precious stones.

Kathmandu shops are overflowing with statues of deities, most of them painfully clumsy and ill-proportioned. Master artisans still exist, turning out images breathtaking in their precision and detail. Shoppers for Buddhas should look for evidence of technical skill (a smooth finish and deep engraving) as well as aesthetic points (a balanced pose and a pleasing expression). Too often the gods appear to be suffering from indigestion or mental deficiency. The best place to shop is Patan, for here you can combine the hunt with glimpses into the tiny, dark ateliers of Mahaboudha, Thaina and Nag Bahal where the statues are made. Look especially along the street north of Durbar Square, and around Mahaboudha. In Kathmandu try along Ganga Path, and of course Durbar Marg.

Paintings

Old Newari painters produced intricately detailed Tibetan-style *thangkas* and the uniquely Newari *paubhas*. Both are painted on flat scrolls and focus on religious themes, generally Buddhist. *Thangkas* are more stylized, using fine lines and brilliant colours to depict Buddhist deities or the geometric designs called mandala. Traditionally they are framed by bands of contrasting silk or brocade. The lines of *paubha* are more flowing and sensuous, and generally depict a single deity surrounded by a border of richly detailed miniatures.

Tibetan-style *thangkas* dominate the modern market, with dozens of shops in Thamel, Freak Street and Bhaktapur. Quality varies wildly, as do prices, and the two are not necessarily commensurate. Educate your eye with art books before you buy to see the potential of this form, though few modern paintings rival the exquisite precision of antiques. Sadly, few ancient examples of this most portable art remain in Nepal. Museums in Los Angeles or Paris have better exhibits than Kathmandu.

Look for graceful, well-proportioned figures and richly ornamented backgrounds. As in statues, facial expressions are a clear indicator of quality. Squinting or cross-eyed deities do not inspire devotion. Salesmen may try to justify a high price by pointing to the gold paint used on a *thangka*, or claiming it is painted with stone-ground colours. More important than these claims, which may or may not be true, is that the overall composition is pleasing and the proportions of figures harmonious.

Beware of artificially aged *thangkas* smoked over wood fires or bordered with ragged cloth. It is highly unlikely you'll find a genuine antique in a Thamel shop, or along trekking trails for that matter (the villagers of Tarkeghyang, along the Helambu trek, are notorious for the trunkloads of 'family treasures' they sell every year). Exquisite antique *thangkas* are available on Durbar Marg, for a price. Indigo Gallery above Mike's Breakfast in Naxal sells good modern *thangkas*. Crude but charming modern renditions of Newari *paubhas* are produced by a few painters: visit B B Thapa's gallery in Ekantakuna, Jawalakhel.

An inexpensive and colourful alternative to *thangkas* are the vigorous line and tempera paintings of doll-like deities intertwined with flowers and foliage, created by the women of Janakpur in the Terai. These designs are traditionally used in courtship rituals, when women send their betrothed paintings bursting with fertility symbols. Hastakala in Kopundol has a good selection of paintings produced through the Janakpur Women's Art Project.

Tibetan Carpet Primer

It is ironic that a non-indigenous craft, introduced by penniless refugees, should become Nepal's biggest export, principal source of foreign exchange and largest industrial employer. Tibetan carpets have moved far from their traditional origins, evolving into a durable, distinctly modern product. Hand-knotted, of lush, durable wool, in a fascinating array of traditional and modern colours and designs, they are a remarkable value and one of the most popular buys for shoppers visiting Nepal.

Carpets developed out of the wool-rich culture of Tibet: the barren plains of the high Tibetan Plateau are difficult to farm, but sheep and yaks graze on the emptiest expanses. Carpets were eminently practical devices, used to cover beds and sitting benches, never as floor coverings. The finest pieces were used to decorate lama's thrones.

Old traditional carpets are one-of-a-kind, reflecting the individuality of their creators, who drew on a shared stock of designs and colours. Patterns include medallions, elaborate floral designs, and a menagerie of fantastic creatures—dragons, phoenixes, tigers, and turquoise-maned snow lions. Others are geometric: dizzying chequerboards, intricate latticework, 'frog feet' and cruciforms. Tibet's Buddhist orientation appears in the eight auspicious symbols, the lotus and the *dorje*, the thunderbolt symbol of immortality. A more unusual design is the tiger skin, representing the freeing of the ego, and appearing as a flayed skin or in abstracts of subtle stripes. All these are rendered in the brilliant bold colours Tibetans adore.

'Old' in the context of Tibetan carpets is not that old: most traditional carpets date from this century. The term refers to style rather than age, and encompasses everything pre-1959. Today Kathmandu is an international headqarters for the Tibetan rug trade, old and new. Old rugs make their way into Nepal via pilgrims or private sellers, or are smuggled in by antique dealers well aware of the high prices their pieces will fetch in the world market.

The Tibetan carpet entered the modern world with the influx of refugees fleeing the 1959 Chinese crackdown in Tibet. At the Jawalakhel Handicraft Centre, founded with Swiss assistance, master-weavers from the Tibetan town of Gyangtse taught the craft to others. The Swiss emphasized the use of handspun yarn and quality dyes for a uniform appearance. Slowly, the modern Tibetan carpet, or rather the Tibeto-Nepali carpet, was born.

Modern carpets are woven using traditional techniques, but designs have been adapted to the demands of the European marketplace. It's difficult to recognize any connection between the brilliant, bold traditional carpets and the subtly patterned pastels of new ones. Virtually the only common link that remains is the compound border, using the 'key' or 'thunder' pattern found across Asia, or designs interpreted as clouds, waves or mountains. Western decorators want rugs to harmonize with existing furnishings; thus there is a demand for muted pastels and natural wool, though a few bright-hued abstracts are being woven, some according to computer-generated patterns.

The old tradition of vegetal dying relies on rhubarb for yellow and gold, lac (from the dried egg sacs of insects) for magenta and pink, madder for red, tea for brown, and indigo (mixed with urine, and the most dificult of all to stabilize) for blue. A tremendous range of hues can be produced from each substance, depending on preparation, and while vegetal dying is a more complex and volatile process, it yields richer and more subtly varied hues than chemical dyes. The latter were introduced in Tibet in the late 19th century through India and were quickly adopted. Most traditional carpets on the market, as well as most new ones, are chemically dyed, regardless of what the dealer says. Mystique aside, there is little obvious difference, though vegetal dyes are less stable and can fade in sunlight.

High-quality wool is the Tibetan carpet's principal selling point. The Tibetan aboriginal sheep produces a superbly lustrous, resiliant wool ideal for carpets. Most of it is brought down from Western Tibet, packed onto the backs of sheep or goats—and the unstable supply means most carpets are a mix of Tibetan and New Zealand wool. Theoretically the proportions are 50-50, but often the percentage of cheaper, cleaner New Zealand wool is increased. The wool is generally handspun, creating a varied texture that contributes to the carpets' unique appearance, though machine spinning is becoming more common in Nepal.

The yarn is then hand-knotted onto a large upright loom strung with a cotton warp. The knot density averages 40-60 knots per square inch, low when compared to other Asian carpets. The use of the senna loop, dating back to ancient Egypt, allows intricate patterns even with this low count

Few weavers are Tibetans nowadays. Many are Tamangs from the hills surrounding the Valley, drawn by the rare opportunity of wage employment. They sit cross-legged before looms, swiftly knotting according to a pattern sketched out on graph paper, then tamping down each row with a wooden mallet. Weavers are paid by the amount they produce: it takes 120 hours to weave a 1.6-square-metre carpet.

The finished carpet is clipped to emphasize the contours of the pattern, then chemically washed—a recent innovation which has been blamed for contributing to water pollution in the Kathmandu Valley. (Perhaps more serious is the amount of scarce water consumed in the carpet washing process). The carpet industry has also been criticized for employing child labour, though the term is difficult to define in Nepal, where a carefree childhood ends by the age of six and girls are married, and often mothers themselves, by the time they are sixteen. What is certain is that the carpet industry directly employs some 18,000 workers, most of them otherwise unskilled women. By some estimates, 250,000 people are directly and indirectly involved in the business.

Other problems are quality control and how to avoid market saturation and over-production. Of late it appears that every other new building going up in the Valley is a carpet factory. Exports have more than quadrupled since 1986-7, to 2.3 million square metres in 1991-2. About half of all exports are to Germany, with another 40 percent going to the UK and Switzerland.

Woodcarving

Woodcarving is another art which the Newars raised to dazzling heights, and one that has suffered in translation into souvenirs. The delicate wooden lace adorning the Valley's old houses and temples is justifiably famous. Dozens of pieces are skilfully fitted together to form a single window or *torana*. Window grills of interlocking strips are particularly lovely, with a near-infinite variety of patterns, and door jambs, lintels, brackets, frames, entablatures and pillars are all carved with lavish motifs. Most dramatic are the figures of deities carved onto the slanting roof struts supporting the pagoda's stacked roofs. Small vignettes below display scenes of daily life, and the notorious erotic carvings beloved of tour guides.

Unless you plan to ship home an entire old window or doorframe, there is little of superior quality available. Woodcarvers make adequate small statues of deities, toys, picture frames, jewellery boxes, miniature struts and windows, and some beautifully carved rocking horses. Tachapal Square in Bhaktapur is a good place to shop.

Potters' Square, Bhaktapur

Jewellery

While Kathmandu is not a major gem-buying centre, it offers bargains in semi-precious gems and worked silver. Indigenous stones like tourmaline, garnet and aquamarine are medium quality and cheap. Imported stones include lapis lazuli and smooth green malachite from Afghanistan, and huge chunks of turquoise and coral favoured by Tibetans. Imitations of all exist, so shop carefully. The best places are Thamel and New Road, or the stores around Boudhanath for turquoise.

Gold and silver jewellery is sold by the *tola*, approximately 11 grams. The price, set by the government, is no bargain, but the fine workmanship is virtually free. Nepalis themselves view jewellery as an investment as much as adornment, and prefer soft 24-karat gold. Silver is very good value. Delicate filagree work, deep-carved designs and etching are performed by jewellers who anchor the piece with their toes. Jewellery shops sell hollow silver beads by weight and string them into necklaces. Shop in Thamel, or seek out one of the tiny dark cubbyholes scattered throughout the old city.

The bead bazaar or *potey pasal* behind Indra Chowk displays shimmering strands of tiny glass beads in all the colours of the rainbow. Married Hindu women wear them in necklaces set with a ridged golden cylinder. Most of the merchants here are Muslim, descendents of 18th-century vendors invited into Nepal to sell their wares. The necklaces, bracelets, belts and earrings are inexpensive and easy to carry, and make wonderful gifts. You can buy ready-made or custom-order colour combinations.

Clothing

Cheap cotton skirts, trousers and shirts are widely available in Thamel. They are not particularly durable but will extend your wardrobe for the length of the trip or trek. Knitted sweaters are another popular item, but don't be fooled by salesmen insisting they're made of yak wool. Again, they are inexpensive and useful but wool quality is often poor and they have a tendency to develop huge holes once you've staggered home with them. Handicraft shops have the best quality sweaters.

Thamel shops are stocked with T-shirts embroidered with flaming dragons or baleful Buddha eyes. Some proclaim 'No Rupees. No Change Money. No Hash. No Problem'. They would be worth the purchase if they did indeed deter hustlers. Boutiques on Durbar Marg offer more stylish and expensive garments: Mandala specializes in handpainted silks; Wheels in creatively used local materials, including raw silk and *dhaka* cloth.

Women visitors may wish to try local wear, like the Tibetan style *chuba*, a long sleeveless dress that ties at the waist. It is available around Boudhanath and nicest in raw silk. The two-piece *shalwar kameej* is a comfortable, practical outfit consisting of baggy drawstring pants, tight at the ankle, topped by a knee-length shirt. It comes in bright embroidered cottons or silk in a variety of styles. The ready-made ones tend to be gaudy, but a local tailor can sew one up from material of your choice in a day or two.

Pashmina, made from the silky inner fleece of the Himalayan sheep or goat and similar to cashmere, is made into cloud-light, warm shawls and scarves. Shop carefully around Indra Chowk (beware of acrylic), or visit Everest Pashmina in Gyaneshwar. Nepalese Silk Products in the Balaju Industrial Estate has *pashmina* in an array of gorgeous colours.

Bhutanese Textiles

Since the tiny Himalayan kingdom of Bhutan admits only a few thousand tourists a year, Kathmandu is a major marketplace for Bhutan's unique hand-embroidered textiles. Originally worn as garments, these rectangular pieces make wonderful wall hangings and bedcovers. The more expensive older pieces are usually dark blue or white, embroidered with handspun raw silk thread in natural shades of black, blue and red. Newer pieces are embroidered with chemically dyed acrylic thread in a rainbow of colours. Shop at Zambala and Dragon Boutique Corner in Thamel, or the stores around Boudhanath.

Antiques

Most of the interesting antiques are Tibetan: ritual artifacts, jewellery, *chang* cups and copper teapots, carpets, painted wooden chests, *thangkas* and embroideries. The best and most expensive shops are along Durbar Marg, where shopping resembles browsing through a museum, with serene deities and ancient *thangkas* all around. The statues here are generally new, but exquisite. Karma Lama's Ritual Art Gallery and Mohan's Curio Arts are among the best. Shopkeepers keep their finest wares in a back room and bring them out only for discerning buyers. Prices are no bargain, but the goods are top quality.

The Department of Archaeology requires that all *thangkas*, statues, old carpets and antiques be checked for historic value before being taken out of the country. There is a ban on exporting items over 100 years old. To avoid problems, get a certificate of approval from the Department of Archeology on Ram Shah Path in the National Archives Building, a little south of Singha Durbar.

Miscellany

Some of the most attractive items are simple, traditional brass household utensils: polished plates, vessels for water and *rakshi*, old grain measures, and ritual articles like incense burners and elaborate little oil lamps (*sukunda*). Chainpur Brass in Kopundol sells old brass, but cheaper and more fun is the cluster of shops in Bhaktapur's main bazaar, just past Taumadhi Tol at the beginning of the bazaar.

Handwoven cloth, once commonplace, has virtually disappeared before an onslaught of cheap machine-made cotton. You can still find the black, red-bordered *hakuwa patasi* worn by Newari peasant women, the red and black block-printed cotton used for shawls and blouses, and colourful geometric *dhaka*, used in making the national hat, the topi. Thick, brilliantly coloured Nepalese silk is occasionally available. Handwoven woollen blankets worn by the Bhotia women of northern Nepal are often impregnated with the smell of yak butter and wood-smoke. They are dyed in natural hues and woven in traditional patterns according to region.

A souvenir guaranteed to impress is the *khukri*, the curved knife wielded by the stalwart Gurkhas. While elaborately decorated versions are sold on the tourist market, the real article is simple, unembellished and wicked, kept in a wooden sheath. It can sharpen a pencil or lop off a goat's head with equal ease. And of course there's Khukri brand rum, in a *khukri*-shaped bottle.

Smaller suitcase-stuffers include Tibetan incense and prayer flags (look around Boudhanath), small clay figures from Potter's Square in Bhaktapur, masks and puppets modelled on ritual dancers, and charming rag dolls in Nepalese dress. For a wide array of inexpensive goods visit handicraft shops, which have low fixed prices for colourful cushion covers, block-printed fabric, whimsical wooden toys (including authentically gaudy renditions of Tata trucks), sweaters, clothing, brass and pottery. There are at least half a dozen on the Kopundol road on the way to Patan: Dhukuti and Hastakala are particularly worth a stop. A cut above in terms of both price and quality is Pasal on Durbar Marg, which showcases handicrafts from India.

Shopping for Buddhas

I embarked upon these adventures in shopping in the company of Nancy, the friend with whom I had recently travelled in Tibet. Known for her infectiously buoyant personality, Nancy had recently joined the ranks of the walking wounded. She had fallen in love (or 'merged', to use her favored phrase) with an exquisite statue of the goddess Tara. The Tara had been one-of-a-kind, breathtakingly beautiful, but a bit beyond her means. Nancy had deliberated and, all but convinced, decided to sleep on it. Unfortunately, a somewhat more experienced buyer entered the shop a few moments after she left. Nancy rushed back first thing the next morning, bristling with those natural amphetamines that permeate the bloodstream just before a large and important purchase—only to discover that her Tara had just been given a one-way ticket to Dusseldorf.

This crushing disappointment coloured to an alarming extent the way that Nancy and I went about our rounds. There was a need for non-attachment, to be sure; but also a prerequisite of knife-like resolve. It was as if, here in this distant, exotic land, we were compelled to raise the art of shopping to an experience that was, on the one hand, detached and almost Zen—our ultimate goal was, after all, enlightenment—and on the other hand, tinged with desperation, like shopping at Macy's or Bloomingdale's during a one-day-only White Sale: viciously predatory, and laced with the fear that the choicest Buddhas would be gone, snatched up if we hesitated too long, or neglected to visit each and every shop the very day that new work was due to arrive. Because in spite of deceptively vast quantities of statues displayed in the windows and on tattered blankets covering the sidewalks outside of the major hotels, most are chintzy rubbish; the ill-conceived abominations of a tourist trap industry!

Some archetypes! If these were real humanoids, they'd be barred from military service: club-footed, triple-jointed, bug-eyed, eleven-toed, elephant-eared abominations with monkey-long limbs ending in pawlike appendages, with bronze or copper flashing festering like mould under the armpits: the kind of thing you wouldn't even want to use as a paperweight. Some were so ill proportioned, they flew so hard in the face of anatomy, that I had to wonder if the artists had even seen a human being before. The statues reminded me of those old European drawings of elephants and rhinoceroses, based on distant sightings or wild rumour.

And then there were the copies. Back in 1984, when I was shopping for my first Ganesh, I found a very handsome one copied from a statue in the National Museum. By now, though, all those first-generation duplicates had ben sold. The copies made from the copies were also gone; as were the copies made from the copies made from the copies. And with each consecutive recasting, you can be very sure that something had been lost in the translation.

For example: imagine taking an original Rembrandt drawing, and photocopying it on a primitive machine. You now put the flawed copy back on the glass, copy that, and repeat the whole process another three or four times. Come the fifth generation, you're holding something that looks more like a Franz Kline than a Dutch Master. Likewise, by the time Nancy and I encountered them, the 1987 model Buddhas were little more than crude lumps of bronze heaped into vaguely recognizable postures. Their feet and fingers exhibited the terminal stage of leprosy while the faces—those all important,

Detail, Swayambhunath Stupa

so-serene Buddha faces—looked like they'd just gone twelve rounds with Jake LaMotta.

But I'm making it all sound like a hopeless quest, and that's nowhere near the truth. Because every so often, in one of maybe three or four very exclusive shops—and not in the front foyer, but concealed in musty back rooms—we would discover a statue that made me sigh with a feline growl of primal longing. These were statues that crossed the Pygmalion line and seemed fully infused with life. Half-closed eyes, perfectly centred, and just a hair downcast; the corners of the mouth curving up, so, so subtly, into what might be a smile. That smile is more than an invitation; it's the whole party.

Those statues are few and far between, hidden in drawers and cupboards, wrapped in rice paper and string, but always outlandishly expensive, and reserved for some Japanese or German buyer. We were lucky enough to even see them; the mere knowledge that these statues existed, that the Nepalis still created objects with this much grace and power, was a truth reserved only for the most persistent, impulsive collectors; people who would kill for a really good Buddha.

And so it got to the point where we shopped with consummate single-mindedness of purpose. We would look only at the best. Often we would enter a shop and, barely glancing at the inferior products on the shelves, demand instantly to be taken into the back room to see the newest, the latest, the most expensive work. We were the élite; the ones who knew the veins and arteries of the business. We were connoisseurs of Buddhas, of Taras, of Manjushris; and we begged not to be insulted by clumsy or sloppy workmanship.

And here I beheld the first of many twisted Zen truths pretzelled throughout this crazy koan called Shopping for Buddhas: only through the yoga of true pushiness, only by being relentlessly pushy in the most charming possible way, would I ever find the prize that I was seeking: a Buddha that really said something; or, a Buddha that really said nothing—and said it loudly enough for me to hear.

Jeff Greenwald, Shopping for Buddhas, *1990*

PLACES TO VISIT

The Kathmandu Valley

Cresting a low range of hills, which runs along the valley, we at length came in sight of Katmandoo. This is another most remarkable view, and a very beautiful one. A picturesque quaint-looking temple, and a cluster of red wide-eaved houses, profusely adorned with carved woodwork, form a pretty foreground; in the plain below is a broad river, on the opposite bank of which stands the town, with its numberless Chinese-looking temples, the brasswork with which they are ornamented glittering in the sun...

[*Francis Egerton*, Journal of a Winter's Tour in India: with a Visit to the Court of Nepaul, *1852.*]

Swooping down upon the Kathmandu Valley in a plane one sees the Valley as the gods must see it, floating disembodied in the air. It is a riveting panorama: a fertile green bowl, cut by the shimmering tracks of sacred rivers, set with the geometric patterning of fields and punctuated by Swayambhunath's golden spire and the stacked roofs of pagodas. The compact row houses of Newari villages spread out below as clearly as a map. Matchbox houses and tiny trees dot the patchwork fields, and tiered terraces of green and gold rise up the steep sides of the encircling hills. Beyond, blue hills fold off into the hazy distance, an ocean of frozen land lapping against the Valley rim. They climb up to the Himalaya: shockingly, unnaturally high mountains towering on the northern horizon like a stage set propped up to delight the eye.

The Kathmandu Valley is an unexpected oasis, a green oval nestling beneath the highest mountains on earth. Measuring 24 kilometres east to west, 19 kilometres north to south (12 by 15 miles), it is small enough to walk across in a single day. Yet within its confines are thousands of monuments, shrines, temples, stupas and palaces, including seven UNESCO World Heritage Sites, the densest such concentration anywhere on earth. The Valley is not simply a showcase of old art and architecture, but a living, vibrant entity, nourished by old traditions and customs which continue, miraculously, to this day.

Traditionally it was an assortment of city–states ruling over smaller villages, and the three old kingdoms of Kathmandu, Patan and Bhaktapur remain Nepal's main attraction, apart from the incredibly high mountains.

Even today, 60 percent of the Valley is countryside, most of it intensively farmed by traditional methods. The rural ambience creeps into the city, as flocks of ducks waddle across the central Tundikhel, recalcitrant goats are dragged across crowded streets, and sacred cows amble amidst urban gridlock.

The Valley is the traditional homeland of the Newari people. They have left their mark everywhere, in its well-tilled fields and magnificent art and architecture. The Newars are an urban people at heart, and their highly developed sense of aesthetics is apparent in the intensely organized environments of the old towns, where public and private space blend to harmoniously support one of the highest population densities in the world.

The old cities are vertically-oriented human warehouses, people piled upon people in tiny rooms. A single two-storey home might shelter 30 family members spanning four generations. The thick-walled houses of reddish baked brick stay warm in winter, cool in summer. They are decorated with finely detailed woodcarvings, the distinguishing mark of Newari architecture. In the cities the houses are three or four storeys high, and are joined together in solid rows, punctuated at intervals by open squares housing temples, water taps and sunken baths.

Urban layout reveals the ancient concept of city as mandala (sacred diagram). Towns are organized as reflections of the universe, sanctifying and ordering daily life within them. At the centre of town—the symbolic if not actual centre—stands the old royal palace, surrounded by a panoply of shrines and temples. These Durbar Squares form the main attraction of each city, and because they were created over the centuries by kings competing to produce the most magnificent assemblage, there are certain similarities. Each has its gilded statue of a great king kneeling on top of a pillar, its elaborately carved royal bath, its richly decorated temples to the Malla patron goddess Taleju.

Communities are arranged around this central core according to social status, with the highest castes living closest to the sacred centre and the lowest on the peripheries. The outskirts of town are bordered by the shrines of fierce, protective deities. This urban townscape is the product of a rich and highly developed traditional culture. The old system worked: even if it didn't always meet Western standards of material wealth and social equality, it was well-integrated and stable, tested and refined over centuries of communal living.

Kathmandu Valley

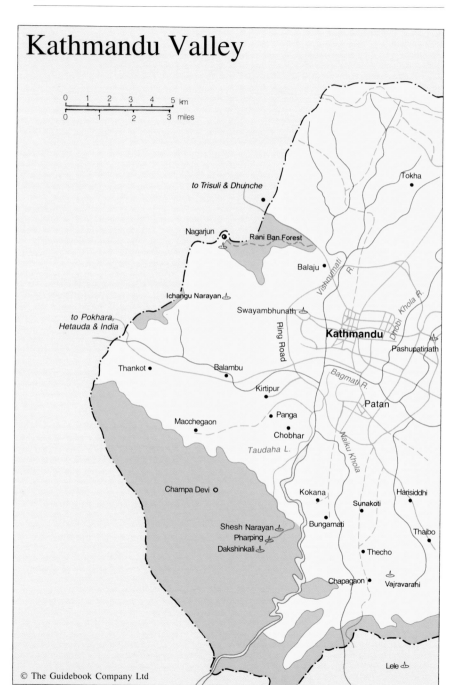

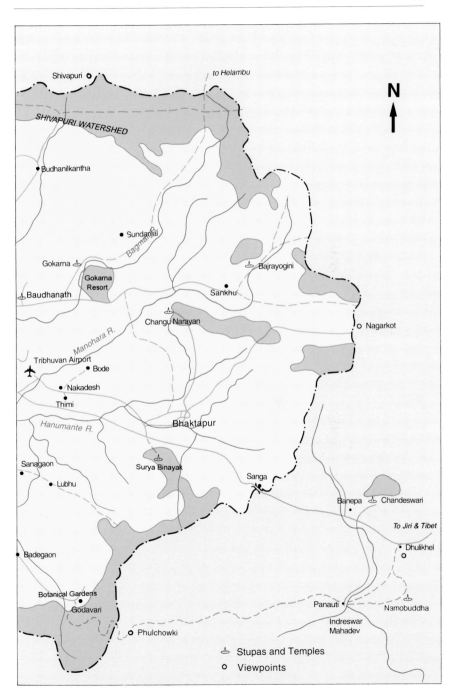

Shivapuri

to Helambu

N

SHIVAPURI WATERSHED

Budhanilkantha

Sundarijal

Bagmati

Gokarna

Bajrayogini

Gokarna
Resort

Baudhanath

Sankhu

Changu Narayan

Manohara R.

Nagarkot

Tribhuvan Airport

Bode

Nakadesh

Thimi

Hanumante R.

Bhaktapur

Sanagaon

Surya Binayak

Lubhu

Sanga

Banepa   Chandeswari

To Jiri & Tibet

Badegaon

Dhulikhel

Botanical Gardens

Godavari

Panauti

Namobuddha

Phulchowki

Indreswar
Mahadev

⚑ Stupas and Temples

o Viewpoints

Modern Times

The Valley's unique culture remained practically untouched up to the end of Rana rule in the early 1950s, the sum total of 1,500 years of continuous cultural development. Even the Gorkha invasion caused little disruption: the conquerers were simply absorbed into the ancient system. But 20th-century technology and values have been more successful in undermining ancient cultural traditions.

Rising expectations and increasing modernization have supported a flood of immigrants into the Valley, who overstrain already under-funded public services such as electricity supply and garbage collection. Clean drinking water and adequate sewage disposal remain a dream, and air pollution has become a most unpleasant reality in Kathmandu. Chaotic traffic blocks the streets, and is doing more than anything else to destroy the once leisurely pace of life.

The outward manifestation of this cultural erosion appears in the crumbling *pati*, perilously leaning old homes, and decrepit temples with skeletal roofs visible everywhere. The old tradition of maintaining public buildings to earn religious merit is dying away, and there is simply too much for the already besieged Department of Archaeology to preserve single-handed. Foreign donors have stepped in to save the most spectacular temples and palaces, and the US-based Kathmandu Valley Preservation Trust is active in restoration work, especially in Patan, but essential local support has been seriously weakened, especially with the nationalization of the *guthi*, the communal Newari associations traditionally responsible for temple upkeep.

Art theft is another threat to the Valley's unique culture. Being an open-air museum has its disadvantages. By some estimates perhaps half Nepal's ancient art has disappeared, most of it in the last 40 years, sold off to collectors, dealers and museums. Torn from their settings and encased behind glass in temperature-controlled galleries, the statues, sculptures and *thangkas* are diminished, robbed of the meaning which gave them life. Townspeople have learned to protect their ancient stone sculptures by cementing them down or caging them behind padlocked metal grilles, but thieves still chisel the images out, sometimes sawing off only the head in grisly dismemberment. Poor documentation, weak law enforcement and the tremendous amount of money involved mean that the smugglers usually get away with it.

More broadly, the old ways are crumbling, replaced by new values in which material acquisition figures high on the agenda. Young Nepalis, already alienated by the miserable job prospects which follow even a college education, find little relevance in seemingly outdated rituals. Their influences are Star TV and Hindi movies; their cultural heroes Michael Jackson and Rambo. Not surprisingly, participation in festivals is becoming more rowdy than religious. Traditional Newari culture has been further diluted by the recent influx of immigrants, weakening the Valley's indigenous customs.

It's difficult to find anyone to blame for the changes assaulting Kathmandu: the process is too vast, too amorphous. Property values are simply too high for owners to resist knocking down old houses and raising multi-storey concrete boxes (and it's doubtful if objecting purists want to actually live in those quaint old thatched-roofed buildings). The green fields that used to extend even into the city are being paved over to produce a new crop of buildings. Farmers earn a tidy profit from the sale of their suddenly valuable land, but they lose their identity and way of life. Urban sprawl punctures the sacred dimensions of the mandala. Kathmandu is already written off as lost, and Patan has begun the same process of change. Bhaktapur remains the most traditional and peaceful of the three old kingdoms, and the old ways linger in the villages dotting the still rural countryside. A way must be found, and quickly, to harmoniously combine development and tradition, because there is no turning back the clock. Regardless of what the future brings, the real miracle is that living examples of an ancient culture have survived into the waning years of the 20th century.

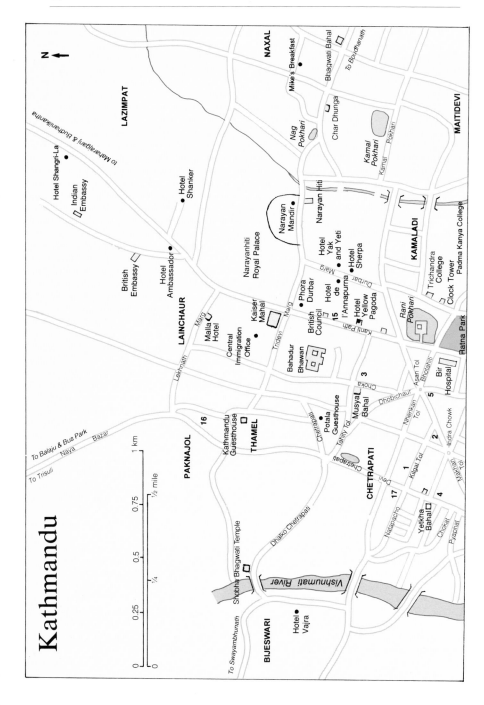

Kathmandu

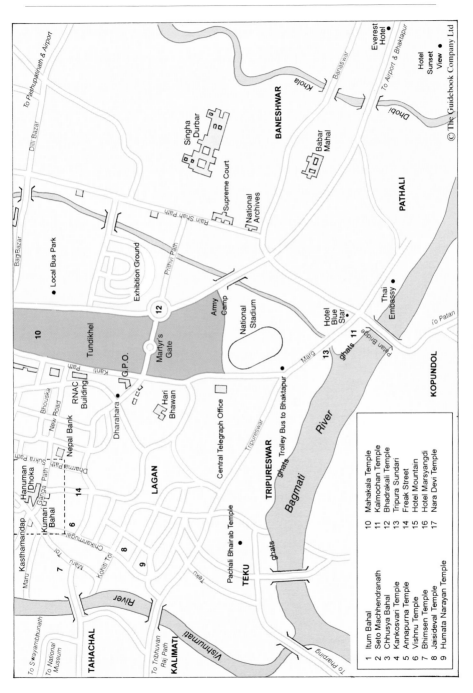

© The Guidebook Company Ltd

1 Itum Bahal
2 Seto Machhendranath
3 Chhusya Bahal
4 Kankosvari Temple
5 Annapurna Temple
6 Vishnu Temple
7 Bhimsen Temple
8 Jaisideval Temple
9 Humata Narayan Temple
10 Mahakala Temple
11 Kalmochan Temple
12 Bhadrakali Temple
13 Tripura Sundari
14 Freak Street
15 Hotel Mountain
16 Hotel Marsyangdi
17 Nara Devi Temple

KATHMANDU

Kathmandu is an upstart youth of a city, brash yet full of growing pains, unsure of its rapidly changing self. The contrast of modern and traditional can be almost painful. Blaring taxi horns mingle with the tinkle of silvery puja bells, as traffic snarls form behind slow-moving porters labouring behind pushcarts. A wisp of incense is followed by a whiff of sewage. Neatly dressed hill women with gigantic earrings of pure gold brush past budget tourists in patchwork cotton. A half-forgotten festival brings forth a procession of old men bearing an ancient image of a goddess on a palanquin. They pass by a group of young men wearing blue jeans and leather jackets. Modernity is careering in, but tradition is putting up stiff resistance. Taxi drivers still touch their foreheads in respect as they cross the crowded bridge over the sacred Bagmati, and passersby reverently brush their hands against the flanks of a wandering sacred cow.

Kathmandu can be overwhelming, even depressing at times, but it can also be astounding. Focus on the compact old city, an area easily covered on foot. All the major sites and many more obscure ones are described here, but beyond these, try simply wandering down narrow lanes in search of the ancient, interesting and hidden. The best sights are those you discover yourself: a procession of cymbal-clanging old men, a neighbourhood *bhoj* or communal feast distributed on leaf plates, a quiet temple courtyard where children play amidst 1,000-year-old *chaityas*. Much is hidden from the public eye, and much has been lost to the ravages of time and modernization. But so much remains that the loss is sometimes scarcely felt.

Orientation

Although Kathmandu is relatively compact, getting around can be confusing. The situation is complicated by a lack of street names and numbers. Only the largest streets are named; other areas are defined by neighbourhood, and it takes a resident to know where Bangemudha Tol ends and Kilgal Tol begins.

The area of Kathmandu most worth exploring lies in a relatively small stretch along the east bank of the Bagmati River. Most tourist hotels are located at the northern end of this area. Budget and mid-range places are headquartered in Thamel, while the more expensive hotels are on Durbar Marg, Kanti Path, or further north in Lazimpat. The interesting areas of town lie south of this, in the compact narrow streets of the old city. Old

Kathmandu extends from Thamel down through the main bazaar to Durbar Square and further south to Tripureswar. Modern businesses are concentrated around New Road and Durbar Marg. Neighbourhoods to the east and west are mainly residential and not worth intensive exploration, though you'll travel through them *en route* to other sites.

Durbar Square

If Kathmandu is the centre of Nepal, Durbar Square is the emotional centre of Kathmandu. All gravitate here, drawn by this forest of temples and shrines erected over the centuries across from the old royal palace. The square contains more than 50 monuments, most from the Malla era, the oldest dating back 900 years.

The old trail to Tibet once began from here, and Durbar Square is still a major crossroad, chronically and sometimes chaotically busy. Taxis and tempos lurch across the flagstones behind porters bent behind rattling pushcarts. Indian vendors brandish poles bristling with bamboo flutes, little girls tenaciously hawk bangles and postcards, and on red-bricked Basantapur Square, the former site of the royal elephant stables, acres of glittering souvenirs are displayed in a magpie paradise.

The focal point of the square is the old durbar or palace, **Hanuman Dhoka**. The site may well date back to Licchavi times, but the present complex is a Malla dynasty creation, expanded and elaborated upon over the centuries. When the Shah kings moved in they enlarged it, but retained the basic Newari style. They moved out in the mid-19th century to a more spacious complex, and King Birendra now lives in the thoroughly modern Narayanhiti Palace at the head of Durbar Marg. The old palace retains its ritual and ceremonial importance, but no self-respecting king would dream of living in its draughty, dim, low-ceilinged rooms.

A century ago the palace was far bigger, with 40 to 50 courtyards. About ten remain today, many closed to the public. The complex still covers over five acres (two hectares), encompassing three centuries of architectural styles, Malla beneath Shah beneath Rana; all knit together by expert Newari craftsmanship.

By the late 1960s the old Durbar was in danger of collapse, centuries of neglect combining with damage from the 1934 earthquake. It was saved in the 1970s by the Hanuman Dhoka Conservation Project, a joint undertaking between the Nepal government, UNDP and UNESCO.

Restoration focused on Lohan Chowk, with its four towers and the elaborate Vilas Mandir. Crumbling structures were dismantled, strengthened, carefully cleaned and reassembled in accordance with the original plan. The intricate woodwork presented a gigantic challenge: over 20,000 pieces in all, fitted together like jigsaw puzzles without a single nail. A single window in Basantapur Tower was made up of over 500 interlocking pieces, which had to be painstakingly disassembled, numbered, carefully cleaned, then fitted back into place. Stripped of centuries of grime and obscuring paint, the original beauty shines through.

The palace entrance is guarded by a near-faceless effigy draped in a red cape and shaded by a royal umbrella. Hanuman the Monkey King, one of the principal figures in the *Ramayana* epic and a favourite patron of Malla kings, lends his name to the nearby gate (*dhoka*) and by extension to the entire palace complex. The thick paste of *sindhur* and mustard oil smeared over his features protects onlookers from his evil eye, which averts smallpox and other disasters.

Behind him is the famed *dhoka* of beaten and gilded metal, flanked by a pair of lions ridden by Shiva and Shakti, and guarded by an impressively uniformed soldier. A Rs10 ticket grants admission to the palace complex (open 10:30–4:15 daily except Tuesday, and closing one hour earlier in the winter, two hours earlier on Friday).

The doorway leads to **Nassal Chowk**, which over the centuries has served as a royal theatre for dance–dramas, a meeting place for the king and his subjects, and more recently, the coronation site of Shah kings. To the left of the entrance is a black marble sculpture of Narasimha, a half-man, half-lion incarnation of Vishnu, depicted disembowelling a hapless demon. The long verandah behind is the former audience chamber of Malla kings, now hung with portraits of the Shah dynasty. An elaborate gilt image of **Maha Vishnu** embracing Lakshmi, retrieved from the rubble of the 1934 earthquake, is displayed in a glass case along one side.

The courtyard is decorated with some of the most splendid woodcarvings in Nepal, especially the magnificent struts adorning the tall **Basantapur Tower** on the southern edge (look for the incredibly tangled erotic scenes on the strut bases). The top floor of the tower yields a vertiginous view of the palace complex and Basantapur Square outside it, with Freak Street running along the side.

Look for the unusual temples crowning the courtyard rooftops: the five-storey round Panch Mukhi Hanuman, and the secret *agam chen* housing the family deity of the Malla kings. The courtyards beyond Mohan Chowk,

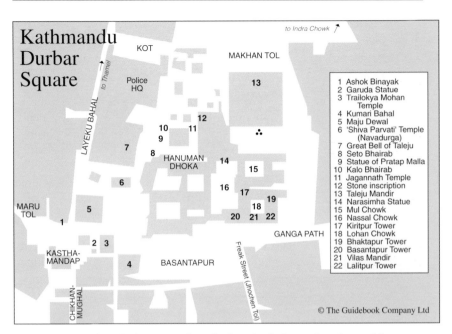

Kathmandu
Durbar
Square

KOT

MAKHAN TOL

to Indra Chowk ↗

to Thamel

Police
HQ

LAYEKU BAHAL

MARU
TOL

KASTHA-
MANDAP

CHIKHAN-
MUGHAL

HANUMAN
DHOKA

BASANTAPUR

Freak Street (Jhochen Tol)

GANGA PATH

1 Ashok Binayak
2 Garuda Statue
3 Trailokya Mohan
   Temple
4 Kumari Bahal
5 Maju Dewal
6 'Shiva Parvati' Temple
   (Navadurga)
7 Great Bell of Taleju
8 Seto Bhairab
9 Statue of Pratap Malla
10 Kalo Bhairab
11 Jagannath Temple
12 Stone inscription
13 Taleju Mandir
14 Narasimha Statue
15 Mul Chowk
16 Nassal Chowk
17 Kiritpur Tower
18 Lohan Chowk
19 Bhaktapur Tower
20 Basantapur Tower
21 Vilas Mandir
22 Lalitpur Tower

© The Guidebook Company Ltd

the residence of Malla kings, and Mul Chowk, dedicated to the goddess
Taleju, are unfortunately closed to the public.

The stone-paved Lohan Chowk to the southeast is open, however, its
corners topped by towers sponsored by former kingdoms of the Valley in
recognition of their unification: copper-roofed **Kirtipur Tower**, octagonal
Bhaktapur Tower, the square **Lalitpur Tower** and the tall **Basantapur**,
Kathmandu's own. Between the latter two is the three-storeyed Vilas
Mandir, 'Temple of Luxury', adorned with finely carved woodwork.

Aficionados of the bizarre will want to glance in the **Tribhuvan
Memorial Museum** ensconced in a wing of the old palace. Exhibits pay
tribute to the grandfather of the current king, who re-established the Shah
Dynasty in 1951. There are royal baby clothes trimmed with stiff gold braid;
pictures from the king's coronation at age five and from his marriage (to a
pair of Rana sisters) at age 13, and trivia from the royal life: stuffed pets,
boxing gloves, a drained aquarium. Newspaper clippings document the
king's bold escape to the Indian Embassy and his return as ruling monarch
in February 1951.

Opposite Hanuman Dhoka is the **Jagannath Temple** built in 1563, its
doors painted with three eyes and a Shiva trident. The luridly painted erotic
woodcarvings at the base of its struts are perhaps the most famous in the

Valley, though more renowned for their prime location than any artistic skill. Across the way, a picket fence protects a stone drinking tank inset into the palace wall. The slab is carved with polyglot verses in praise of the goddess Kali, written in 15 different languages and alphabets, at the command of that most erudite of kings, Pratap Malla. The words 'l'hiver', 'l'otomne' and 'winter' can be distinguished, perhaps obtained from the Capuchin missionaries who briefly settled in the Valley in the 16th century.

Continue north a few steps to admire the towering **Taleju Mandir**, a perfectly proportioned pagoda set atop a 12-stage plinth. Once this was the highest building in the Valley. Its imposing aura perfectly suits its role as the sanctum of the Malla patron deity Taleju Bhawani, a mysterious goddess imported from South India in the 12th century, and supposedly once worshipped with human sacrifice. Apart from the eighth day of Dasain, when it is open to Hindus, only its high priests, the Royal Family and the Kumari may enter the temple compound—a great pity, as it is a superb example of Newari architecture.

Retrace your steps past Hanuman Dhoka, and pass the exquisite triple-roofed **Degu Taleju Temple** sprouting out of the palace's main wing, once a

private shrine for Malla kings. Opposite, crowning a pillar, a gilt statue of **King Pratap Malla** kneels in prayer, surrounded by smaller images of four sons and two of his many wives. This exquisite statue started a trend, as the rulers of the Valley's other kingdoms promptly immortalized themselves on top of pillars raised in their own Durbar Squares.

Across from it is a red-painted wooden lattice screen, behind which glares the ferocious mask of **Seto** or **White Bhairab**. This enormous piece of metalwork was commissioned in 1796 to drive away evil spirits and ghosts. It is displayed once a year during the festival of Indra Jatra, when crowds

Kneeling Garuda, Kathmandu Durbar Square

jostle for a mouthful of the rice beer gushing from a pipe stuck between the Bhairab's teeth. Above is a magnificent **window** of carved ivory and gilt, where kings once sat to view their subjects. Glance across the road at an open shelter holding a pair of **immense drums** dedicated to the goddess Taleju and once beaten during worship at the Degu Taleju temple. Nearby, the steps of the unusual octagonal **Krishna Temple** are a favourite haunt of itinerant fortune-tellers.

Behind, another Bhairab, this one black or **Kalo Bhairab**, is represented. The huge, luridly painted bas-relief receives sacrifices from hill people who remain in awe of it. Supposedly, whoever tells a lie in front of the image will instantly die, a belief once used to wring the truth from suspected criminals.

Move south down the narrow flagstoned road, passing an elaborately carved palace wing housing *thangka* shops on the ground floor. The lane leads into the second portion of Durbar Square, studded with some grand if inactive temples. On the left is a rectangular wooden shrine dedicated to and depicting the nine Navadurga goddesses. Everyone calls it the **Shiva-Parvati Temple**, after the brightly painted wooden images of the deities peering from an upper window. In the autumn, wandering Indian snake charmers perform on the low platform in front, once used for ritual dance performances.

A pair of imposing tall temples dominates the square, one dedicated to **Shiva**, the other to **Vishnu**. Closed to worshippers, they have little of artistic note apart from the massive **stone Garuda** kneeling in front of the Vishnu temple, but the upper levels of their steep tiered platforms provide a fascinating overview of the busy square. The east side of the square is dominated by the dazzling white façade of **Gaddi Baithak**, a turn-of-the-century addition to the royal palace modelled on London's National Gallery.

Across from it is **Kumari Ghar**, the abode of the young Newari girl worshipped as an embodiment of the Hindu goddess Durga. Built in the style of a Buddhist *bahal*, it is adorned with elaborate woodcarvings depicting Hindu mythology. For a few rupees donation, the Kumari will appear in an upstairs window, a self-possessed, regal little girl with enormous kohl-rimmed eyes and pulled-up hair.

Behind the Vishnu temple's stone Garuda looms the massive broad-roofed bulk of the **Kasthamandap**, the ancient temple cum rest-house which gave Kathmandu its name. According to legend it was built from the wood of a single tree, thus its name, Kasthamandapa, 'Pavilion of Wood'. The large, plain structure dates back at least to the 12th century and is probably much, much older, though the current building is a mere five centuries old and has been restored many times. Once it was the starting point of the Tibet trade route, serving as a rest-house for travellers and pilgrims. The ground floor, with its small shrine to Gorakhnath, the patron of the Shah kings, is a favourite venue for religious meetings featuring amplified teachings by Hindu pandits. Also on this square is the beautifully restored **Kabindrapur**, built by Pratapa Malla in 1673, with an image of Nasadyo, the dancing Shiva, inside.

Beside the Kasthamandap is a tiny but very important shrine. **Ashok Binayak**, the abode of the elephant-headed Ganesh, is renowned as one of the Valley's four most auspicious Ganesh temples, and crowds are forever circling it, ringing its bells and ducking inside for a brief blessing. The brightly gilded little pagoda, bedecked with stiffly flying metal pennants, houses a stone image of Ganesh beneath a gilded *ashoka* tree. Across the way is a charming larger-than-life brass image of Ganesh's mount, the rat.

South of Durbar Square

Kathmandu is traditionally divided into two distinctly separate entities, Upper and Lower Kathmandu, with Durbar Square, the dividing line. The ancient rivalry between the two neighbourhoods was vented in an annual rock-throwing festival held on the banks of the Vishnumati River, abolished only in 1846. Wounded prisoners were dragged away by the opposing sides to be sacrificed to the mother goddesses of each quarter.

The main bazaar and major sights lie north of Durbar Square. Few travellers venture south to explore the narrow ancient streets of 'Lower' Kathmandu. Unlike the busy market area to the north, it comprises primarily residences and small shops crowded into ancient buildings, some seemingly toppling before your very eyes.

From the Kasthamandap, follow the left-hand lane down along Kabindrapur, past sweet shops, stores selling bamboo spools for kite string, and crumbling *pati* so ancient that their wooden pillars have virtually disintegrated. The road runs into a square dominated by the 17th-century **Jaisi Deval** temple, dedicated to Shiva. Its principal point of interest is the enormously high, stepped plinth it rests upon. Take the asphalt road to the right and swing back up to **Bhimsen Mandir**, a brightly painted temple dedicated to the patron of merchants. Appropriately, it houses shops on the ground floor. The road from here heads uphill, past cloth shops displaying Indian print bedspreads and gold wedding saris, and eventually leads back into Maru Tol.

Old Kathmandu

The heart of the old city deserves repeated visits at different times of different days. It is a self-correcting course: stay amid the red-brick buildings and avoid the filthy riverbanks and overcrowded main roads, and you're bound to encounter something of interest, though it's difficult to predict exactly what.

Makhan Tol leads from the northern end of Durbar Square, lined with shops selling *thangkas*, souvenirs and Chinese sneakers. It debouches into **Indra Chowk**, a busy six-street crossroad dominated by a rectangular, gaudily tiled temple, **Akash Bhairab**, flanked by leaping griffins. The top floor (open to Hindus only) enshrines a blue Bhairab mask, worshipped with evening hymns; the bottom floor consists of shops. Be sure to look on the opposite side for the **Bead Bazaar**. This narrow passageway is lined with stalls selling the glittering glass bead necklaces beloved by Nepali women. And whoever said Kathmandu was isolated: the merchants are Muslim, and the beads are from Eastern Europe and Japan.

Crowds sweep up the main bazaar road from here, past shops stocked with colourful bolts of cloth from India and China, and second-storey emporiums draped with carpets and bags. Look for a white plaster archway on the left. This is the entrance to **Jana Bahal**, the abode of Kathmandu's beloved **Seto Machhendranath**. The classically proportioned temple is encaged behind iron grilles to prevent further disappearance of its exceptionally fine metalwork, as demonstrated in the elaborate trellis and triple *torana* over the main door. Inside is enshrined the doll-like statue of *Seto* or White Machhendranath, a Newar cult deity associated with the bodhisattva Avalokitesvara. The big courtyard with its assortment of *chaityas* and odd statues is invariably full of worshippers, pigeons and herds of frolicking children.

Duck down the low-ceilinged passageway leading through the rear wall of the courtyard, and emerge at an out-of-use temple stacked high with clay jugs and animal flowerpots. At the corner, streetside barbers give haircuts and shaves to squatting clients, finishing off with a vigorous head massage. **Kel Tol**, the street leading east back to the main road, is lined with more shops selling printed Nepali cotton and fluffy *kapok* used to stuff pillows and quilts. The men loitering about, twanging the single string of their strange wooden implements, are hired to fluff the kapok to an appropriate degree. Back at the crossroads, the doors of a **tile-roofed temple**, sacred to one of the Ajima, bear her symbol, an eye over a full water pot. The exterior has been appropriated by jewellery sellers who display glass bangles, necklaces and the red cotton *chulto* woven into women's braids.

THE KUMARI

In an elaborately decorated building beside Kathmandu's Durbar Square lives a regal little girl worshipped as an embodiment of the Hindu goddess Durga. The tradition is said to have been started in the 18th century by King Jaya Prakash Malla, an intimate of the goddess Taleju. One evening the intoxicated king made a pass at her, and the insulted goddess disappeared. She finally consented to return, but only in the form of a virgin Newari girl of the Sakya caste.

Or so the story goes. Actually the tradition of the Kathmandu Kumari predates Jaya Prakash's reign by at least five centuries and has its roots in ancient Indian practices. There are around a dozen Kumaris in the Valley today, including four in Kathmandu, three in Bhaktapur and two in Patan. Most lead relatively normal lives and are worshipped only occasionally, but most important is the Royal or State Kumari.

High priests search for her amongst small girls of the Sakya clan, looking for a child worthy to serve as a vehicle for the goddess. Traditionally she is supposed to manifest the *battis lakshin*, the '32 perfections', poetically described with comparisons such as 'thighs like a deer, chest like a lion, neck like a conch shell, eyelashes like a cow', and 'voice soft and clear as a duck's'.

A likely candidate is chosen, and her horoscope checked to avoid conflict with that of the king. The final test occurs with her installation ceremony, held on the great eighth day of the Dasain festival. Around midnight, over a hundred buffalo and goats are slaughtered in the old palace courtyard of Mulchowk, and their severed heads, with lighted wicks placed between the horns, are set in rows on the ground. The girl, often no more than three years old, must remain calm at this terrifying sight, circumambulate the courtyard and enter the shrine of the goddess. Then she is taken upstairs for a secret ceremony in which she is purified of all past experience and the goddess fully possesses her body. Attendants dress her in red with golden ornaments, paint a third eye on her forehead and rim her eyes with collyrium. Then she walks on a strip of white cloth—the

Kumari's feet should never touch the ground—to take her place at Kumari Ghar.

Here she lives on the second floor, separated from her family and cared for by attendants. The high priest of the Taleju temple worships her daily, and each day she grants audiences to devotees, both Hindu and Buddhist. Most common are government officials hoping for promotion, and women with sick children or menstrual problems. Seated on her gilt throne, the Kumari looks on while worshippers make offerings and supplications. Her slightest action is taken to be an omen. If she smiles, the worshipper will experience good fortune; but restlessness warns of bad luck, and if she weeps and rubs her eyes, it portends certain death.

In the afternoons the Kumari plays like an ordinary little girl with the children of her caretaker. She seldom ventures outside except on ritual occasions, when she is carried. Her greatest moments are her festival appearances, climaxed by the Kumari Jatra during Indra Jatra, when she is paraded about in a golden chariot before adoring crowds and gives a *tika* to the King of Nepal.

This charmed life continues for years, ending only when the Kumari first sheds blood. A lost tooth or a cut can betoken this fall from Taleju's grace, though sometimes it only occurs with the advent of menstruation. The search commences for a new little girl, and the old Kumari is returned to a family she may hardly know. It is a drastic change in fortune for a girl accustomed to being treated as a goddess and worshipped by the king. A marriage may be arranged for her, but there are few takers for the Kathmandu Kumari, as the husbands of this ex-goddess are rumoured to die young. She lives out the rest of her life in obscurity, supported by a small stipend from the state and memories of her glorified childhood.

Kumari, Patan

The crowd sweeps you further up the street, past shops selling brasswork, plumbing tools and aluminium pots by weight. Pass a small Ganesh shrine, across from a finely carved octagonal **Krishna Temple**, now taken over by sellers of ginger and turmeric, and enter into **Asan Tol**. This ancient bazaar is the true heart of Kathmandu. Until recently it functioned as a fascinating clearing-house for fresh produce hawked by wholesalers who arrived before dawn to stake out a good position. In a misguided effort at urban development, city officials have cleared vendors out of Asan. The result is increased traffic congestion—formerly vehicles could never hope to penetrate the densely packed intersection; now they barely can and there is a marked loss of local colour. Plenty of interest remains on the fringes with the orange-dust-coated vendors of powdered turmeric, an important seasoning in Nepali and Indian food; mountains of fresh ginger, pungent dried peppers and bins of grains in the shops around the side. Age-old shops sell sticky masses of brown *gur* or unrefined molasses, fed to recently calved cows and nursing mothers; cannonball-sized laundry soap of clay mixed with oil of the *neem* tree; stacks of *sal* leaves used for plates in feasts and offerings; bundles of small plaited lamp wicks, clay pots of yoghurt, and bright orange goat meat rubbed with turmeric to repel flies. Of the three temples situated at Asan Tol, by far the prettiest is the lavishly decorated little **Annapurna Mandir**, dedicated to the goddess of plenty, represented by an overflowing silver vessel.

Interesting streets radiate out in every direction from here. Thamel is a few minutes north; Kanti Path a few minutes east, but the best direction for further exploration is west, into the old town. Turn left towards the next intersection, Banghemudha Tol, to find **Wasya Dyo**, the 'Toothache God', who inhabits a slab of wood studded with hundreds of nails. Hammering one in is said to be an assured remedy for toothache sufferers. If this doesn't work, plenty of dentists in the neighbourhood display dentures behind their dusty shop windows.

Turn right and walk north a few paces, past a recently restored 10th century Vishnu temple and an ancient standing Buddha image set into a blue-tiled niche beside a building entrance. A little further down (look for the sign for 'Cujo Dog Training School') is **Kathesimbhu Stupa**, built in the 17th century as a conveniently located replica of Swayambhunath, minus the 365 steep steps. The site itself is even more ancient, as demonstrated by some splendid **Licchavi-era sculptures**. Further north, past shops selling Bhutanese fabric, Chinese brocade and Tibetan prayer flags, is **Thahiti stupa**, ringed with Tibetan-style prayer wheels.

Back at the Toothache God: continue one block west and then turn south, and you'll find the ancient **Naradevi Temple**, dedicated to a fierce Tantric goddess who is placated by blood sacrifice. A king built the shrine in response to her appearance in a dream, and instituted the annual performance of a masked dance troupe in her honour.

Take a left turn and head east at this intersection down **Kilgal Tol**. About 75 metres (70 yards) down the road, look for the entrance to **Itum Bahal**, a vast hidden courtyard harbouring an ancient Buddhist *bahal*, with a superb 16th-century wooden *torana* and some marvellous, if worn, examples of 14th-century woodcarving in the graceful *yaksha* struts. The embossed copperplates on the north wall depict a bit of local folklore in the form of **Guru Mapa**, a child-eating demon persuaded to switch his diet over to an annual sacrifice of buffalo that to this day is delivered by Itum Bahal residents.

Tripureswar and Teku

Hidden behind the busy shops and streets of Tripureswar, a commercial neighbourhood on the road to Patan, the sacred Bagmati River winds past interesting temples, rest-houses, shrines and cremation ghats. This area is seldom explored by tourists, possibly due to the pungent aroma emanating from the polluted river, but the architecture is worth it.

Begin across from the Bluebird Supermarket at the Thapathali intersection. The Mughal-inspired white-domed **Kalomachan** temple was completed under Jung Bahadur Rana, who is said to have hidden the ashes of the victims of the Kot Massacre in the foundations. A gilt statue of King Surendra Bahadur Shah stands atop a pillar in the compound, along with a particularly large and brilliant **Garuda**, but the courtyard lies silent and neglected.

Next door is the imposingly large triple pagoda of **Tripureswar Mahadeva**, built in 1818 for the repose of the ill-fated King Rana Bahadur Shah. Once devout and dedicated to the gods, he went mad with grief when his favourite queen died of smallpox, smashing religious images and denouncing priests. He was packed off to Benares but eventually returned, only to be assassinated in 1806. The temple was raised for the benefit of his soul by a surviving queen. The temple is crumbling and the surrounding buildings are in a state of poor repair, but the atmosphere is peaceful and timeless, with a charm lost in the impeccably restored and varnished shrines of Durbar Square.

Thus A Nation Pretends to Live

Honoured friend,
this is Machapuchare, that is Annapurna,
over there stands the Dhaulagiri range.
You can see them with the naked eye,
you do not need binoculars.
Here I shall open a three-star hotel:
would you kindly make me a loan?

Dear guest,
this is the Koshi and that is the Gandak,
the blue over there is the Karnali.
You may have read in some papers
about the selling of Nepal's rivers.
That was a lie, sir.
Those rivers have given our regions their names,
we plan to generate power from them:
could you give us some help?

Respected visitor,
This is Kathmandu Valley.
Here there are three cities:
Kathmandu, Lalitpur, Bhaktapur.
Please cover your nose with a handkerchief,
no sewage system is possible,
the building of toilets has not been feasible.
Our next five-year plan has a clean city campaign:
could you make a donation?

Min Bahadur Bista, 1989
Translated by Michael James Hutt in Himalayan Voices, 1991

From here it's a ten-minute stroll along the riverside past bathers and laundresses, towards the cluster of interesting temples around **Teku**. First is the unusual triple *shikhara* of **Tindeval**, decorated with fine teracotta figures of protective *naga* and *nagini*. Other riverside shrines hold images of Ram, Sita and Shiva, and there's a fascinating open-air collection of fine stone sculptures of various deities, plus Nandi and a linga, both symbols of Shiva. A quivering old suspension bridge leads to the temple complex of **Rajghat** on the opposite bank. A major cremation ground is located just beyond the bridge at the junction of the Vishnumati and Bagmati rivers, a spiritually auspicious site.

To conclude the tour, walk north towards a huge twisted pipal tree. Its roots embrace the mysterious open-air shrine of **Pachali Bhairab**, an important site for Kathmandu Newars, who visit in force on Tuesdays and Saturdays. Blood sacrifices are offered through the intermediary of **Betal**, a goblin-like creature here depicted as a supine naked corpse rendered in brass. The two roads from here lead back up to Tripureswar Marg, a major thoroughfare with plenty of taxis.

Masked dance, Boudhanath

Central Kathmandu

While Central Kathmandu consists mainly of concrete buildings and busy roads and lacks the character of the old town, it is the site of most offices, shops, hotels and restaurants, making visits inevitable. Below is a guide to enable you to make the most out of the sights you will frequently pass.

Durbar Marg is the premier area in the kingdom in terms of rent, and many airlines and travel agencies have their offices here. The road begins just below **Narayanhiti Royal Palace**, the official residence of the King of Nepal. Inaugurated in 1970, it features a central tower resembling a rocket poised for take-off. A portion of the palace has been opened to visitors. Foreigners are admitted on Thursdays from 1–4 pm for a fee of Rs250 (no children or cameras allowed). A guide escorts visitors up the garishly decorated main stairway and through the reception hall and throne room, with glimpses of stuffed tigers, royal portraits and King Tribhuvan's personal pair of engraved scissors along the way.

Down the road and opposite the palace is the recently restored **Narayan Hiti**, a sunken water tap featuring a pair of *makara* with unusual upward-curving snouts. Across the street, musicians sometimes give evening performances in the peaceful compound of the white plaster **Narayan temple**.

At the opposite end of Durbar Marg a statue of **King Mahendra**, the father of the present king, presides over a traffic roundabout and an occasional goat sacrifice. The road continues past Kathmandu's main mosque (3 percent of Nepal's population is Muslim), especially crowded on Friday afternoons, and the distinctive white clock-tower of **Trichandra College**, a Rana-era leftover. Further down is the huge grassy swath of the **Tundikhel**, the official parade-ground, where you might see displays of military might or more typically a soccer game. A narrow path cutting across its north end hosts a popular open-air bazaar featuring Indian vendors selling clothes, houseware and quack medicines. The corners of the Tundikhel are set with massive bronze statues of mounted Ranas, each weighing an estimated 1,800 kilos (4,000 pounds), and like everything else of the period hauled in over the mountains by teams of porters.

At the lower end of the Tundikhel, Prithvi Path branches off towards **Singha Durbar**, the seat of Parliament and government offices. It was the largest palace in South Asia when it was built in 1901, with 17 courtyards and 1,700 rooms, but this epitome of Rana excess was largely destroyed in a 1973 fire, though the original state rooms and façade remain. The road swings about **Bhadrakali Mandir** to head west, bisecting the Tundikhel and passing **Shahid Gate** (Martyr's Gate), a rather neglected monument to five Rana-era supporters of the banned Congress Party, four of whom were executed for their pains (the fifth, being Brahman, could not be killed and was instead deprived of caste and imprisoned).

The next road we meet is **Kanti Path**. At its corner is the **General Post Office**: a visit at peak hours provides a wonderfully chaotic glimpse of the real Nepal. The slender white tower rising behind is not a minaret but the **Dharahara**, the legacy of a Rana prime minister who wished to awe the populace. Once used as a watch-tower, it is now closed. Nearby, the big Sundhara is a favourite washing and laundry spot for the many old-town residents who live without running water.

Heading north up Kanti Path, the next intersection is **New Road**, its name dating to 1934 when the wide, modern street was built over the rubble of the great earthquake. It is filled with wealthy Nepalis and Indians shopping for clothes, watches and electrical goods imported from Hong Kong and Bangkok. **Bisal Bazaar**, a cavernous multi-storey complex at the end of New Road, boasts Nepal's only escalator.

Continuing north, traffic whizzes past a small but popular **Mahakala Temple** on the right. The black stone image with silver eyes is worshipped by Hindus as a form of Shiva, by Buddhists as a protective deity. Both supplicate him for relief from pain and injury, and conveniently the temple is located across from government-run **Bir Hospital**.

Further up is **Rani Pokhari**, a large artificial pond created in 1670 to please a queen mourning the death of her son. A few decades ago it was a favourite suicide spot for Kathmanduites, necessitating the high fence surrounding it. A bit further, across from the **British Council**, is **Bahadur Bhawan**, a sprawling old palace complex that once housed Boris Lissanevitch's Royal Hotel and now serves as the office of the Election Commission.

Fragments of other Rana palaces are scattered about this neighbourhood, including **Kaiser Mahal** up the street, the abode of the Ministry of Education and Culture and the **Kaiser Library**. This great rainy-day hideaway is worth a visit solely for the decor: stuffed tigers, suits of armour and oil paintings of personages from Shiva to Napoleon. Glass cases display the 35,000-volume personal collection of Kaiser Jung Bahadur Rana who, judging from the titles, was equally interested in obscure wars, English gardening and Hindu philosophy.

THREE HOLY SITES

No visit to Kathmandu is complete without paying one's respects to three compelling, supremely holy sites on the outskirts of town. In perfect if unintentional symmentry, each serves as a sacred shrine for one of the these three great religions of the Valley—Newari Buddhism, Hinduism and Tibetan Buddhism—though each is generally revered by all.

The white stupa of **Swayambhunath**, frequently called the 'Monkey Temple' by those intimidated by its tongue-twisting name, is usually the first visited, as it is an easy walk from Thamel. On the eastern outskirts of town, the Hindu temple complex of **Pashupatinath** and the great stupa of **Boudhanath** can be combined into a single visit. Try to avoid the flat light and heat of midday, when tour buses disgorge, and visit early in the morning or at dusk, the prime hours for puja. Like all the Valley's shrines, these three host interesting rituals on no-moon and full-moon days. Each site has its own special festivals: if your visit coincides, don't miss **Losar** at Boudha, **Buddha Jayanti** at Swayambhu, or **Shiva Ratri** at Pashupatinath.

Swayambhunath

The most important shrine of Buddhist Newars, Swayambhunath is a supremely ancient site dating back to at least the fifth century. Its name, 'The Self-Existent', refers to the magical lotus blossoming from the legendary lake which once covered the Kathmandu Valley. The miraculous light emanating from its golden petals drew gods and men alike to its worship, until a wise man, sensing the coming of the present Kali Yuga or Dark Age, buried the light beneath a stone slab and raised the structure above it.

The whitewashed, richly adorned stupa is wonderfully sited above a small hillock a little west of Kathmandu. While you can take a taxi to just below the top, the 45-minute walk from Thamel is more interesting. The route leads downhill through Chhetrapati, across the sacred Vishnumati River, and past the Hotel Vajra and various small carpet factories and monasteries to the brightly painted gate at the foot of Swayambhu hill. The gate and the **giant prayer wheel** just beyond were donated by the local Tibetan refugee community. Tibetan devotees can be seen circumambulating the hill clockwise, spinning prayer wheels or repeatedly prostrating themselves.

It's a slow climb up 365 worn stone steps, through a shady forest teeming with monkeys, past several groups of **giant stone Buddhas** painted in brilliant orange and yellow. At the top waits the stupa, painted eyes peering from the base of its gilded spire. The platform is littered with votive offerings installed over the centuries, beginning with a gigantic **gilt vajra**, a ritual Tantric implement symbolizing the indestructible nature of ultimate reality, resting on a carved stone base at the top of the steps. Everywhere are small *chaitya* and shrines, some dating back to Licchavi times.

Devotees move clockwise about the stupa, tossing offerings into the five elaborate little gilt shrines set at intervals into the hemispheric dome. These are dedicated to the elemental **Pancha Buddha**, each associated with a different colour, direction and wisdom. Swayambhu's association with these

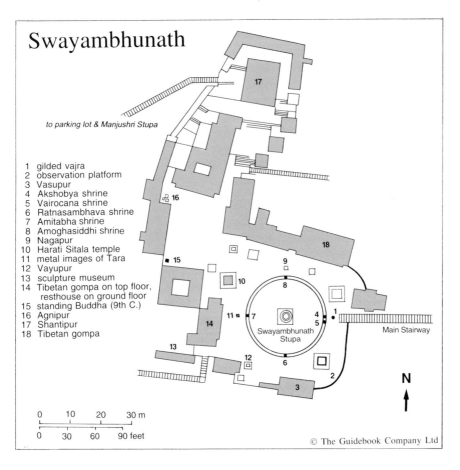

primarily Newari deities has inspired some incredibly dense symbolism. Look for the animal 'vehicles' set in niches below each shrine, and the Buddhas' consorts in smaller shrines alongside them. The Pancha Buddha appear again in the gilt *torana* above the stupa's eyes; the dome is said to embody their combined wisdom, which is the essence of enlightenment.

The same motif reappears in five shrines dedicated to the elements scattered about the compound, beginning with the copper-roofed **Vasupur**, the abode of the earth goddess Vasundhara. Marble-faced **Vayupur** or Wind Sanctuary is impressive enough, but the white rock dedicated to **Agni**, Lord of Fire, is easily missed, as is the simple open pit called **Nagapur**, abode of the water-loving *naga*.

By far the most compelling is **Shantipur**, the 'Mansion of Peace', consecrated to the mystic element, ether. Look for a large beige building down a flight of steps in the northeast corner. Behind its locked doors, the eighth-century tantric master Shantikar Acharya is said to dwell seated in a meditative trance. Paintings of fierce deities guard the entrance, and ancient frescoes depict the legend of King Pratap Malla's descent into the secret chamber to retrieve a magical rain-bringing mandala and break the drought plaguing the Valley.

Other sights around the stupa include a small **museum** with some fine stone sculptures discovered in the area, a superb ninth-century sculpture of a **standing Buddha**, and two lovely metal images of the bodhisattva goddess **Tara**, set behind metal grilles to deter thieves. The beautifully proportioned little pagoda nearby is the abode of the Hindu goddess **Sitala**, who serves both as the protector of children and the sender of smallpox. Devotees placate the goddess with offerings of duck eggs, lighted lamps, grain and incense, and mothers carry their babies inside for blessings.

Swayambhu also has two small Tibetan *gompas* with typically colourful shrines open to the public, the first above an open rest-house where families prepare offerings to Sitala. The second, a yellow building in the northeast corner, holds an enormous gilt **Shakyamuni Buddha**, and a statue of a modern saint: the 16th **Karmapa**, head of the Kargyu sect, who died in 1981 in the US.

The stupa's viewing platforms offer sweeping vistas of Kathmandu's huddled red-brick buildings, surrounded by dwindling fields. The view is best at dusk on a clear day, when the Himalaya rise rose-tinted in the north. Full-moon nights, when the stupa is illuminated with tiny butter lamps, are another good time to visit. A smaller hillock to the west holds a stupa dedicated to **Manjushri**, the bodhisattva who drained the Valley's legendary lake.

Pashupatinath

The essence of Hinduism, three millenia of unbroken tradition, coalesces in this temple complex, littered with shrines, sculptures and statues raised over centuries to the glory of the great god Shiva. Pashupatinath is one of the most important Shiva sites of the subcontinent, and a visit here crowns the traditional pilgrimage to Shiva's four holiest temples.

Busloads of Indian pilgims descend on Pashupatinath in the winter months, building to a crescendo around the boisterous festival of Shiva Ratri (usually February). Nepali devotees come throughout the year to worship Shiva in the form of Pashupati, 'Lord of the Beasts', an ancient Indian cult which today survives most prominently in Nepal. Lord

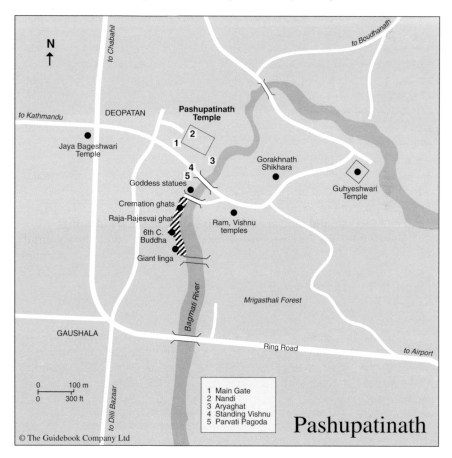

N

to Chabahil

to Boudhanath

to Kathmandu

DEOPATAN

Pashupatinath Temple

Jaya Bageshwari Temple

Gorakhnath Shikhara

Guhyeshwari Temple

Goddess statues

Cremation ghats

Raja-Rajesvai ghat

Ram, Vishnu temples

6th C. Buddha

Giant linga

Bagmati River

Mrigasthali Forest

GAUSHALA

Ring Road

to Airport

0   100 m
0   300 ft

to Dilli Bazaar

1 Main Gate
2 Nandi
3 Aryaghat
4 Standing Vishnu
5 Parvati Pagoda

Pashupatinath

© The Guidebook Company Ltd

Pashupati is the country's official protector, invoked in royal speeches and cited on treaties and pledges. Shiva symbolism appears everywhere at Pashupatinath, in stone bulls representing his mount Nandi, in the trident, and in the omnipresent linga, his special symbol, representing the generative power of the universe.

Shiva is present also in Pashupatinath's fluctuating population of sadhus, wandering Hindu devotees who have renounced the strictures of caste and normal custom, and beg to meet their minimal daily needs. Some perform austerities or smoke incredible quantities of *ganja* (marijuana). Sadhus may wear splendid orange robes or appear naked and smeared in ashes from the cremation ground. Some are genuine devotees, even saints; others are rogues, charlatans, or misfits who can't fit into society in any other way. Nepalis as well as tourists find them bizarrely fascinating.

Pashupatinath is on the eastern edge of town, a stone's throw from Tribhuvan International Airport (the runway is built on former grazing ground for its sacred cows). The site is sanctified by the presence of the Bagmati River, Nepal's answer to India's sacred Ganges. Indeed, the Bagmati is said to be connected to the Ganges by an underground stream, and a ritual bath here is said to ensure release from the cycle of samsara. The river, barely a trickle in the dry winter season, is horribly polluted, but the faithful still submerge themselves the ritually prescribed three times and take the recommended sip of holy water.

Pashupatinath dates to the fifth century (the oldest inscription is dated AD 477), but as usual the site is much, much older. Royal donations over the centuries have reworked the temple far beyond its original form. The present main shrine, a two-roofed gilt pagoda, dates from the reign of Pratapa Malla, but even it has been ceaselessly improved with gifts, including elegant doors of *repoussé* silver and a giant bull with silver hooves and golden tail, donated by a Rana prime minister as atonement for accidentally shooting a cow on a Terai hunt.

Inside the temple is enshrined the sacred black stone **linga** of Pashupatinath, each of its four sides carved with a different aspect of Shiva. A special subcaste of South Indian Brahman priests tend to it in a daily cycle of ritual bathing, dressing and offerings. For reasons of ritual purity only they may touch it. Non-Hindus are not allowed in the compound, though nothing prevents a discreet peep through the gate. The main (western) entrance, surmounted with a plaster relief of Shiva as Yogesvara, provides a good view of the year of the above-mentioned bull. The best overall view of the compound is obtained from the opposite side of the Bagmati.

Even without access to the main temple there is plenty to see at Pashupatinath. The sprawling complex is littered with ancient sculptures, like the hefty goddesses **Bachhlesvari** and **Lakshmi** set in a compound near the central footbridge. The western *ghat* in particular is a veritable museum, with a **sixth-century Buddha** draped with drying laundry, a gigantic 1,500-year-old linga, and rambling old courtyards where pilgrims and squatters cook and wash and live.

It's worth stopping midway across one of the narrow twin bridges spanning the Bagmati to survey the scene. Naked little boys frolic in the murky river, and monkeys scamper across the hermit dwellings cut into the cliffs upstream. More often than not a cremation is being conducted on the western bank: Pashupatinath is Nepal's most auspicious site for Hindus, and cremation here is said to ensure release from samsara. The three square platforms downstream are for the general public, while **Aryaghat** upstream is reserved for royalty and distinguished personages. Funeral ceremonies are conducted by male relatives clad in white, the colour of mourning. The ritual's dignity and eerie beauty is somewhat marred by the crowds of tourists busily photographing and videotaping the final disposal of some family's loved one.

More temples and shrines lie on the river's east bank, where according to legend Shiva once roamed as an antelope in **Mrigasthali Forest**. Climb the broad stone stairs to a shady glen dotted with more shrines and Shiva images. The fierce red-bottomed monkeys lurking about will plunder your lunch if you're not careful. From behind a large ochre *shikhara* enshrining the footprint of the great yogi **Gorakhnath**, steps lead down to the **Guhyeshwari Temple**. One of 51 *pitha* or sacred sites dedicated to Shiva's consort Sati, it too is extremely holy and is closed to non-Hindus. From here you can cross the Bagmati on a footbridge and hike north up a dirt road (none too clean towards the end) to Boudhanath, a 20-minute walk.

Boudhanath

—about three and a half miles from Kathmandu is a peculiar village called Bodhnath. This village is built in a circle round an immense Buddhist temple ... This place is a favourite resort of the Bhotiyas and Tibetans who visit the valley in the cold season, and many of the houses are occupied as jewellers' shops wherein are manufactured peculiar amulets, armlets, necklaces, etc. which the Bhotiyas wear in great profusion.

—Daniel Wright, History of Nepal, *1877*

Seven kilometres east of the city centre, the great stupa of Boudhanath serves as a magnet for Buddhist pilgrims from across the Himalaya. In recent years it has become a focal point for Tibetan refugees and a vibrant centre of Vajrayana Buddhist teachings, but its history goes back to at least the fifth century when, according to legend, a lowly poultry-keeper asked the local ruler for as much land as could be covered by the hide of a buffalo. Granted this seemingly innocuous request, she cleverly cut the skin into strips and used it to girdle an immense plot. Ruefully surveying the site, the king said something like 'Permission once given cannot be taken back'. To this day Tibetans call the stupa **Jarung Kashor**, the gist of the king's remark.

The huge whitewashed dome is said to enshrine the relics of Kasyapa, a leading disciple of the Buddha. Tibetans believe these relics multiply and are occasionally manifested in the form of tiny white pellets emitted by the stupa and treasured by devotees. The stupa's size alone is imposing enough (the diameter exceeds 100 metres, 300 feet), but more striking is the sense of presence apparent from the moment you enter the gate and come beneath the disquieting stare of its painted eyes. Buddhists consider it an extraordinarily powerful site, able to fulfil all wishes, and the pilgrims flocking here in the winter travel season add to the colourful scene: women from Dolpo and Mustang wrapped in striped woollen blankets, Ladakhi women in elaborate turquoise-trimmed head-dresses, Bhutanese in their embroidered *gho* and *kira*. Authentic high-plains Tibetans are easily identified by their Chinese sneakers and wide-eyed stares, but the local Tibetans are more sophisticated. The women still wear turquoise and silver jewellery, and striped aprons but the men have adopted Western dress, except for Losar, when they appear in brocaded fur hats and magnificent *chubas*.

Everyone circles the stupa, moving clockwise in the ancient ritual of circumambulation. Boudha is a miniature showcase of Buddhist practices such as this. Mornings and evenings the entire community pours out to do *kora*, chanting and praying, spinning prayer wheels or fingering prayer beads, the most devout performing full-length prostrations around the stupa. Itinerant monks chant prayers with great vigour, supported by donations from passersby hoping to increase their stock of religious merit. Shops on the ground floors of the tall houses ringing the stupa sell ritual implements, souvenirs and Tibetan artifacts (or 'Tibetan', as the case may be). Zoning of a sort is preserving the visual harmony of the immediate neighbourhood, though the original old thatch-roofed houses are fast disappearing.

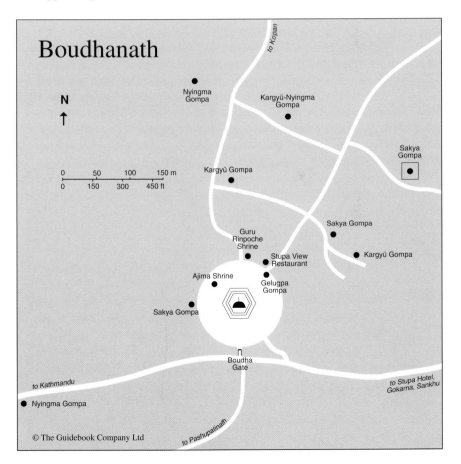

Stairs leading up to the stupa's tiered base are at the western end, across from a small whitewashed building housing a shrine to the eighth-century tantric wizard **Guru Rinpoche**, its old frescoes soot-stained from hundreds of flickering butter lamps. Opposite, built into the wall girdling the stupa, is a tiny temple enshrining a silver image of a **Newari Ajima**. In the small courtyard behind is a row of ancient stone images, many of them Hindu, and a gigantic prayer wheel housed in a separate room. Buddhist holy men often set up camp here, performing elaborate rituals.

From here, flights of stairs lead up to the stupa's triple-tiered base, each level offering a different perspective of the surrounding countryside, now engulfed by new monasteries and carpet factories. The topmost level circles the stupa itself, its base inset with 108 niches containing ancient stone images of deities.

The stupa is an embodiment of Buddhist principles rendered in concrete form, serving as an ultimate symbol of enlightenment. Its massive white dome is periodically whitewashed, then splashed with buckets of saffron-tinged water heaved in great arcs to create a contrasting lotus pattern. Buddhist families sponsor the painting process to earn merit for deceased members, and it is entertaining to watch the workmen flinging their buckets across the dome and touching up the enigmatic eyes.

The route to Boudha passes the smaller but equally ancient stupa of **Chabahil** which, unadorned with later contributions, is much closer to its original form than Boudhanath. (It is said to have been built from the bricks and earth left over from Boudha's construction.) The stupa grounds are scattered with ancient *chaitya*, sculptures and architectural fragments dating back to the Licchavi era. Peer through the door of a small brick building at the rear to glimpse a lovely sculpture of **Padmapani Lokesvara**.

Nepali Temples: Sacred Architecture, Sacred Space

Nepali art is the art of the Newars, and the finest examples of this glorious outpouring are the temples of the Kathmandu Valley. Stacked-roof pagodas punctuate urban skylines with their graceful balanced silhouettes, each one a different variation on a basic theme. The form is well over 1,000 years old—a seventh-century Chinese scholar visiting Kathmandu reported 'multi-storeyed temples so tall one would take them for a crown of clouds'—but fire, earthquakes and the ravages of time have taken their toll, and the oldest temples existing today date from the mid-16th to mid-18th century.

Some scholars believe these multi-roofed towers are the prototype of the pagoda form that eventually spread across Asia. The inspiration for their form is variously attributed to mountains, the silhouette of branching pine trees or the multi-storeyed Himalayan house. The ground plan of temples is based on sacred *yantra*, mystic designs depicting the cosmos in a pattern of alternating circles and squares. Like a mandala, temples unite the mundane with the sacred, serving as a bit of heaven come to earth.

Temples tell a story through images, symbols and in their very form. The building formula follows a set traditional standard. Builders, like artists, remain anonymous, working not to express an individual vision but to duplicate traditional forms. Within the boundaries of set formulae they are free to become inspired, but again inspiration is not thought of as an individual quality but as a divine gift.

Temple materials are a brilliant blend of the earthy and the ethereal. The simplicity of red brick and dark, strong *sal* wood is lightened by lavish metal ornaments, 'jewellery' for the gods. These take the form of tinkling bells and lacy borders of beaten metal, banners and tridents and the pataka—a segmented metal banner streaming down from the highest roof, serving as a sort of runway for divine power. The roofs of the most lavish are adorned with gilt sheeting, a symbol of purity and an enormously expensive undertaking. Somehow all these diverse elements combine to form an exuberant, joyously beautiful whole. Newari art is unashamedly baroque, scrolling over empty spaces with swirls and arabesques, but its excesses are always harmonious.

The heavy, stacked roofs are supported by massive carved struts, depicting the various forms of the deity which reside within, or protective guardians or sometimes on the very oldest temples slender *yakshas*, nymphs from the most ancient mythology. Their bodies are sensuous, vital and delicately detailed, their expressions serenely dignified, human and yet something more. Look closely at the small scenes beneath the main figures, where the carver took liberties not permitted in portrayals of the gods. Here are scenes of daily life, gruesomely imaginative renderings of the torments of the various hells, and erotica ranging from the crude to the sublime. There is nothing unusual in its appearance on a temple: it taps ancient fertility symbolism. More inventive explanations have been developed to suit European mores, like the theory that they were installed to repel the prudish goddess of lightning, cited by Daniel Wright in 1877 and repeated ever since.

The identity of a temple's divine tenant is advertised by the struts surrounding sculptures (the animal mount kneeling in front is a sure indicator), and the *torana*, a tympanum of carved wood or beaten metal mounted above the main door. The central figure depicts the resident deity, surrounded by figures from Indian mythology, usually the Kirttimukha ('Face of Glory') at the apex and a pair of *makara* (sea serpents) at the bottom corners. Spaces between are filled with swirls of foam or flames, strings of pearls and lush foliage. Often a pair of *naga*, snake deities, encircles the building protectively, forming a symbolic boundary between the sacred and profane.

The lavish decorations are all external. The deity dwells in an image set in a small, dark ground-floor shrine which often is not meant to be entered. A priest may serve as intermediary for worshippers standing in the doorway, or worshippers will duck in for a brief moment of private devotion. Daily worship or puja is an individual matter in both Hinduism and Buddhism.

The Buddhist **stupa** and the smaller *chaitya* have similarly intricate imagery embedded in their forms. They evolved from the burial tumuli of ancient India, and are often used to enshrine sacred relics. Many distinct styles of stupas and *chaitya* are derived from the original. In the northern border regions are Tibetan stupas, called *chorten*, literally 'support for worship'. They serve as tangible symbols of the Buddha's enlightened mind.

The stupa's components represent the cosmos: the base represents earth, the dome water, the spire fire, the tip air, and the *bindu* or topmost point, ether. The 13-storey gilded spire culminating in a filigreed pinnacle symbolizes the stages to enlightenment. The largest stupas, like Boudhanath, embody giant mandalas, with rounded domes set on stepped square plinths, but this perspective is only manifest when viewed from above.

A uniquely Nepali touch are the eyes painted on the base of the spire. Their expressions vary from stupa to stupa: some appear to be squinting; others seem wise or compassionate, or mildly contemptuous, or, in the most frequently used adjective, 'all-knowing'. Some say these are the Buddha's eyes; others believe they are associated with the protective eyes painted on doorways all over Kathmandu. The Nepalese number '1', a graceful squiggle, serves as the nose of the face, and as a reminder of unity.

Chandesvari Temple, Banepa

PATAN

The old kingdoms of Kathmandu and Patan have become Siamese twins, sprawling into a single amorphous mass—but what a difference in character. From Kathmandu's Durbar Square to Patan's is a distance of barely four kilometres (two and a half miles), but the two cities are worlds apart. While Kathmandu has slipped irrevocably into the noise and bustle of the modern world, Patan clings to the old ways. Time seems to have stopped here on these quiet, cool byways lined by tall old buildings. From an upper storey dangles a string of *gundruk* (dried greens), or a freshly laundered sari streaming down in a bright banner. Look up, and almost always a pair of equally curious eyes is looking down, surveying the street from an elaborately carved window.

Over the past few decades urban sprawl has gobbled up the farmland once separating Patan and Kathmandu. Only the Bagmati River divides them now, and the crowded suburban neighbourhoods in between provide little of interest. But the old city remains sheltered from the forces of change buffetting Kathmandu. Most of Patan's 100,000 people are Newari, about a third of them farmers, another substantial portion artisans. Patan's metalworkers in particular are renowned for the ease with which they manipulate their unyielding material into fluid images of gilded bronze.

Patan's long and distinguished history as one of Asia's great Buddhist centres remains in the many *bahal, chaitya* and shrines scattered about the town, many 600 or 700 years old and in danger of collapse. Its classical name, Lalitpur, the 'Beautiful City', refers to its reputation as a metropolis endowed with hundreds of exquisite temples.

History

The legend claiming Patan as the most ancient of the Three Kingdoms is difficult to substantiate, though it doubtless has an element of truth. The four '**Ashoka stupas**' set at the cardinal points of the old town were supposedly built at the command of the Buddhist emperor who visited in the second century BC. It is doubtful whether Ashoka ever visited the Valley, but the squat white domes above grassy hillocks are undoubtedly ancient.

Patan rose to prominence while Kathmandu was still just a collection of villages. By the seventh century it was one of the great Buddhist cities of Asia, a meeting point for Indian, Chinese and Tibetan scholars and monks. They lived in *bahals*, quadrangles set about central courtyards which formed Patan's old neighborhoods. As Hinduism grew, Buddhism waned.

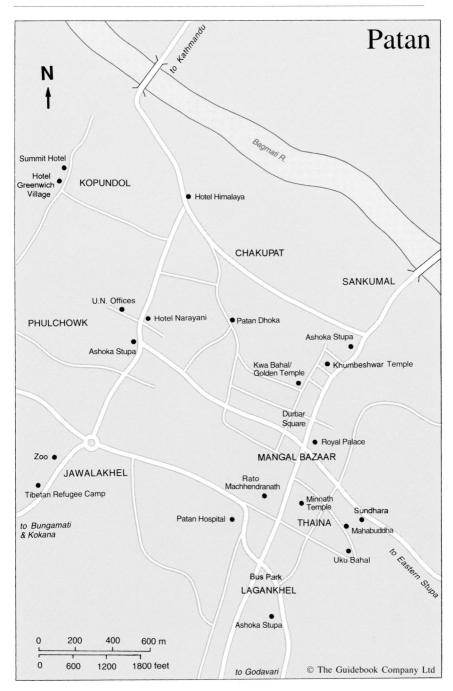

Patan

N

to Kathmandu

Bagmati R.

Summit Hotel
Hotel
Greenwich
Village
KOPUNDOL

Hotel Himalaya

CHAKUPAT

SANKUMAL

U.N. Offices
PHULCHOWK
Hotel Narayani
Patan Dhoka
Ashoka Stupa
Ashoka Stupa
Kwa Bahal/
Golden Temple
Khumbeshwar Temple

Durbar
Square

Royal Palace

Zoo
JAWALAKHEL
Tibetan Refugee Camp
to Bungamati
& Kokana

MANGAL BAZAAR

Rato
Machhendranath

Minnath
Temple
Sundhara
Patan Hospital
THAINA
Mahabuddha

Uku Bahal
to Eastern Stupa

Bus Park
LAGANKHEL

Ashoka Stupa

0	200	400	600 m
0	600	1200	1800 feet

to Godavari

© The Guidebook Company Ltd

The Buddhist priesthood became a hereditary caste, and the *bahals* evolved from monasteries into trade guilds of families sharing the same caste and profession. As their population expanded, the *bahals* sent out offshoots, their number swelling to over 150 today.

Medieval Patan was a large and wealthy kingdom which extended even beyond the fertile southern Valley. Ruled by a series of feudal lords, it was annexed to Kathmandu in the late-16th century. The Malla kings who ascended the throne brought Patan to its fullest glory, and most of its present monuments and temples date to the 17th century. Following the Gorkha conquest of Kathmandu, Patan was largely forgotten. It remained a quiet backwater, to the detriment of economy but to the advantage of present-day visitors who find a relatively intact traditional society—perhaps the Kathmandu they were hoping to find.

Do not be put off by the ride to Patan Dhoka, which is 20 minutes by bicycle and possibly longer by taxi in rush hour. The single crowded bridge spanning the Bagmati does not help matters; neither does the traffic roaring down the Kopundol road. But once you pass through the old plaster city gate it's a different world altogether.

Durbar Square

This is the greatest of all the Three Kingdom's Durbar Squares, a perfectly spaced and balanced forest of temples, pagodas, shikaras, massive bells, statue-topped pillars and the finest stone temple in all Nepal. Buildings of disparate styles erected centuries apart somehow blend into a magical harmony. Late at night, with the old stone temples lit by oil lamps, or early on a winter's morning shrouded in mist, the complex exhibits an almost otherworldy serenity.

Begin at the southern end, at the intersection of **Mangal Bazaar**, Patan's main shopping area. The flat rooftop of the row of stores across the way provides splendid views of the square's bell-fringed pagoda roofs, backed on clear days by the snowy bulk of Langtang.

The **old royal palace** runs along the east side of the square, its massive façade pierced by doors leading into courtyards still exhibiting details of the 17th-century original. Since the defeat of the Mallas this palace has been left undisturbed, and is far less altered than the Kathmandu Durbar.

The first courtyard is **Sundari Chowk**, 'Beautiful Square', its entrance flanked by statues of elephant-faced Ganesh, Narasimha disembowelling a demon and Hanuman, the Monkey King, red-smeared to veil his evil eye.

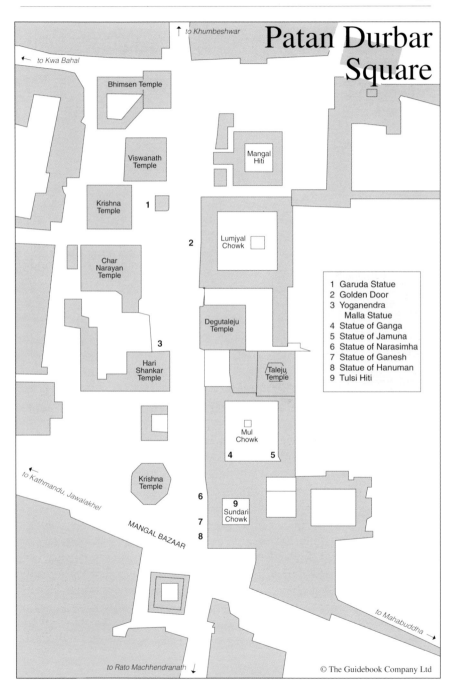

Patan Durbar Square

to Khumbeshwar

to Kwa Bahal

Bhimsen Temple

Mangal Hiti

Viswanath Temple

Krishna Temple   1

Lumjyal Chowk

2

Char Narayan Temple

Degutaleju Temple

3

Hari Shankar Temple

Taleju Temple

Mul Chowk

4   5

to Kathmandu, Jawalakhel

Krishna Temple

6

9
Sundari Chowk

7

8

MANGAL BAZAAR

1   Garuda Statue
2   Golden Door
3   Yoganendra
     Malla Statue
4   Statue of Ganga
5   Statue of Jamuna
6   Statue of Narasimha
7   Statue of Ganesh
8   Statue of Hanuman
9   Tulsi Hiti

to Mahabuddha

to Rato Machhendranath

© The Guidebook Company Ltd

Inside, the intricately carved windows, columns and doors are among the best in the entire palace. At the centre is the **Tulsi Hiti**, an exquisitely carved sunken stone bath dating to 1646. Rimmed by a pair of protective *naga*, its curved oval walls are set with a double row of images of Tantric deities, carved in stone and cast in gilt metal. Even the conch-shaped waterspout is a work of art, topped with gilt figures of Vishnu and Lakshmi astride a Garuda. Above, there is a small stone replica of the Krishna Mandir in the square outside. Nearby is a massive stone slab said to have served as the bed of the saintly King Siddhi Narsingh Malla, who prayed here after his ritual bath.

The central and oldest courtyard, **Mul Chowk**, is dedicated to the Malla's patron goddess Taleju. The small triple-roofed pagoda perched atop the southern roof marks the Taleju Temple, with a lovely *repoussé* door and an exquisite 1715 *torana*. The graceful goddesses guarding the entrance, **Jamuna** astride a crocodile and Ganga seated on a tortoise, are representations of India's holy rivers.

Next is **Lumjyal Chowk**, 'Courtyard of the Golden Window', named after its splendid gilded entrance. Just north of the palace is **Manga Hiti**, an ancient sunken water tap still in use. Water pouring from the mouths of three stone *makara* is collected in metal jars by small girls who stagger back with them to their homes.

Turn now to admire the square's assembly of temples. **Bhimsen Mandir**, dedicated to the patron deity of merchants, is appropriately well-endowed with a marble façade, and silver and gilt struts. The plates, pots and brooms nailed up under the eaves are offerings to ensure the well-being of deceased souls. Beside it stands **Vishwanath Mandir**, a 17th-century pagoda dedicated to Shiva that collapsed without warning in the 1990 monsoon. It has since been restored, though the massive stone elephants guarding the steps are somewhat the worse for wear.

Krishna Mandir is pure poetry wrought from weighty stone, inspired by a dream of the wise King Siddhi Narsingh Malla, who saw Radha≈Krishna in union at the place. Its *shikhara* spire is surrounded by airy colonnaded porticoes, an unusual combination carried off with great élan. Bands of delicately carved friezes depicting scenes from the Mahabharata and Ramayana adorn the lintels, and the gray stone and gilt ornaments harmonize perfectly. In front of the temple, atop a stone pillar kneels a noble **gilt Garuda** waiting to serve his master, Krishna, one of the ten incarnations of Vishnu. The sound of bells and music floats from inside: unlike most purely formal Durbar Square temples, Krishna Mandir is regularly used.

The resolutely squat **Char Narayan Mandir** beside it is the oldest temple on the square, completed in 1566 and largely ignored today. The small base scenes carved on the wooden struts display some particularly imaginative couplings of men, women and beasts.

Set above a pillar in imitation of the other Durbar Squares, a gilt image of **King Yoganendra Malla** kneels in prayer, facing the triple roofs of the palace's main Taleju temple. This 17th-century king renounced his throne after the death of his favourite son and wandered off as a sadhu. He told his grieving people they would know he was alive as long as the face of the statue was bright and untarnished, and the small bird remained atop the cobra's head. They took him at his word, and for over a century after his disappearance a bed was laid out nightly in the palace for his return.

The square is completed by another large **three-storey pagoda**, this one jointly dedicated to Shiva and Vishnu, a massive **bronze bell** dedicated to Taleju and an unusual eight-sided stone *shikhara*, a favourite seat for porters waiting for work.

Exploring Patan

Patan's quiet streets offer innumerable walks, and it's difficult to get *too* lost as the old city is barely three square kilometres (1.9 square miles) in area. Taking Durbar Square as the central starting point, ancient temples and interesting old *bahal* beckon at every turn. Remember that courtyards are public property shared by up to a dozen or more families, and feel no shyness about ducking through the low doors to examine an interesting stupa or statue. Often these unplanned encounters lead to more interesting meetings.

North Patan: Khumbeshwar, Sankhumal and Kwa Bahal

The road leading north from Durbar Square passes several crumbling old pagodas currently being restored. A red brick lane curving to the left leads to the slender five-storeyed pagoda of **Khumbeshwar**, Patan's oldest and tallest temple. The name means 'Lord of the Water Pot', one of the 1,008 epithets of Shiva. Khumbeshwar is considered the god's winter home (in the summer he moves to Mount Kailash in Tibet). When originally constructed in 1392 the temple was a two-storeyed pagoda; the upper three roofs were added in the 17th century. A small rectangular shrine on the south side houses the goddess **Bagalamukhi**, the dreaded sender of cholera.

The spring-fed water tank here is the scene of a boisterous annual *mela* held on Janai Purnima (usually the August full moon). Worshippers crowd into a pavilion raised in the middle of the tank to lavish flowers, red powder and grains of rice on an embossed silver linga specially displayed for the day. Crowds of young boys frolic in the sacred water, which is said to be connected by underground channel with the pilgrimage site of Gosainkund, several days' walk north of Kathmandu.

A few hundred metres north, down the main road, is Patan's northernmost **Ashoka stupa**, a gleaming half-hemisphere of white plaster, its shape echoed by the mounds of grain drying on the brick-paved courtyard. A bit further down the road ends at **Sankhumal**, an exceedingly ancient stretch of sacred *ghats* along the Bagmati. Seldom visited by tourists, this tranquil area contains overgrown monuments, crumbling temples and giant statues. You can wander back in the approximate direction of Durbar Square through fields and backstreets.

Another must is **Kwa Bahal**, known as the '**Golden Temple**' to tourists and the street urchins who escort them there. A five-minute walk northwest of Durbar Square, the temple's gilt and silver façade is embossed with elaborate details: a tiny frieze of scenes from the Buddha's life, various Buddhas and bodhisattvas, elephants, lions and snakes slithering off the second-storey roof. Strange statues abound in the courtyard, including a pair of squatting monkeys contemplating spiked jackfruit.

The amount of wealth on display here is quite astounding. In days past, rich Newari merchants would donate a portion of their profits from the lucrative Tibet trade for the temple's upkeep, and wealthy donors continue to sponsor it even today, accounting for its exceptionally good condition. Tibetan influence is visible also in a ground-floor shrine to Tara, in the prayer wheels rimming the main courtyard, and in the second-floor temple with its Buddhist frescoes and maroon-robed monks. The steady flow of tourists streaming in and out oddly does not disturb the rhythm of daily life; they are a part of it.

South Patan: Mahabuddha and Machhendranath

Ten minutes southeast of Durbar Square, **Mahabuddha**, the '**Temple of 1,000 Buddhas**', fills up an entire courtyard with its towering *shikhara* composed entirely of embossed terracotta plaques. It is said to have been raised by a 17th-century pilgrim in imitation of the great stupa of Bodh Gaya in India. The resemblance is vague at best, but Mahabuddha has its own charms, like the thousands of tiny Buddhas and intricate floral designs covering the entire monument. A nearby shrine dedicated to the Buddha's mother Maya Devi was constructed from tiles left over when the edifice crumbled in the 1934 earthquake.

Mahabuddha is at the centre of a metalworking neighbourhood of tiny ateliers and shops specializing in statues of Buddhist deities. Ratna Jyoti Shakya, whose shop is in the southeast corner of the courtyard, is particularly helpful in explaining the intricate *cire perdue* or lost-wax casting process.

A few steps past the Mahabuddha entrance at the end of the road stands the richly decorated **Uku Bahal**, described in written records that go back to AD 1117. Its members are the local gold and silversmiths who keep it ritually active and well-preserved. The courtyard houses a menagerie of fantastic metal beasts—horned horses, *garuda*, and lions—plus figures of kneeling donors immortalized in worship, and an imperious Rana general. Look for the subtly beautiful ancient carvings of nymphlike *yaksha* on the struts along the courtyard's rear wall.

The street in front of Uku Bahal runs through the old metalworking quarter of **Thaina**. Here the air rings with the tap-tap-tap of hammers on metal, as caste artisans fashion water pots, statues, urns and jugs in their dark, cramped ateliers. It leads back to the main road of **Mangal Bazaar**, the traditional old market area.

Turn north down the main road and a few minutes later enter the large temple compound on the left. The brightly painted shrine is dedicated to **Minnath**, an ancient local deity who eventually became associated with the bodhisattva Padmapani. Many Newar deities began as such animistic powers: later absorbed by Buddhism, they retained their ancient characteristics.

The prime example is the famous **Rato Machhendranath**, or **Bunga Dyo**, a strange flat-faced idol ensconced in a 17th-century pagoda across the street from the Minnath temple. This Red Machhendra, as opposed to Kathmandu's Seto or White Machhendra, has a long and convoluted history, beginning as a local godling and evolving into the compassionate bodhisattva Padmapani. Still later he became associated with the wandering Tantric master Machhendranath.

His principal devotees are Buddhist Newars, particularly farmers, who implore him for rain. His doll-like image is paraded annually in Patan's biggest and most jubilant festival, dating back to the 13th century. All through the increasingly hot spring, Machhendra is slowly pulled through the streets by groups of men heaving and hoing on the ropes of a great wooden chariot topped by a towering bamboo spire. The procession culminates in early June at Jawalakhel with the Bhoto Jatra, the showing of Machhendra's tiny jewelled vest; an occasion which is attended by the king himself. If all goes as it should, the first drops of the monsoon are expected to fall at exactly this moment—and often, eerily, they do.

The Festival of Red Machhendra

The car is a huge, unwieldy structure, with massive wheels, on the solid spokes of which are painted in distinctive colours the eyes of Bhairab or Shiva. Surmounting this is the chamber containing the deity, built up in the form of a column, somewhat resembling a Maypole, and between 60 and 70 feet high. This construction is only dragged for a distance of about a mile and a half, but this short journey ordinarily occupies at least four days, as certain prescribed halts are made, and neither is the car itself nor are the roads adapted for easy progression. The scene is a wild and barbaric one. Through the narrow streets overhung by wooden balconies crammed with excited groups of onlookers, or across the great open square, the platforms of all the picturesque buildings forming vantage grounds on which the crowds congregate, the car, dragged by over a hundred willing devotees, makes its triumphal tour. As these panting individuals become exhausted, so their places are taken by others from the packed mass of spectators, who, grasping one of the many ropes attached to the large under-beams or shafts, joyfully contribute their share to this portion of the ceremony. The superstructure of the car, overlaid with plates of copper gilt and surmounted by a metal umbrella with gay streamers and ribbons, sways until it almost overturns as the groaning wheels bump over the uneven pavement of the city, or sink deep into the soft soil of the roadway outside, but willing hands cling manfully to the guide ropes and thus accident is averted. Like a great ship staggering through a heavy sea—its curved prow terminating in a gilt figurehead of Bhairab, and apparently forcing its way through the seething mass of humans who like billows surround it in one capacity and another—the great god Matchhendra in his car, with strain and cry makes his annual journey. On a staging somewhat resembling a deck the officiating priests take their stand, and, like sailors, cling valiantly to the oscillating structure. A procession naturally accompanies the car, elephants gaily painted and caparisoned move ponderously along, bearing in their gold and silver howdahs the royalties of the State. Bands make joyful, if somewhat barbaric, music on tambourines, cymbals, trumpets, conches, and drums, while bevies of girls carrying garlands of flowers enliven the proceedings with song and dance. Other attendants bear great bells on poles, golden umbrellas, incense burners, fly-whisks, banners, and all the insignia of the great deity to whom they are doing honour. And so for four days and often longer, moving from place to place, this unique ceremony is maintained with shout and song, religious enthusiasm, feasting and rejoicing, until the final portion of the complete and complicated ritual is accomplished and the god is returned to his temple at Patan, where he remains in state until the following year.

Percy Brown, Picturesque Nepal, *1912*

Festival of Red Machhendra, Kathmandu

BHAKTAPUR

The ancient city of Bhaktapur nestles amidst the Valley's best farmland, 15 kilometres (nine miles) east of Kathmandu. Bhaktapur's rich fields, farmed by Newar Jyapu peasants, produce immense cauliflowers and the highest rice yield in the country. Bhaktapur is the most traditional, the most agrarian and the most Newar of the Valley's three ancient kingdoms. Even today, you can meet people in its backstreets who speak not a word of Nepali.

Once upon a time—from the mid-12th to the late-15th century—Bhaktapur was the capital of the entire Valley. With the subsequent fragmentation into three kingdoms and the rising importance of Kathmandu, the city was left to dream in peace. Its most ambitious residents leave for nearby Kathmandu; those who stay prefer the traditional ways that Bhaktapur embodies.

The old trade route to Tibet remains the town's main artery, its quiet brick-paved curves unmarred by traffic and lined with richly decorated temples, houses, shrines and fountains. Bhaktapur began as a series of villages, which gradually grew together into a unique urban environment. Better than any other place in the Valley, it preserves the ambience and charm of a medieval Newari city. Each caste-based neighbourhood has its own square, its own water source, its own temples. Private quarters may be dark and cramped, but people are rich in public space, and the open squares are living exhibits of all the mundane activities of daily life: people spinning wool, throwing pots, husking grain, nursing children, pounding chillies, hammering jewellery, selling vegetables. In a hundred years, perhaps, Nepal will be forced to recreate Bhaktapur in a historical park run by costumed employees, but for the present it remains genuine. A visit here will restore faith in the possibility of a tranquil urban existence, and inspire admiration for the Newars' traditional culture and their superb mastery of urban spaces.

Although accommodation in Bhaktapur is limited, an overnight stop here is worth considering simply because it reveals the city in different moods and lights. Bhaktapur is far more tranquil than Kathmandu, and in many ways more interesting. Even 24 hours here can be remarkably restorative.

Getting There

Bhaktapur lies down the Chinese-built highway to Tibet, about an hour's bicycle ride from Kathmandu. The trolley bus from Tripureswar ends at the southern edge of Bhaktapur, requiring a crossing of the smelly but sacred Hanumante River. Most vehicles take the side road just after the Hanumante bridge and head up a forested hill into town, passing the local version of Loch Ness: a vast slimy pond called **Siddhi Pokhari**, said to be inhabited by a terrifying serpent—the justification for it not having been cleaned for centuries.

Most tourists enter through Durbar Square and pay Rs50 admission for the privilege, but it's more interesting to follow the old trade route, which commences at an arched gate guarded by a pair of stone lions. The quiet road, lined with fine houses and beautifully carved temples, leads into Taumadhi Tol, just a few minutes' walk from Durbar Square.

For a splendid overview of Bhaktapur, go past the turning a few miles down the Tibet road to see the city nestled in the surrounding countryside, the smooth lines of its huddled rooftops broken by towering temples set against the gleaming backdrop of Himalayan peaks.

Durbar Square

Tucked away in the western corner of the city, Bhaktapur's Durbar Square is relatively unintegrated into daily life. Once the most beautiful of all the Three Kingdoms, it was devastated in the great earthquake of 1934 and is now a shadow of its former self, with odd blank spaces ruining the once masterful composition. Still, it remains imposing, and with grand temporary additions, recently served as the set for Bertolucci's film 'The Little Buddha'.

The **old royal palace** flanking the north side of the square once had 99 courtyards: six remain, most of them closed to the public. The **National Art Gallery**, housed in a renovated old wing, displays over 200 exquisite paintings from the 13th century on, including palm-leaf manuscripts, *thangkas* and restored frescoes decorating the walls of King Bhupatindra's private quarters (open 10 am–4 pm daily except Tuesdays).

A few steps further glitters the famed **Golden Gate**, hailed by an early visitor as 'the most exquisitely designed and finished piece of gilded metalwork in all of Asia'. It is dedicated to the Tantric goddess Taleju, whose temple lies in a courtyard beyond, and who appears as the central figure in the elaborate gilt *torana*. Finely detailed *repoussé* images of deities line the doorframe. Though the workmanship is superb, what astounds is the sheer quantity of wealth displayed.

A gilded statue of **King Bhupatindra Malla** kneels on a pillar opposite, dignified and solemn, his hands folded in prayer. The gateway marks the entrance to the supremely sacred **temple of Taleju**, hidden around the corner in a separate courtyard. It is closed to non-Hindus, and you must be content to peer through the guarded doorway at the richly ornamented courtyard, reportedly the finest in the Valley. When leaving, look for the **old royal bath** half-hidden in a crumbling courtyard. Once lit with oil lamps for the king's evening ablutions, it is overgrown with ferns, but the beautiful gilded metal spout remains, along with a *naga* standard set in the bathing pool.

Back in the main square is the imposing **Palace of 55 Windows**, built in 1697. In one, note historical chronicles, the king placed a single pane of glass carried in from India as 'an object of wonder for the people'. The palace once sprawled far beyond here, but the 1934 earthquake has left only an enormous empty plaza to the east, littered with the bases of giant temples.

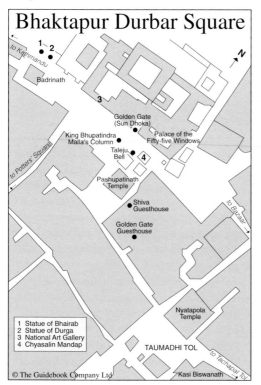

Chyasalin Mandap, the elegant little 'Eight-Sided Pavilion' across from the palace, was originally a viewing point for nobles observing festivals and rituals. Destroyed in the 1934 earthquake, it was recently reconstructed with assistance from Germany. Local workmen cleverly fitted together new wood-carvings with the remaining fragments, rubbing the whole with linseed oil to achieve the patina of age. Making a rather obscure aesthetic point, the steel reinforcements used to earthquake-proof the structure have been deliberately left exposed.

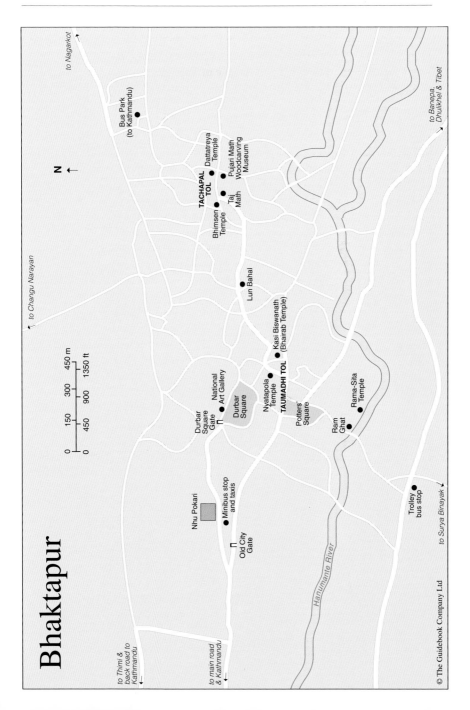

Bhaktapur

Behind it is an old sunken water tap, and behind this a large **Pashupatinath Temple**, supposedly a replica of the sacred original, but minus the gilt roof and silver doors. Struts show Shiva and characters from the Ramayana; at the bottom are small erotic scenes. Follow the narrow souvenir-lined street leading off behind here to Taumadhi Tol.

Taumadhi Tol

Far more than Durbar Square, this is the central square of Bhaktapur, tightly woven into daily life and rituals. The square is dominated by the towering Nyatapola Temple, at 30 metres (98 feet) the tallest temple in Nepal. Poised atop a five-storey plinth, its five-tiered roofs soar upwards, a paragon of balanced form and grace. It was built in 1702 in record time after the king himself carried three bricks as an example for his subjects. Inside dwells an extremely secret Tantric form of the goddess Durga. A special family of priests tends the temple, which may be entered only by the king.

The steep staircase is lined with massive stone guardians: first the brawny wrestling brothers Jai and Patta Malla, said to have possessed the strength of ten men, followed by elephants, lions, griffons and minor deities, each ten times stronger than the last. The series culminates in the powerful tantric goddess hidden inside, about whom rumours are legion. Not even her name is certain: some call her Siddhi Lakshmi, some Bhairabi, some Durga; all, in the ultimate analysis, the same.

This powerful temple is counterbalanced, ritually and aesthetically, by the unusual rectangular **Kasi Biswanath** on the eastern side. Fantastically gilded, it houses a once unruly Bhairab who reportedly calmed down after the Nyatapola's goddess was brought in to offset him. The deity is worshipped as a tiny 10-inch-high gilded image set in a niche in the ornate façade. The entrance is behind, via the *dyochem* of **Betal**, a hobgoblin who accompanies Bhairab on his annual chariot ride, in the form of a metal mask on the prow. A troublesome and malignant being, Betal is worshipped for half an hour a year as part of the Bisket festival; the rest of the time he is tied, face down, to the topmost roofbeams of his temple.

Potters' Square

A five-minute detour south of Taumadhi leads to the fascinating neighbourhood of **Talako**, home to the potter caste. The heavy old wooden wheels have been for the most part replaced by weighted truck tyres which spin faster. Guided by skilled hands, the cones of wet black mud are shaped and smoothed into yoghurt bowls, washbasins, giant grain storage jars and tiny oil lamps. All around the square, pots lined up in symmetric patterns dry in the sun, waiting for a final firing in temporary kilns of heaped straw. Nearby shops sell whimsical souvenirs: tiny animals, candlesticks, ashtrays and flowerpots. Bargain hard, remembering that they are essentially baked mud.

To Tachapal Tol

Back at Taumadhi, follow the winding brick road east through the city's **main bazaar**, a fascinating walk past tiny shops selling sweets, cloth, brass, toys and fruit. The route passes various water taps, ancient water tanks and temples, most of them neighbourhood shrines dedicated to Ganesh, the god of luck. Bhaktapur's intimate relationship with the land is visible even in this city centre, in the heaps of grain and brilliant red chilli peppers spread out on straw mats to dry in the sun. The blessed absence of traffic makes the experience particularly pleasurable.

In about 15 minutes you'll reach Tachapal Tol, another large square which marks the old centre of town, dating back to perhaps the eighth century. It is lined by richly decorated *math*, nine in all, the densest concentration of these Hindu monasteries in the Valley. Formerly they housed religious communities of ascetics and yogis, but descendents of the original inhabitants took them over long ago as private residences. Several of Tachapal's old *math* have been converted into handicraft shops, and one into a restaurant.

At the east end the broad-roofed **Dattatreya Temple** ranks among the Valley's oldest shrines, dating back to 1427. A former rest-house for pilgrims, it still houses wandering sadhus, especially around the Shiva Ratri festival. Dedicated to an unusual three-headed combination of Brahma, Vishnu and Shiva, it is guarded by gigantic sculptures of the wrestling Malla brothers. Look for the tiny wooden image of Indra peering from an upstairs window which was hoisted up by tipsy revellers one Indra Jatra.

Behind the temple, once attached to it but now separate, is **Pujari Math**, built in the 15th century and restored with German funding as a wedding present for King Birendra. Its wealth of elaborate carvings include the famous **Peacock Window** down the narrow side alley and a courtyard decorated with cavorting wild boars, monkeys and *makara*. Inside is the **National Woodcarving Museum**, with a small collection of statues and old temple struts (open 10 am–4 pm daily except Tuesdays, admission Rs10). The same hours are observed by the less interesting **Brass and Bronze Museum** across the street.

More Exploring

Bhaktapur offers alternative possibilities to wander beyond the standard stroll outlined above. Explore the warren of ancient *tols* or neighbourhoods, each inhabited by a different caste and guarded by local deities. There is no traffic, no dust, no pushing and shouting, only a steady tide of pedestrians flowing down the brick lanes. The wide streets north of Tachapal are particularly good for wandering, lined with temples and water tanks, and crowded with curious people. The bathing and cremation *ghats* along the sacred but filthy Hanumante River on the southern edge of town are fascinating, if you can tolerate the stench.

The surrounding countryside is prime territory for walks: uphill to **Nagarkot**, or the easy two-hour stroll through fields and small villages to the ancient temple of **Changu Narayan**. **Surya Binayak**, a small hilltop temple about 20 minutes walk south of the trolley bus terminus, is one of the Valley's four great Ganesh sites. Worshippers crowd here bearing Ganesh's favourite offerings…radishes, *doob* grass, milky-sweet *ladoo*—to beseech special favours: business success, the health of a weak infant, a good husband. As is usual for Ganesh, the unlucky days of Tuesdays and Saturdays draw the biggest crowds.

Thimi

Returning to Kathmandu, take the back road through Thimi, a large Newari village built on a raised plateau surrounded by a sea of fields. The town's main artery, accessible only on foot, runs north–south, linking a series of temple-studded squares. Most prominent is the gilt-roofed pagoda dedicated to **Balkumari**, a Tantric mother goddess worshipped for rain, for children and for health. Dozens of coconuts are nailed up on the temple façade in an offering peculiar to her. The goddess is paraded about in a palanquin each April during Nepali New Year in a riotous festival. Thimi's traditional specialities, papier—mâché masks and pottery, are sold in shops on the eastern outskirts of town.

AROUND THE VALLEY

Probably the most common mistake visitors to Kathmandu make is to neglect the surrounding countryside. The three main cities and the holy sites of Swayambhu, Boudhanath and Pashupatinath all make the must-see list, but the rest of the Valley gets short shrift. However long or short your stay, make an effort to get out and explore, as some of your most rewarding experiences are to be found here. Distances are not great and transport is easily arranged (the best options are taxi or bicycle, combined with judicious amounts of walking). Kathmandu may be increasingly noisy, crowded and polluted, but over half the Valley remains farmland, and in its rural hamlets traditional life continues virtually unchanged.

Out in the countryside, you get a feel for the subtly shifting rhythms of seasons and crops. During the monsoon the paddy-fields begin as a sea of floating mirrors, carpeted with the incredibly vibrant green of growing rice. Slowly the grain ripens into gold and is cut by hand, to reveal the textured brown of fallow earth. Soon enough the land is covered with winter wheat and flowering mustard, its golden blossoms vibrant in the crisp winter sunlight; this is then harvested and another crop planted, in an endless cycle.

In the clear light of autumn and winter the brilliant colours astound the eye, with vistas of ochre-washed houses with marigolds and banks of scarlet poinsettias in front, surrounded by fields of dazzling yellow mustard. The distinctly rural character adds to the local architecture: tall brick Newari houses adorned with strings of drying chillies or bitter greens, or the ochre-and-white mud-walled houses of caste Hindus or Tamangs, their thatched roofs overrun with flowering squash vines. Rocky outcrops and high ridges are the favoured sites for the most ancient villages: they were easy to defend, with the additional benefit of conserving flat farmland. Some, like Pharping and Kirtipur in the South Valley, were once fortress–fiefdoms in themselves, and retain a wealth of shrines and ornate architecture.

Ambling down the roads and trails, you never lack company. Here comes a bunch of schoolchildren in neat uniforms who, sighting a foreigner, commence with the mantra so common among Nepali children: 'One pen! One pen!', or 'one rupees!'—neither of which should be acceded to. Next is a woman toting a plump infant with kohl-ringed eyes and silver anklets, followed by a man with swinging double baskets of vegetables suspended from a bamboo shoulder pole—a device used only by Newars. Then a line of women bent over beneath giant loads of leaves for fodder, or hay for drying, or firewood, followed by some young girls lugging heavy metal *gagri* filled with water for washing, cooking and cleaning. It doesn't take long to realize that the endless cycle of backbreaking labour, as in most of the Third World, falls most heavily on Nepali women. In addition to the time-consuming duties of running the house, cooking meals and caring for children, women put in most of the labour involved in tending to the fields and processing the harvested crop. You will find them out in cheerful groups, weeding or planting or harvesting according to season. At ploughing time the men step in, directing their slow-moving oxen with abrupt shouted commands, or attacking the heavy clay soil with the *kodali*, a backbreaking short-handled hoe.

Most of the Valley is served by slow and crowded local buses and minibuses, but these are not recommended as transport. Either rent a bicycle or hire a taxi for half a day or a day. If you're hiking, the driver can drop you off and pick you up several hours later at your destination. Bring water, plus a bottle of iodine with dropper to treat more along the way, and snacks or picnic fare. Available sustenance is generally limited to soft drinks, tea, biscuits and snacks in local teashops.

Important shrines and interesting villages are described below, arranged by area rather than any preferred ranking. The best map for in-depth exploring remains the old Schneider map of the Valley, available at local bookstores.

North and East Valley

Balaju

This ancient pilgrimage site, now one of Kathmandu's very few public parks, lies a few kilometres north of Thamel. It centres around a line of 22 carved stone *dhara* from which sacred water spouts. Crowds of devotees flock here for ritual bathing on astrologically auspicious days, most notably the April full moon.

Balaju was originally a pleasure garden for Malla kings: from here, Prithvi Narayan Shah launched his successful 1768 assault on Kathmandu. Today it is a popular weekend picnic site for Kathmandu's middle class. The landscaped garden is adorned with some extraordinary sculptures, most notably a fine seventh-century **Sleeping Vishnu** set in a pond, a smaller contemporary of the famous image at Budhanilkantha. Among the many Hindu and Buddhist deities depicted here, look for a 16th-century image of **Harihara**, a rare hybrid of Vishnu and Shiva, bearing the wheel and conch shell of the former and the trident of the latter.

Budhanilkantha

Seven kilometres north of Kathmandu lies the **Sleeping Vishnu**, more properly Jalasayana Narayana, 'Narayan Lying on the Waters'. The massive stone image is inspired by the ancient Hindu creation myth which describes Vishnu slumbering on the primordial ocean, floating unconscious above the coils of the great serpent Ananta, until Brahma unfolds from his navel in the form of a lotus, inspiring all creation. Budhanilkantha's image, consecrated in AD 641, is the largest and most awe-inspiring of all the Sleeping Vishnus in the Valley. Carved from a single massive block of black stone, Vishnu floats gently in the waters of the tank, seemingly dreaming, a half-smile on his lips. Devotees toss flower petals, coins and red powder onto the image and bow humbly at its feet, while morning and evening Brahman priests perform elaborate rituals.

Vishnu and his water tank are set in an old courtyard, ringed by an ugly cement fence and surrounded by subsidiary shrines and bells. The kings of Nepal have avoided viewing this image on pain of death ever since King Pratap Malla had a prophetic dream. The name has nothing to do with the Buddha: *budha* or *burha* means 'old' in Nepali; *nil* 'blue', and *kantha* 'throat'—thus 'Old Blue Throat', referring to the time Shiva drank a draught of poison which burned his throat blue. Exactly what this has to do with Vishnu is unclear, but the waters of the tank in which the god rests are said to be magically connected with the Himalayan lake of Gosainkund, where Shiva sought relief from the burning poison.

Gokarna Mahadev and Sundarijal

At the sacred confluence of three rivers a few kilometres east of Boudhanath stands the 14th-century temple of Gokarna Mahadev, sacred to Shiva. The temple, which boasts some fine **woodcarvings**, and its surrounding buildings are among the best-maintained in the Valley, thanks to a UNESCO restoration effort in the early 1980s. The compound holds a unique collection of recent but well-rendered sculptures of various Hindu deities, plus an eighth-century **Parvati** in a small shrine.

Just beyond is the small Newari village of **Gokarna**, while across the river and reached by a separate road is **Gokarna Jungle Resort**, a commercial enterprise situated in an old Rana game reserve. The lush woods here are the largest remaining fragment of the subtropical forest which long ago carpeted the Valley floor. They are best explored on the backs of swaying elephants, available for rent by the hour. There is a minor admission charge, and hiking is free.

The road past Gokarna Mahadev ends several kilometres further at the foot of Shivapuri mountain. About 20 minutes' climb up a flight of steep stone stairs is the waterfall called **Sundarijal**, 'Beautiful Water', a popular picnic site. The cascade can be impressive in early autumn, but don't bother going in the dry spring season.

Changu Narayan

The supreme example of Nepalese temple architecture is generally agreed to be the ancient hilltop shrine of Changu Narayan, located about six kilometres (3.75 miles) east of Boudhanath on the road to Sankhu. (It can also be reached by taxi, or on foot from Bhaktapur.) The site is a contemporary of Swayambhunath, Pashupatinath and Boudhanath, and rivals them in importance, but despite its historical significance, it is little-known and seldom visited by tourists.

Climb up the ancient stone steps leading to the top of the hill. A large square courtyard embraces the classical broad-roofed pagoda, this latest version dating from the early 18th century. It is richly decorated with painted woodwork, with an incredibly extravagant assemblage of gilt *repoussé* work adorning the main doors. The principal image is kept hidden from non-Hindus, but all around in a casual open-air assemblage are superb sculptures of Vishnu in his many forms, any one of which would arouse the envy of a museum director. Look for **Vishnu Vikranta** striding across the universe, Vishnu aboard the winged Garuda as **Vishnu Vaikunthanata** (this image appears on the back of the Nepalese ten-rupee note), and best of all the eighth-century **Vishnu Vishvarupa**, inspired by the *Mahabharata* description of Vishnu in his Universal Form. The god stands with ten heads and multiple arms, displaying his full glory to a host of adoring divinities; below is an image of the Sleeping Vishnu floating on the cosmic ocean.

More images are littered about, including a plump kneeling **Garuda** and behind it, engraved on a stone column, the **oldest inscription** in Nepal, *circa* AD 464. Nearby, **gilt votary images** of Kathmandu's King Bhupalendra Malla and his mother, the queen regent, kneel in a wrought-metal cage. (Devout donors often funded statues of themselves kneeling in perpetual prayer before a favourite temple.) Shrines to Krishna, Shiva and the Ashta Matrika complete the complex. The small village of **Changu** below remains virtually medieval. The opposite side of the hill is used as pastureland and is a good picnic site, with views of the sprawling fields below and the Manohara River snaking off into the distance. Bhaktapur lies two hours' walk away, a wonderful stroll through rolling countryside and rural villages.

Sankhu

The Boudhanath road ends at the peaceful village of Sankhu. Tucked away in the eastern corner of the Valley, this Newari settlement seems nearly forgotten. Once it was an important halting place on the Tibetan trade route, and the wealth that passed through contributed to its fine old buildings. Some of the older houses still boast ornate rococo plasterwork, part of the Rana-era mimicry of European architecture. The town is said to be arranged in the form of a conch shell (*sankhu*), hence its name.

A flagstoned pilgrim path heading north of town leads to an ancient site of Buddhist power, occupied for the last few centuries by the temple of the tantric goddess **Vajra Yogini**. This is the most important of the Valley's four shrines to this powerful Buddhist deity, worshipped by Hindus as a manifestation of Durga. Set in a pine forest halfway up the hill called **Manichaur**, the 17th-century shrine features a lovely metal *torana* depicting the goddess. The principal image is kept hidden away inside, along with some rare old sculptures. Buddhism prescribes blood sacrifice, but Hindu devotees get around the restriction by offering goats and chickens at a boulder on the pathway below the temple.

South Valley

Kirtipur

The layout of this ancient Newari town typifies the fortress mentality of the frequently besieged Valley fiefdoms. Huddled on top of a high ridge a few kilometers south of Patan, Kirtipur is easily defended. Gorkha troops attacked it on three occasions during their 20-year siege of the Valley, finally succeeding in 1766. For their pains the conquerors exacted a bloody revenge, cutting off the noses of every male over the age of 12 and changing the town's name to Naskatipur, 'City of Cut Noses'. This ancient grievance may possibly explain the town's rather grim atmosphere and unfriendly people.

Kirtipur also typifies the urban orientation of Newari villages. The flagstoned streets are lined with once-elegant, now crumbling houses, closely huddled together. The lower reaches of town, known as the 'New

Bazaar', include a string of shops selling modern goods and an oddity for Nepal: a **Theravada Buddhist temple** with tapering roof, built with donations from Thailand.

The old town is spread along the top of a dumbbell-shaped hill. The older and more dilapidated eastern section clusters around the 16th-century **Chilamchu Stupa**. In the middle of the hummock is the impressively well-proportioned rectangular temple of **Bagh Bhairab**, 'Tiger Bhairab'. Legend relates that shepherd children once carelessly discarded a toy tiger they had fashioned of clay. Bhairab took possession of the image and proceeded to devour their flock. Local people also worship the resident deity as **Ajudya**, the grandfather god. The temple is supremely ancient, dating back to AD 1090, and the compound holds some incredibly old sculptures, such as a row of five well-worn mother goddesses from the fourth century, and a roughly contemporary **Shiva–Parvati** image.

The mainly Hindu western portion of town is in better condition than the eastern, with houses and *pati* inset with some exceptional woodcarvings. It terminates in a hillock topped by a tall pagoda dedicated to **Uma≈Mahesvara**, Shiva and Parvati. The steep flight of steps is flanked by elephants bearing spiked saddles to discourage local children from play. You can obtain an excellent view of the Himalaya from this high vantage point.

The Dakshinkali Road

If you have time for only one excursion, this is arguably the most interesting, offering a diverse assortment of villages, temples and holy sites. The road leads past the Tribhuvan University Campus and the Kirtipur road. One kilometre further, a flight of stone steps leads up a steep pine-forested hill into the ancient town of **Chobhar**. This Lichhavi-era settlement is seldom visited by tourists as no road reaches up here, which does wonders for its charm. In the centre is a lovely temple to **Adinath Lokesvara**, the Buddhist embodiment of compassion: his image is an exact replica of Patan's red-faced Rato Machhendranath. A profusion of pots and pans is nailed up under the eaves, offerings donated by newlyweds hoping to ensure a happy marriage, or children a deceased parent's comfort in the afterlife.

Below the village and across the road, the sacred Bagmati rushes through the narrow defile of **Chobhar Gorge**, its rock walls scarred by earthquake fault lines. It is spanned by a still functioning iron suspension bridge manufactured in Glasgow in 1903, shipped to India and carried over the hills by porters. On the riverbank stands one of the Valley's four great Ganesh shrines, the 17th-century **Jal Binayak**. Worship here is said to bring wisdom and strength of character, perhaps explaining why this temple is less popular than, say, the wealth-granting Chabahil Ganesh. Jal Binayak is also worshipped to avert water-related disasters.

Ganesh is worshipped as a naturally manifested unsculpted image, a giant boulder encased in a gilt collar, that only vaguely resembles an elephant's head. He appears more distinctly in a plaster plaque on the temple façade, which shows him seated in the lap of his father, Shiva. The temple struts depict his companions, the Eight Bhairabs and the Eight Matrikas, with clever erotic scenes inset below the principal figures.

A little further down the road is the pond called **Taudaha**, the fabled abode of the naga king who guards the Valley's wealth. Manjushri is said to have ensconced him here in an underwater golden palace after draining the Valley's waters. Though small, the pond is said to be unfathomably deep, foiling efforts made in the last century to retrieve the fabled wealth in its depths.

Pharping, a former small fiefdom, now a minor village, is surrounded by several immensely holy sites, both Hindu and Buddhist. Stop first at the roadside site of **Shesh Narayan**, a series of clear sacred pools set in a beautiful little grotto. Up a stone stairway, opposite a vividly painted **Tibetan monastery**, is one of the four main Vishnu shrines in the Valley, called variously **Shesh**, **Shikar** or **Shekha Narayan**. Set in a rock overhang, the small temple is a skilful blend of natural and man-made elements. Its 15th-century image of Vishnu Vikrantha, the Wide Strider, was stolen several years ago and has been replaced by a glossy new sculpture.

A trail, difficult to discern at times, winds around the hill from here, passing a little gilt-roofed pagoda dedicated to the Buddhist protectress **Vajra Yogini**, built in the 17th century and still in fine condition. On the rear side of the hill (accessible also by road) are several more-recently built **Tibetan monasteries**, the lowest enshrining an image of the bodhisattva Tara said to be slowly and miraculously manifesting from the rock. With typical Valley syncretism, local Hindus worship the image as the goddess Saraswati. Most of these *gompas* are Nyingma, members of the 'Old School' sect, revering the eighth-century Tantric master Guru Rinpoche, who introduced Buddhism to Tibet. Climb the steps past them to an extremely sacred rock cleft where Guru Rinpoche is said to have left his head and handprints in the rock. The topmost monastery is built around the **Asura Cave**, revered as Guru Rinpoche's meditation site. The grassy hilltop beyond makes a fine if somewhat steep setting for a picnic beneath strings of fluttering prayer flags.

Sleeping Porter

On his back a fifty-pound load,
his spine bent double,
six miles sheer in the winter snows;
naked bones;
with two rupees of life in his body
to challenge the mountain.
He wears a cloth cap, black and sweaty,
a ragged garment;
lousy, flea-ridden clothes are on his body,
his mind is dulled.
It's like sulphur, but how great
this human frame!

The bird of his heart twitters and pants;
sweat and breath;
in his hut on the cliffside, children shiver:
hungry woes.
His wife like a flower
searches the forest for nettles and vines.
Beneath this great hero's snow peak,
the conqueror of Nature is wealthy
with pearls of sweat on his brow.
Above, there is only the lid of night,
studded with stars,
and in this night he is rich with sleep.

Lakshmi Prasad Devkota, 1958
Translated by Michael James Hutt in
Himalayan Voices, 1991

Farmer's sickle

The road ends at the 22-kilometre mark, at the bloody and ancient open-air shrine of **Dakshinkali**, the Valley's premier site for animal sacrifices. Originally dedicated to a mother goddess, it was transferred a few centuries ago to the Hindu goddess Kali. 'The Black One' is not a winsome creature: her grinning, hideous image, wielding a skull cup and sword, squats over a corpse (symbolizing her victory over Time). She is surrounded by companions: the Ashta Matrikas, Ganesh and Bhairab. Kali is merely another aspect of the great goddess Durga, appearing in gruesome form to battle with evil.

Her shrine draws hundreds of thousands of visitors each year, many of them Indian tourists. On Tuesdays and Saturdays, the most auspicious days for blood sacrifice, the site takes on the cheerful atmosphere of a temple *mela*. The shady stone path leading in is lined with villagers selling offerings and treats: buffalo-milk yoghurt, flower garlands, fresh farmer's cheese and giant pumpkins, this last used as a substitute offering by those too poor to afford the standard chicken or goat. The gaiety contrasts oddly with the bloody scene at Kali's shrine, where caste butchers slit animals' throats, then drag the carcasses off to a nearby stream to be eviscerated. The meat is delivered to the sacrificial donor and frequently becomes the basis for a family picnic on a nearby hillside.

Bungamati and Kokana

These two charming Newari villages are among the nicest sites in the entire Valley for a stroll, lying about an hour's walk south of Patan, down the level gravel road running from Jawalakhel. Traditional society here remains relatively intact, with neighbourhoods organized by hereditary occupational castes, each with their own *guthi* and *bahal*. The men of Bungamati are known for their skill in woodcarving, and carpet weaving has spread here too, providing work for women.

The white plaster *shikhara* in the centre of town is the part-time abode of Rato Machhendranath, the rain-bringing patron of Buddhist Newars. Six months of the year he dwells here (thus his alternate name **Bunga Dyo**, God of Bunga); the rest of the time he is enshrined in Patan. Crumbling shrines are dotted about the large open courtyard, and all about are vignettes of agriculturally based village life, which is carried out largely in public. Fortunately for visitors, Bungamati's residents have not yet been overexposed to tourism and are wonderfully friendly. Ten minutes northwest, via a path cutting through fields, lies the smaller village of Kokana, really just a single exceptionally wide main street culminating in a square with a large temple dedicated to the mother goddess **Shekali Mai**.

Godavari

The South Valley is dominated by the looming bulk of Phulchowki, at
2,765 metres (8,427 feet) the highest of the peaks ringing the Valley. Its
lush climate and exceptionally high rainfall once supported large
cardamom plantations; today the main attraction is the Royal Botanical
Gardens.

The paved road that leads here passes through the Newar town of
Harasiddhi, notorious for the human sacrifices once offered in its temple.
Twenty kilometres (12.5 miles) down are the **Botanical Gardens**, 24
hectares of pleasantly landscaped green lawns, flowers and trees collected
from across the country. The site is peaceful except on weekends when
families and groups of students flock here for picnics. A bit further down
the road is Godavari Kunda, a sacred spring flowing through carved stone
taps into a stepped pool, the mythic source of South India's Godavari River.
A giant *mela* held here every 12 years draws thousands of pilgrims.

Returning, look behind **St Xavier's School** (a prestigious Jesuit-run
institution) for a tranquil 17th-century pagoda dedicated to **Pulchowki Mai**,
the ancient mother-goddess associated with the lush mountain rising
behind. No doubt she, like local environmentalists, is disturbed at the
marble quarry ripping an ugly scar into the mountainside directly across
from her temple.

Over the Rim

Around Banepa

Over the Valley's eastern rim and down the Chinese-built highway to Tibet
lies a pastoral countryside of tiered rice fields dotted with Newari villages,
imbued with old ways and old culture. This is the former domain of the
Kingdom of **Banepa**, once a powerful rival to Kathmandu, Patan and
Bhaktapur. Today Banepa is a dusty, noisy little bus-stop of a town, though
the old town off the main road retains some interest, primarily in the great
wall fresco of a fanged and blue-faced Bhairab at the **Chandesvari temple**.

The old medieval village of **Nala** four kilometres (2.5 miles) northwest
of Banepa is even more remote and unchanged. Despite the level dirt road
leading to it, visitors seldom explore its peaceful streets. The centre of town
is dominated by an unusual **four-storey pagoda** dedicated to the goddess
Bhagawati, embodied in a weathered 12th-century image.

Dhulikhel

The principal destination in this direction is **Dhulikhel**, 32 kilometres (20 miles) from Kathmandu. This old Newari town was once a stop on the old trade route to Lhasa, and the wealth which passed through manifests itself in its impressive old buildings, many of them now leaning precariously, and propped up with beams. The town remains over half Newar, with a mercantile orientation. There are various **Hindu temples**, and budget guest-houses catering to travellers who stay here overnight to catch sunrise views of the Himalaya from the **hilltop Kali shrine** south of town. A few other elegant resorts found along the main highway are nice places for Himalayan sunset-views with dinner.

Dhulikhel's attractions are fairly low-key, but worthwhile when combined with walks in the surrounding countryside. Overnighters or early-starting day-trippers can make the two-hour hike from here to the hilltop stupa of **Namobuddha**. The small whitewashed monument is said to enshrine the relics of a virtuous local prince who, moved by compassion at the sight of a starving tigress, fed himself to her, piece by piece. Tibetan Buddhists revere this peaceful site, flocking here to string up bright prayer flags and spin the encircling prayer wheels. A very bumpy dirt road leads up here, but it's nicer to hike, returning in a loop to Dhulikhel or perhaps continuing on to Panauti.

Panauti

This ancient Newar village, another former mini-kingdom, has far more charm than the unappealing bus park at the entrance to town would first indicate. The quiet streets behind are lined with prosperous old buildings. The masterpiece is the **Indresvar Mahadev** temple to Shiva, dating back to 1294. Severely damaged in the 1988 earthquake, it is now being restored with financial assistance from France. Study the finely carved original struts: slender, graceful figures that represent the best of Nepalese woodcarving.

Close behind, at the sacred confluence of the Roshi and Punyamati rivers, is a charming collection of old shrines and rest-houses. This pilgrimage site hosts an annual *mela* involving ritual bathing in chilly mid-January. Panauti is well worth a visit, either hiking from Dhulikhel (two hours), via Namobuddha (four hours), or driving direct from Kathmandu (it lies at the end of a seven-kilometre paved road branching south from Banepa).

Mountain View Points

A pilgrimage to one of the hilltop viewing points ringing the Valley is nearly obligatory for visitors, though with altitudes nearing 3,000 metres (9,000 feet and above) it seems ridiculous to call these peaks 'hills'. It is impossible to single out any one as the best, as all close-up Himalayan views are magnificent, but Nagarkot probably has the most expansive views (apart from **Daman**, which lies beyond the Valley).

What you see, if anything, is subject to the whims of the weather. The Himalaya can hide for weeks on end, then miraculously emerge one day, usually after a night of rain has cleared the air, or a stiff afternoon wind blows away the clouds. Views that are clouded at midday often cooperatively clear up for sunsets and sunrises. Fortunately the mountains are frequently clear in the autumn and winter months. Remember that the winter morning mist doesn't veil the peaks: ascend early and you'll see the mountains shining above the cloudy lake of the Valley below.

Staying overnight at a hilltop resort maximizes the chances of superb views, and provides a break from Kathmandu's increasingly relentless urban grittiness. Nagarkot and Kakani have overnight accommodation; also see the section on **Dhulikhel**, which has several up-market resorts with mountain views. Day hikes to Shivapuri, Nagarjun or Phulchowki also yield mountain views; indeed, an extensive stretch of Himalaya can be seen from virtually anywhere in the south Valley.

Wide-ranging, classic perspectives are available from mountain flights run by RNAC, Everest Air and Necon Air daily in season (US$99 per person). From Pokhara, Everest Air's 'Annapurna Air Trek' glides at eye level along the Annapurna and Dhaulagiri ranges. The ultimate is a helicopter flight (about US$160 an hour per person). The wrap-around windows and lower flying altitude provides truly spectacular views of the dramatic hill and mountainscapes. The 90-minute flight to Langtang drops passengers for a brief stop into the very heart of the mountains: undoubtedly an easier route than trekking.

This small, popular hill resort of **Nagarkot**, perched on a ridge 32 kilometres (20 miles) east of Kathmandu commands sweeping views of the Himalaya. Five of the world's ten highest peaks (Everest, Lhotse, Cho Oyu, Makalu and Manaslu) are visible from here…distant, to be sure, but still awe-inspiring, floating in the rosy light of dawn or sunset. Nagarkot itself is not even a village, just a scattering of lodges ranging from simple budget dormitories to neat little brick bungalows. It's all well above Kathmandu's hurly-burly and very low-key, though there's not much to do here besides eat, admire the views and stroll about the steep hillside long ago denuded of forest. Returning, there's a great array of mainly downhill hikes: to Sankhu, Changu Narayan, Bhaktapur, or Nala and Banepa.

Kakani is a tiny village perched on the northwest Valley rim, about 30 kilometres (19 miles) from Kathmandu. It offers unforgettable close-up views of the Central Nepal Himalaya, especially the elephantine bulk of Ganesh Himal. The best viewing point is the back lawn of the quaintly decrepit Taragaon Resort, which has basic rooms and simple meals (or bring your own picnic and order drinks). As added entertainment, you can watch recruits at the police training centre below practice lathi charges and other crowd-control methods. Kakani is a favourite with mountain bikers, lying a few kilometres off the paved, not-too-steep Trisuli highway.

The closest of all the Valley's surrounding peaks, the green hump of **Nagarjun**, looms northwest of Swayambhunath. Its name is that of a Buddhist Indian sage who is said to have meditated in a cave on its slopes. Another legend relates that from Nagarjun's summit a bodhisattva tossed the lotus seed that blossomed into Swayambhunath.

Nargarjun's fine forests of oak and rhododendron were once a Rana hunting preserve called Rani Ban, Queen's Forest. Today they are a protected sanctuary sheltering wild boar, deer, even a few small leopards. The main entrance is up the Balaju road, not far from the water gardens. There are two routes to the grassy 2,096-metre (6,388-foot) summit: a fairly easy five-kilometre ridge trail and an unpaved but usually motorable road of about 25 kilometres. At the top are a few picnic shelters, some small whitewashed stupas and a metal viewing tower strung with Tibetan prayer flags. From the top, Tibetans toss out coloured slips of paper printed with prayers, which slowly flutter down on the breeze. Nagarjun is a holy site for Tibetan and Newari Buddhists, who on weekends and festivals come here for elaborate family feasts, puja and some discrete gambling. It provides an excellent overview of the Kathmandu Valley, and on a clear day the Himalaya are visible from Annapurna all the way to Sikkim.

As the main watershed for Kathmandu, **Shivapuri** is protected by a conservation project that has halted woodcutting and has evicted most of the farmers on its slopes. The resulting natural regeneration is supporting the return of the tremendous biodiversity typical of midland Nepal. One study of Shivapuri found 129 varieties of mushroom, 50 types of birds and a species of dragonfly formerly unknown to science.

The gravel road looping around the mountain in a figure of eight is a favourite route for mountain biking, but the pleasantest option is the four-hour hike up to the summit, starting from the guard-post marking the entrance to the preserve. Follow the road up past tumbling streams to a steep trail branching off up to the Buddhist nunnery of Nagi Gompa. Sherpa, Tamang, Newari and Tibetan women of all ages study and pray here in a peaceful communal setting.

Above the *gompa* is a steep prayer-flag studded ridge; conquer it, and be rewarded by an easier passage through increasingly lush oak and rhododendron forests. The upper reaches are old-growth forest, degraded but pristine, a rarity in Nepal. The trail passes near the dripping springs of Bagdwar, the legendary source of the Bagmati River and a sacred pilgrimage site. The springs are set in a lovely overgrown clearing adorned with crumbling *chaitya*. Shivapuri's grassy 2,732-metre (8,327-foot) summit lies less than an hour beyond and provides some fine Himalayan views, though these must be experienced in the company of the Nepalese Army soldiers posted here. Camping is possible on the mountain, and local companies run two- or three-day Valley Rim treks between Shivapuri and Nagarkot.

With its high rainfall and varied altitude, the green peak of **Phulchowki** is the lushest and most ecologically diverse of all the mountains ringing the Valley. Orchids and ferns abound, and in the spring waves of blossoming rhododendrons unfold at increasingly high altitudes.

Access begins behind St. Xavier's School at Godavari in the extreme south Valley. A graded but unpaved road leads to the summit. If you're on foot, avoid the twisting road and take the faster foot trails which start behind the school. It's a three- or four-hour climb to the top. On the summit is a shrine to Phulchowki Mai, the mother goddess of the mountain, a communications tower, a small army post, and, if you're lucky, a 320-kilometre (200-mile) Himalayan panorama stretching from Annapurna to beyond Everest.

THE HILLS

The Hills are the geographic and cultural heartland of Nepal, the home of the dominant Hindu castes who have shaped the nation's ethics, language and culture. The term 'Hills' is a distinct understatement. Rising from 1,500 to 4,300 metres (5,000 to 14,000 feet), these ridges would anywhere else rank as mountains. The tremendous altitudinal variation fosters enormous diversity, both biological and cultural. Researchers have barely begun to scratch the surface of the immense variety of ecosystems, but anthropologists have long noted how greatly the people of one valley differ from the next.

The rugged terrain ensures variety, but it also makes development difficult. Farming families scratch a subsistence livelihood from small scattered terraces carved out from the steep slopes, growing rice if irrigation allows, corn or millet on the drier fields. Family plots are fragmenting as the population increases, forcing people to feed more mouths on less land. Forests supply firewood and fodder, vital to household economies, but as supplies dwindle people must walk further to obtain what they need. Roads, schools, hospitals, pharmacies and electricity are all in short supply. Life in the Hills is hard and relatively short, and this is unlikely to change soon. While roads and the ensuing modernization have penetrated a few regions, it is highly unlikely they will ever reach most areas.

Pokhara

Nepal's biggest tourist destination after Kathmandu, the Pokhara Valley is an extraordinarily beautiful place. The green valley, dotted with half a dozen lakes, is lower and warmer than Kathmandu, its gentle climate nurturing all sorts of flowers: cacti, giant poinsettias and a profusion of flowering vines and creepers. This lush semi-tropical setting is backed by some of the world's highest peaks: Dhaulagiri, the Annapurna massif, Manaslu, Himalchuli, and most spectacular of all, the soaring, twisting spire of Machhapuchare, the 'Fishtail'.

Pokhara lies in the very heart of Central Nepal, and its population is representative of the ethnic patchwork of the region. Hindu castes now dominate the original Gurung inhabitants, whose large slate-roofed villages still dot the countryside. Once, Pokhara belonged to the independent Kingdom of Kaski, and on the surrounding hilltops stand the ruins of ancient stone fortresses (*kot*), waterless and lonely, but virtually impregnable.

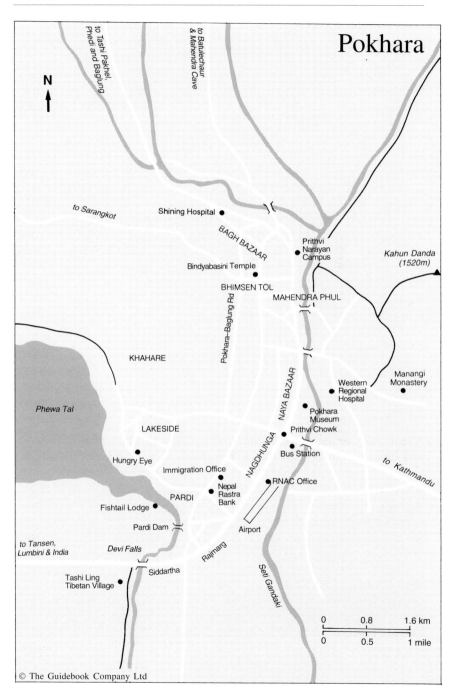

Pokhara

N

to Tashi Pakhel,
Phedi and Baglung

to Batulechaur
& Mahendra Cave

to Sarangkot

Shining Hospital

BAGH BAZAAR

Prithvi
Narayan
Campus

Kahun Danda
(1520m)

Bindyabasini Temple

BHIMSEN TOL

MAHENDRA PHUL

Pokhara-Baglung Rd

KHAHARE

NAYA BAZAAR

Manangi
Monastery

Western
Regional
Hospital

Phewa Tal

LAKESIDE

Pokhara
Museum

Prithvi Chowk

NAGDHUNGA

Hungry Eye

Immigration Office

Bus Station

to Kathmandu

RNAC Office

Nepal
Rastra
Bank

PARDI

Fishtail Lodge

Pardi Dam

Airport

to Tansen,
Lumbini & India

Devi Falls

Rajmarg

Seti Gandaki

Tashi Ling
Tibetan Village

Siddartha

| 0 | 0.8 | 1.6 km |

| 0 | 0.5 | 1 mile |

© The Guidebook Company Ltd

Pokhara serves as a major launching point for treks in the popular Annapurna region, and offers lazy R & R to weary returned trekkers. Trekking need not be a major event: there are some excellent two- to five-day trips outside of Pokhara. The Pokhara Valley itself provides glimpses of rural Nepal, with its shambling brown-eyed water buffalo, smiling women bent beneath haystacks of fodder, ochre-washed thatch-roofed houses and an all-pervading sense of tranquillity.

Sights

The town is sprawling but largely undeveloped, with neighbourhoods scattered far apart from one another. The centrepiece of Pokhara is the beautiful lake of **Phewa Tal**. Most travellers get no further than hypnotic **Lakeside**, a little Never–Never Land of lodges, restaurants, and souvenir shops stretched out along its eastern shore. Dedicated to budget hedonism, Lakeside seems to exist in a 1960s time warp: restaurants play Cat Stevens and Simon & Garfunkel, and serve 'magic mushroom' omelettes. Lakeside runs into **Pardi** (sometimes called Damside), a newer tourist neighbourhood at the south end of the lake, more yuppie than hippie. The old bazaar of **Bagar** is several kilometres away from these, the ugly new

Phewa Lake, Pokhara

town of **Mahendra Phul** lies in another direction, and the bus park and airport in yet another. Transport between areas consists of disorganized local buses and unmetered taxis (which require a price to be set *before* getting in). The relatively flat terrain and minimal traffic make Pokhara ideal for cyclists, and both mountain and regular bicycles are available for rent.

Pokhara's attractions are suitably minor, focusing not on culture, but on gem-like scenic vignettes. Three-kilometre-long **Phewa Tal** is Pokhara's principal attraction, offering warm (if polluted) waters for swimming, or better, boating in the brightly painted wooden rowing boats for hire at several points around Lakeside. Few things in life can beat lazing about here with a picnic lunch and a good book, admiring the mountain views reflected on the lake's placid surface. Energetic boaters can row to the simple restaurant-cum-teashop on the opposite shore, or down to Pardi and back. The little gilt-roofed **Varahi temple** on the small wooded island opposite Lakeside is an appealing destination. On Saturdays, crowds of worshippers row out here to clang bells and sacrifice animals to the boar-headed goddess.

Further afield is the old bazaar area called **Bagar**, its shady streets and big old mud-walled houses a flashback to the past. Shops sell an interesting

Village, Pokhara region

jumble of gold, cloth, rice and soap, all the necessities of a Hills provisioning outpost. This largely Newari neighbourhood developed when Pokhara was a major junction on the old trade route, involving barter of Tibetan salt and wool for lowland grain and goods. On the roads outside town you may still encounter clopping mule caravans decked with jingling bells, remnants of this old tradition.

Atop a shady hillock in the centre of town is the **Bindyabasini temple**, dedicated to the goddess Durga. The shrines here are architecturally unremarkable (the originals were destroyed in a 1949 fire), but in the winter marriage season they are crowded with newlyweds seeking the goddess's blessing. The **Pokhara Museum**, a little past the bus station off the Naya Bazaar road, has mildly interesting exhibits of the region's diverse costumes and customs, while the **Annapurna Museum** on the university campus covers natural history.

There are a number of destinations for day trips, beginning with **Sarangkot**, the bald summit north of Phewa Tal, offering superb views of the Annapurnas and Machhapuchare (the best time is early morning). It's a steep two-hour hike up from the lake, or take a taxi up the new road and walk the last 20 minutes. The trail heading west from here, through Kaski and **Naudanda**, is the old beginning of the Annapurna trek. Everyone now takes the new Baglung Road up to Naya Phul, leaving the trail peaceful. Walk a few kilometres down it for views of Machhapuchare's twin summits (from Lakeside they merge into a single peak). The new road also makes it easy to stop overnight in the charming riverside village of **Birethanti**, which has a number of good lodges and offers promising short hikes.

North of Pokhara is the village of **Batulechaur**, where minstrels belonging to the *gainey* caste are happy to perform for video cameras and tape-recorders (negotiate the fee first). A little further down the road is **Mahendra Gufa**, an enormous limestone cave once considered the abode of Nidhini, a female demon who dined on local cattle. Today it's been adopted by a local school, which charges a small entrance fee to permit visitors to explore the dim interior.

Pokhara's several **Tibetan settlements** were founded by refugees who flooded into Nepal following the 1959 Chinese invasion of Tibet. The prosperous Tibetans now-weave carpets and sell tourist trinkets (the women are particularly tenacious). The largest and most interesting settlement is **Tashi Pakhel** near Hyangja, about 90 minutes' walk northwest of the old bazaar on the bank of the Seti Gandaki River. Here there's a carpet factory, plenty of handicraft hawkers and a new *gompa*. Another settlement, **Tashi**

Ling, is near **Devi Falls**, a minor attraction in itself. The Pardi Khola cascades here into a deep sinkhole, impressive in the wet season or shortly thereafter.

The Pokhara Valley is dotted with lakes, the most important, after Phewa Tal, being **Begnas Tal**, a good 15-kilometre (nine-mile) bicycle ride east of town. More peaceful than Phewa Tal, it is a popular picnic site for residents, who embark for the opposite shore with a soon-to-be-barbequed goat aboard. Boatmen will paddle you about the lake or to the ridge of **Panchbhaiya Danda** dividing Begnas and **Rupa Tal**. Climb it up for views of the Himalaya and the twin lakes.

Gorkha

This small hill town assumes a ritual importance far beyond its size as the birthplace of Prithvi Narayan Shah, the 18th-century unifier of Nepal and founder of the present ruling dynasty. Gorkha is relatively easy to reach, only 20 kilometres (12.5 miles) off a paved spur from the main Pokhara–Kathmandu road. Despite the easy access few tourists stop here, except as a starting point for treks into the Ganesh Himal and the Manaslu circuit.

Gorkha was one of many petty hill states to be taken over in the mid-16th century by Hindu warriors advancing from Western Nepal. It remained obscure until the advent of Prithvi Narayan Shah, a skilful and intelligent leader determined to conquer the rich kingdoms of the Kathmandu Valley. It took him 26 years, but he succeeded, backed by a force of indomitable peasant soldiers that so impressed the British that they dubbed them Gurkhas after the original small kingdom.

The modern town of Gorkha is small, somewhere in between a village and a full-fledged town. It is essentially a hill trading post, the narrow stone-paved streets filled with villagers who have come down to buy salt, cloth, pots and other necessities. The lanes are steep and hilly, preventing the entry of motor vehicles, hopefully forever.

The immense square building in the centre of town is **Tallo Durbar**, the 'Lower Palace' (as opposed to the Upallo Durbar on top of the hill). Built in the mid-18th century, it served as the seat of local administration. The building with its fine woodwork was recently restored, and a history museum is planned for the vast interior.

Gorkha's main sight, the old **Shah palace**, broods above a hill overlooking the town. It is a stiff half-hour climb up a seemingly endless stone staircase, but frequent teashops ease the pain (bring lots of drinking water). The exertion is worth it, not least for the sudden, fabulous Himalayan panoramas revealed from the hillocks surmounting both sides of the ridge: mountains from Annapurna to Ganesh Himal, at the centre the spectacular Himalchuli. A royal helipad on the palace's western side expedites the king's ritual visits to his ancestral home.

The palace is smaller than the ornate durbars of the Kathmandu Valley, but remains a fine example of Newari woodwork and architecture, unspoiled by Rana-era additions. It seems the Gorkhas preferred to concentrate on warfare and let their conquered people do the building, thus preserving traditional styles long past the dates of conquest. Constructed during the reign of Ram Shah (1606–36), it was expanded by successive rulers. The palace's tremendous historic and ritual significance explains its excellent condition (it was recently restored yet again).

There are plenty of erotic strut carvings, especially in the small lower palace called the **Raj Durbar**, the old living quarters, sanctified as the birthplace of Prithvi Narayan Shah. Adjoining it is **Kalika Durbar**, centred around a powerful Kali temple which is the scene of frequent animal sacrifices. Worshippers prostrate themselves in devotion in front of the locked doors, which are opened only on the eighth day of each lunar fortnight. This section of the palace is the holy of holies, with police posted to prevent tourists from entering and ritually defiling it.

The palace complex abounds with other shrines to Hindu deities, including Shiva, Guyheswari, and a 'cave' shrine down a short flight of steps which is sacred to Gorakhnath. This 12th-century yogi is said to have lived and meditated here; gradually he was deified into a cult figure and patron of the Shahs. He is linked with Shiva, obvious from the array of tridents inside.

Having viewed the palace, the nicest thing to do is to sit on the shady *chautara* alongside it at **Hanuman Bhanjyang**, marked by a stone statue of Hanuman brandishing an axe, and watch the procession of local people, *doko*-laden porters, and the occasional trekking group pass by. The surrounding countryside is pure Nepali middle Hills, blazing hot by April but ideal for a winter trek.

Tansen

Located on a hillside a few kilometres off the Siddhartha Highway between Pokhara and Bhairawa, Tansen is definitely off the beaten track. This attractive little hill station boasts a marvellous climate (credited for the fine complexions of its exceptionally good-looking women), a lively ambience and remarkably friendly and open people.

Despite these charms and its location as a natural halt in the course of a Pokhara–Lumbini trip, Tansen remains nearly totally devoid of tourists. Most of the foreigners coming here work at the local missionary hospital, and people will naturally assume you do as well.

Tansen is the largest of the trading posts established by Newars in Nepal's middle Hills. It lies in the middle of Magar country, an ethnic group usually described as one of Nepal's most appealing peoples. The town is the old capital of the Kingdom of Palpa, the last of the independent kingdoms of Nepal, annexed only in 1806.

Built on the southern slope of a hill rising above the Madi Valley, Tansen comprises a maze of narrow lanes lined with red-brick buildings set with carved woodwork. It remains an important bazaar town, with hill

Bridge over the Bhote Kosi, Sagarmatha National Park

people coming in to buy cooking oil, salt, tea, cloth and other provisions, and to enjoy the teashops and sociability. The quiet streets resound with the clack of the loom: Tansen's boldy patterned *dhaka* cloth, used for topis and shawls, is considered the finest in Nepal.

The centre of town is dominated by the rambling pink **Tansen Durbar**, the former seat of the Rana governor, today housing government offices. Behind it is a **temple to Bhagwati**, and further east the exceptionally fine **Amar Narayan temple** to Vishnu, where drums, bells and horns are sounded in worship each morning and evening.

Srinagar Danda looms up behind town. Hike up to the 1,525-metre (4,648-foot) summit for a Himalayan panorama extending from Kanjiroba to Langtang. The hilltop was once the site of an ancient fortified city, but all that's to be seen today are a few old Rana summer cottages and a pine plantation that makes an ideal picnic site.

Probably the best day trip out of Tansen is the all-day hike to the eerie, abandoned **Ranighat Palace** built on a bluff overlooking the Kali–Gandaki River. It was built at the turn of the century for the wife of a Rana governor of Palpa: unruly Ranas were often exiled to high positions in remote districts like this. Another choice is the 13-kilometre (eight-mile) hike to the bazaar town of **Ridi**, with its important **Rishikesh Mandir**. Tansen also serves as starting point for treks into idyllic countryside dotted with friendly Magar villages: typical mid-Hills territory but virtually unspoiled, unlike the territory around Pokhara.

On the Roads

To start with, there are very few of them: apart from the flat Terai, Nepal was simply not made for roads. This point is proven anew each monsoon, as heavy rains trigger landslides and wash away bridges, blocking traffic on certain routes for weeks at a time. Foreign aid has boldly pushed forward a few tentacles of asphalt, which offer slow driving but spectacular scenery. If trekking is off the agenda but you'd like to see more of Nepal, consider the day's drive along the **Arniko Rajmarg** to the **Tibetan** border, or to the magnificent viewing point of Daman on the old **Tribhuvan Rajpath**.

The 115-kilometre Arniko Rajmarg follows the old trade route linking Kathmandu to Lhasa, and is named after a 13th-century Newari artist employed in the court of Kublai Khan. Its construction by China in the mid-1960s generated dark mutterings that it was 'wide enough for one tank'.

Frequently damaged by landslides, it has not proved the important trade link it was touted to be, but it passes through some spectacular scenery. The best, of course, lies across the border as the road climbs, and climbs, and climbs, up to the Tibetan Plateau—but that's a different story.

The road arcs out of the Kathmandu Valley, passing through small villages like Dhulikhel, Lamosanghu and Barabise into increasingly dramatic and landslide-beset terrain. The upper reaches follow the gorge of the **Sun Kosi**, the 'River of Gold'. The village of **Tatopani** is a good stopping point. Here are several teashops and low-grade lodges, and boiling hot water from natural springs gushing out of five stone taps. A few minutes further is **Kodari**, an unremarkable collection of bamboo huts that is the last settlement in Nepal. A 'Friendship Bridge' spans the river (here called the Bhote Kosi), guarded at one end by friendly Nepali troops, and the other by stiff-faced young Chinese soldiers in baggy green uniforms. You'll need a Chinese visa to get past them and to the official border crossing, the booming little trading post of **Khasa** visible high up on the opposite hillside.

The grand prize for comprehensive Himalayan views goes to the tiny village of **Daman**, perched on a ridgetop about three hour's drive from Kathmandu down the **Tribhuvan Rajpath**. This narrow, twisting road was the first highway to link Kathmandu and India when it was completed in 1956. Most drivers prefer the faster route through Mugling, leaving the Rajpath for an occasional truck or bus, and enthusiastic mountain bikers. Only 75 kilometres (46 miles) away, Daman makes a good if strenuous overnight bicycle trip from Kathmandu.

The highway twists down from **Thankot** on the Valley's eastern rim, descending in a series of hairpin bends to **Naubise**, then branching off to wind through sparsely inhabited hills and the broad **Palung Valley**. Daman itself is a dozen or so houses and an imposingly ugly concrete viewing tower run by the government for the few tourists who come this way. Facilities are limited (a picnic lunch is advised, as the only food is basic *dal bhat*), but the views are unbeatable: a 386-kilometre long slice of the Himalaya stretching from Dhaulagiri to Kangchenjunga. As usual you'll be gambling with clouds and weather; an overnight stay is recommended to ensure clear views, though accommodation is less than deluxe.

TIBETAN MONASTERIES AND LAMAS

Fuelled by the Tibetan exodus of the late 1950s, Boudhanath has become one of the great centres for Tibetan Buddhism in exile. All the four principal sects have built elaborate monasteries or **gompas** here, sponsored by an increasingly prosperous local community. The largest boast elaborate shrines (*lhakhang*) decorated in the exuberant colours favoured by Tibetans. Usually these are open to the public.

The entrance porch typically bears paintings of the gigantic, fierce-looking Guardians of the Four Directions and a diagram of the universe according to traditional Tibetan cosmology. Most interesting is the Wheel of Life, a complex diagram depicting the six realms of samsaric existence—one each for the beings of hell, animals, hungry ghosts, humans, *asura* and gods—all held within the grip of the devouring Mahakala, Great Time.

Leave your shoes outside the door and proceed clockwise about the interior of the *lhakhang*, vividly painted with frescoes of deities and divinities. The altar bears giant gilt images of deities particular to the sect, lit by flickering butter lamps (vegetable oil is usually substituted. In front lie offerings of plastic flowers, water bowls, fruit and sweets. Everything is richly adorned, from the carved and painted wooden pillars to the ceilings hung with elaborate banners of multicoloured brocade.

Among Boudhnath's most impressive *gompas* is **Ka-Nying Shedrup Ling** (the big white monastery behind the stupa). **Shechen Tennyi Targey Ling**, the big yellow *gompa*, is perhaps the finest monastery outside Tibet, built under the sponsorship of the Bhutanese royal family. The yellow **Sakya monastery** a few steps from the main gate on the stupa circuit holds a 10-metre (35-foot) high image of Maitreya, the Buddha of the future age, encrusted with turquoise and coral.

Gompas are best visited during daily prayers or one of the great empowerment ceremonies (*wang*) usually held around Losar. Maroon-robed monks, some as young as six or seven, sit for days in the great hall chanting texts and prayers. Their recitation is punctuated by cacaphonous music from cymbals, drums and *kangling* (trumpets made from human thigh bones). Ritual masked dances held in monastery courtyards draws the entire community for days of pageantry.

English-speakers frequently refer to all Tibetan monks as 'lamas', but the term is properly used only for a religious teacher, who may or may not be a monk. Lamas are highly revered for their advice in spiritual and practical matters; ideally they serve as meditation instructors, though most Tibetans are content to venerate them and ask for advice on practical matters. The principle of reincarnation means the lama population is relatively stable: old ones die and are reborn in new incarnations. Lama Yeshe, the founder of Kopan, is believed to have taken rebirth as the son of a Spanish disciple, and in 1993 the new incarnation of Dudjom Rinpoche, the head of the Nyingma sect, was enthroned at Boudhanath following his discovery as a two-year-old in a local Bhutanese family.

It's ironic that visitors to Nepal, which proudly proclaims itself 'the world's only Hindu kingdom', are frequently more interested in Tibetan **Buddhism**. Among the best access points is the **Himalayan Yogic Institute** in Maharajganj (tel 413 094), which hosts frequent lectures and workshops on Buddhism. HYI is affiliated with **Kopan Monastery**, a small monastic community situated above a hillock about 45 minutes north of Boudha. Some of Boudha's lamas are also accessible to visitors, and many of the younger ones speak English.

RHINOS AND TIGERS

Chitwan's most popular large inhabitant is the greater Asian one-horned rhinoceros (*gaida*). Indeed, the park originated in the 1960s as a preserve for this bulky animal which can weigh up to two tonnes. Contrary to the rhino's armour-plated appearance, its thick, rough, folded skin is vulnerable to spears and bullets. Because it has no sweat glands, the rhino spends much of its time wallowing in rivers, coating its hide in mud to protect itself from the sun and insects.

Rhinos are vegetarian, but they tend to be solitary and suspicious creatures, especially mothers with young. An exceptionally small brain may account for their unpredicatable and illogical nature. Rhinos can't distinguish immobile objects beyond 30 metres, but they compensate for their poor vision with a highly developed sense of hearing and the ability to scent a human 800 metres away. They are prone to blind charges on possible aggressors and are surprisingly agile for their bulk, capable of swivelling, turning and charging again: though sometimes their poor vision leads them to charge a tree. To escape a rhino charge, run zig-zag or drop an item of clothing which the animal will hopefully pause to investigate.

Its weak point is the horn rising from its snout, actually a mass of densely compressed dermal fibres. This mysterious appendage has no known use—rhinos use their tusks for defence—but high demand for it as an antipyretic in Chinese medicine makes the rhino vulnerable to poachers. Local people have their own uses for rhino products: a rhino-skin bracelet provides protection against evil spirits; rhino dung is a laxative, while rhino urine cures tuberculosis. British hunters noted that rhino hide made 'capital water buckets', while the horns were carved into cups and khukri handles.

Unlike the highly visible rhino, the Royal Bengal tiger (*bagh*) is secretive and elusive. Park visitors seldom sight one: the most you can expect is a pawprint or a muffled roar from the bush. The tiger is the keystone of wildlife conservation efforts as it preys on a wide variety of herbivores. Preserving its habitat thus saves everything else beneath it on the food chain.

Once there were eight species of tiger in Asia: today there are five. Three or four thousand, a little over half the current total, are Indian tigers, sometimes called Royal Bengal tigers. These majestic creatures are found in Nepal, Bhutan, Bangladesh, India and parts of Burma. Nepal, particularly Chitwan, boasts some of the best tiger territory in Asia, but the park's population of 70 adults would strain its resources to the limits, were it not for the presence of the adjoining Parsi Wildlife Reserve, opened in 1984. Combined with India's Valmili Tiger Reserve across the border, there are 1,875 square kilometres (723 square miles) of tiger territory.

The Terai

A remarkably flat, low-altitude strip running along Nepal's southern border, the Terai contradicts the national image of mountains, mountains and more mountains, but it's doubtful the country could exist without it. Constituting less than a fifth of Nepal's total area, the Terai has over half the arable land, produces 60 percent of the grain and is home to nearly half the population.

Seldom wider than 48 kilometres (30 miles), with an average altitude of 150 metres (492 feet) above sea level, the Terai can be divided into two regions: the flat **Outer Terai** running along the Indian border, and the **Inner Terai**, a higher, bumpier zone sandwiched between two sets of Himalayan foothills, the Siwalik and Mahabharat ranges. Geographically, the Terai is an extension of India's great Gangetic Plain, and its customs and languages are heavily influenced by Indian culture. Its peoples include Bhojpuri, Maithili and various smaller Indo-Aryan groups speaking Sanskrit-based languages, or frequently Hindi. The indigenous residents are the Tharu, a handsome, gentle people who tend to be dominated by later arrivals. All these ethnic groups are largely ignored by tourists as well as by the mainstream Bahun-Chhetri who run Nepal, but they constitute about a quarter of the total population.

Until the 1950s the Terai was largely undeveloped, protected by a particularly virulent strain of malaria, and by the Ranas' desire to isolate Nepal from outside influences. The only permanent residents were the Tharus, who possessed a degree of natural immunity to malaria. Other Nepalis avoided the fever season, and those forced to cross the Terai did so as quickly as possible. The disease's mosquito-born transmission mechanism was unknown at the time, and it was thought to be caused by noxious vapours rising from standing water.

Most of the region was covered by great tracts of tropical deciduous forests, among the last remnants of a prehistoric swath which once extended from Pakistan to Burma. Lush grasslands and forests of fine hardwood *sal* trees growing up to 40 metres (131 feet) in height harboured a dense and diverse wildlife population. The ruling Ranas used the Terai as their personal hunting grounds. A single 1938-9 hunt to entertain the Viceroy of India netted 120 tigers, 38 rhinos, 27 leopards and 15 bears.

In the 1950s a malaria eradication programme (later downgraded to malaria control) opened up the Terai to settlement. The next 30 years saw a huge internal population shift, as marginal farmers from the crowded Hills flooded onto the flat, rich fields. The Terai now houses 47 percent of

Nepal's population, along with most of the country's roads and industry. Much of the original forest has been levelled in the process, and the formerly open region is reaching saturation.

In many ways the Terai resembles India. Slim, dark-skinned women balance water jugs on their heads and walk with incredible grace and ease down the dusty roads. White oxen with blue and green painted horns pull

rickety wooden-wheeled carts, and the trucks are tinselled and painted with images of deities, veritable rolling temples of transport. In the busy, hot street markets, heaps of oranges scent the air, and bright cloth and bangles, animals and people crowd together in a sensory overload of sights, smells and shouts. The peaceful, flat countryside comes as a welcome escape, brilliant green rice paddies shimmering in the heat. Terai cities like Biratnagar and Bhairawa tend to be unlovely, dusty and squalid, but Chitwan National Park and the peaceful sanctuary of Lumbini, the Buddha's birthplace, are worth visiting.

The Terai is best visited in autumn or winter, when clear days reveal startling vistas of the distant Himalaya rising behind flat fields. The period following the annual grass-cutting season in January is considered the best for viewing wildlife. Things get unpleasantly steamy after March, with highs exceeding 36°C (96°F), and the monsoon can be a non-stop torrent.

Chitwan National Park

Bits and pieces of the Terai's primeval forest and rich wildlife have been preserved in a number of national parks and game preserves. Royal Chitwan National Park was the first, created in 1973 to protect rapidly dwindling tiger and rhino populations. The park's 932 square kilometres (360 square miles) of *sal* forest and rolling grasslands support a unique variety and abundance of wildlife. In 1984 it was declared a UNESCO World Heritage site.

Nestling in the Rapti Valley, the largest of the broad flat *dun* valleys of the Inner Terai, Chitwan shelters an incredible concentration of creatures: wild boar and wild cattle (*gaur*); impressively large sambar deer, plus barking, spotted and hog deer; langur and rhesus monkeys, leopards, jungle cats, foxes, jackals, wild dogs and hyenas. River-banks are home to two types of crocodile: the sinister-looking marsh mugger and the rare *gharial*, named after the bulbous extension on its long snout which resembles a *ghara* (the ubiquitous subcontinental water jug). The rare Gangetic dolphin still swims in the waters of the Narayani River, and over 400 species of birds are found in the park. Chitwan's fame is based on two exotic species: the greater one-horned rhinoceros and the Royal Bengal tiger. Its most dangerous animal is the lesser-known sloth bear, an agile and unpredictable creature which attacks with fiercely curved claws.

From a sleepy backwater the park has developed into a major tourist attraction, drawing about 15,000 visitors each year. Luxury lodges inside the park provide top-class accommodation, while several dozen budget lodges clustered near the village of **Sauruha** on the park's eastern end offer a less-polished and less-expensive experience.

Though it harbours an astonishing variety and abundance of wildlife, Chitwan is hardly a pristine sanctuary. Hundreds of thousands of people live in the Rapti Valley, which was the site of a model resettlement programme in the early 1960s. In the early years of that decade, 22,000 villagers were moved to create a rhino preserve which eventually became the park. They were resettled in villages along the park's northern border, with strict orders not to touch its resources. Technically, villagers are allowed in only 15 days a year to collect grass (more on that later), but of course they do enter the park illegally to obtain firewood and fodder.

Understandably this has created conflict and resentment. People living on the park's fringes can't understand why they are being deprived of the resources—wood, grass, hunting and grazing grounds—that were their ancestors' for centuries and theirs until recently. In addition, they are angered by the destruction of their carefully tended crops by marauding boar, deer and rhinos—protected animals they can only scare away with stones and shouts. Each year a few villagers are killed by charging rhino or the more dangerous sloth bear. The temptation to poach is increased by the high prices rhino horn and tiger bone bring in Southeast and East Asia, where they are valued ingredients in Chinese medicine. Eleven Chitwan rhinos were slaughtered in 1993, along with five tigers, despite the fact that the park is guarded by more than 1,000 Nepalese soldiers.

The park also benefits the local economy, however, and not only through the obvious example of tourism-related jobs. A broader-based illustration is the high-quality grass which, due to over-harvesting, has virtually vanished from outside the park. Local people are allowed into Chitwan for two weeks each January to cut as much as they can carry out. They use it as thatch and to make household products, or sell it to the local paper factory. Spurred by such examples, administrators are shedding the old 'park-as-fortress' mentality and are attempting to cultivate a non-adverserial relationship which will benefit both the park and the people living around it.

Sights

A Chitwan stay revolves around various ways to view wildlife. Guests in the expensive lodges inside the park will have a pre-arranged schedule of activities adjusted to their personal tastes. Independent travellers in Sauruha's cheaper lodges can do essentially the same things, though more effort must be put into organization.

The first stop should be the well-designed Visitor's Centre at Sauruha, open 8 am–5 pm daily. Exhibits explain the quirks of indigenous flora and fauna, with emphasis on the most interesting big beasts like rhinos.

Chital or Spotted deer, Chitwan National Park

Elephant rides are deservedly the most popular activity. These huge shambling beasts exert a mysterious fascination with their incongruous combination of clumsiness and agility, strength and gentleness. Rides can be arranged through the government stables (tickets are sold at the window across from the Visitor's Centre). Mounting platforms are provided to expedite the climb aboard. Sit behind the *phanit* or elephant driver, and don't be surprised at the degree of lurch: elephants are ponderous beasts with a pronounced roll to their walk. Their height, plus the fact that other animals respect them, makes them an ideal vantage point for game viewing. The *phanit* urges the beast on by drumming a constant tattoo behind its ears with his knees and feet. Occasionally a recalcitrant elephant will be brought into line with a mighty whack on the head.

While aboard, try to imagine the invitation-only **elephant polo tournament** held at Tiger Tops every December. Jodphur-clad socialites and minor celebrities compete aboard their lumbering mounts, though it's sometimes hard to find the ball beneath the vast girth.

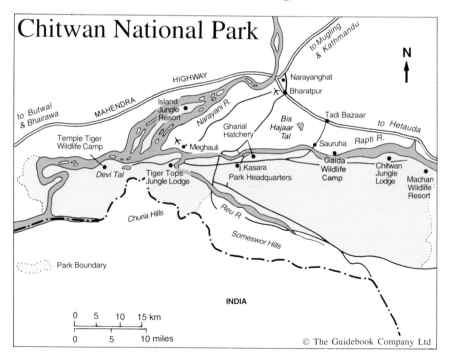

Chitwan National Park

© The Guidebook Company Ltd

Luxury resorts give regular briefings on elephant trivia at their private stables, or you can visit the government-run **Hatisar** (elephant stables) down the road from the Visitor Centre. The animals here are fed concentrated rations of molasses, salt and grain wrapped into football-sized bundles of grass, consuming over 100 of these a day. The **Elephant Breeding Centre** four kilometres west of Sauruha houses 22 beasts, including a few younger pachyderms. As a point of curiosity, elephant lives closely parallel human: they don't start work until around age 15, when they embark on a 40-year career, followed by 10 years of retirement.

Another favourite is **dugout canoe trips** down the Rapti River, best taken early in the morning before things heat up. There are invariably plenty of birds and local fishermen, and possibly a marsh mugger crocodile basking on the banks like a log. The standard trip is a 45-minute float followed by a two-hour **jungle hike**, which may offer sightings of monkeys, and quite possibly a heart-thumping glimpse of a rhino (your guide will advise you on emergency procedure if a rhino lowers its head and signals a charge: climb a tree or run in big zig-zags). However, the strip of jungle across the river from Sauruha is so over-trafficked that you may encounter only other tour groups…one good reason for staying in the in-park lodges. Still, virtually any walk becomes interesting when taken with a local guide who is constantly pointing out things you'd otherwise be certain to miss: animal tracks and spoor, the uses of plants, and local traditions.

Other options, usually only undertaken on longer visits, include a **jungle jeep ride**, either to the bird-frequented lake of **Lami Tal** or more commonly to park headquarters at **Kasara Durbar**, 20 kilometres from Sauruha inside the park. This provides the opportunity for more game spotting and a visit to the nearby **Gharial Breeding Centre**, where these endangered long-snouted crocodile are raised in a protected environment before being released.

Moving beyond the park, visitors can cycle or walk two hours to **Bis Hajaar Tal** ('20,000 Lakes'), a series of small ponds in a forest teeming with birds and wildlife. The tidy **Tharu villages** around Sauruha are also worth exploring, the smooth-walled mud homes stacked high with grass in the winter harvest season.

After-dark entertainment at Chitwan is limited, particularly as there's no electricity. The bigger lodges sponsor performances of the traditional **Tharu stick dance** by troupes of local men, incongruously clad in gym shoes.

On the Pokhara Trail

The track along the Yamdi River is a main trading route passing through rice paddies and villages on its way west ot the Kali Gandaki River, where it turns north to Mustang and Tibet. Green village compounds, set about with giant banyans and old stone pools and walls, are cropped to lawn by water buffalo and cattle; the fresh water and soft shade give them the harmony of parks. These village folk own even less than those of Pokhara, yet they are spared by their old economies from modern poverty: one understands why 'village life' has been celebrated as the natural, happy domain of man by many thinkers, from Lao-tzu to Gandhi. In a warm sun children play, and women roll clothes on rocks at the village fountain and pound grain in stone mortars, and from all sides come reassuring dung smells and chicken clatter and wafts of fire smoke from the low hearths. In tiny yards, behind strong stiles and walls, the clay huts are of warm earthen red, with thatched roofs, hand-carved sills and shutters, and yellow–flowered pumpkin vines. Maize is stacked in narrow cribs, and rice is spread to dry on broad straw mats, and between the banana and papaya trees big calm spiders hang against the sky.

A canal bridged here and there by ten-foot granite slabs runs through a hamlet, pouring slowly over shining pebbles. It is midday, the sun melts the air, and we sit on a stone wall in the cool shade. By the canal is the village teahouse, a simple open-fronted hut with makeshift benches and a clay oven in the form of a rounded mound on the clay floor. The mound has a side opening for inserting twigs and two holes on the top for boiling water, which is poured through a strainer of cheap tea dust into a glass containing coarse sugar and buffalo milk. With this chiya we take plain bread and a fresh cucumber, while children playing on the shining stones pretend to splash us, and a collared dove sways on a tall stalk of bamboo.

Peter Matthiessen, The Snow Leopard, 1978

Other Terai Parks and Reserves

The destinations described below are largely undeveloped and visited only by the doughtiest independent travellers, but they are good choices if you want to be on the cutting edge of adventure travel in Nepal.

Kosi Tappu Wildlife Reserve, located in the flood plain of the eastern Terai's great Sapt Koshi river, was created to protect a herd of rare wild buffalo (*arna*). It also shelters spotted deer and monkeys, and serves as an important point for migrating Asian water birds. Park headquarters is at **Kusaha**, from where canoes ferry visitors into the reserve. At 155 square kilometres (60 square miles) it is small enough to explore on foot.

Royal Bardia National Park in Western Nepal is a less developed and arguably more authentic alternative to Chitwan. The terrain is similar: 1,000 square kilometres (386 square miles) of forested hills and grassy *bhabar* (flatlands) cut by water channels. A former royal hunting preserve gazetted as a park in 1988, Bardia is inhabited by crocodiles, hordes of birds and nearly 50 species of mammals, including antelope, monkeys and a thriving rhino herd transplanted from Chitwan. Tiger Tops, which runs a lodge here, touts it as an excellent place to view the Royal Bengal tiger. The 50 adult tigers in the park are apparently less wary than in Chitwan. As a last alternative, baiting…staking out a live goat as a meal…may bring forth a beast; Bardia is the only place in Nepal where tiger baiting is allowed. The best season for a visit is October–May. Bardia is reached in 12 hours by road from Kathmandu or, preferably, by flying to **Nepalgunj**.

Tucked away in the extreme wild west of Nepal, **Royal Suklaphanta Wildlife Reserve** protects one of the largest remaining grasslands (*phanta*) typical of this dry region. A former game hunting area, Suklaphanta is noted for its huge herds of swamp deer, tigers, and the very rare wild elephant, including a gigantic bull with a 22-inch-wide footprint which is probably the largest Asian elephant alive. This area is very, *very* remote and not equipped to deal with independent travellers…not that you're likely to make it all the way out there on your own. Visitors should make advance arrangements at the Kathmandu office of the only lodge in the reserve (*see* **Accommodation**).

Bhairawa and Lumbini

The most popular border crossing between India and Nepal, **Bhairawa** is hardly attractive. Its hot, dusty streets are more reminiscent of India than Nepal, and travellers passing through here are intent either on reaching **Sunauli**, the border post four kilometres south, or a more hospitable Nepali town like Pokhara or Kathmandu.

The frequently missed local attraction is **Lumbini**, the birthplace of the **Buddha**, 22 kilometres (14 miles) west of Bhairawa in the midst of flat, emerald-green fields. In truth there's not much to see in Lumbini either: the chief point of interest is the intense sense of peace pervading the place. One of four great Buddhist pilgrimage sites, it draws pilgrims from Japan, Thailand, Sri Lanka and Korea in far greater numbers than either Nepalis or Westerners.

The Buddha, Siddhartha Gautama, was born around 543 BC into the royal family of Kapilvastu, a small independent kingdom on the vast Indian plain. His mother, Mayadevi, was travelling to her parents' home when labour commenced in the shady grove of Lumbini. Legend relates that the baby was delivered painlessly from her right side, his birth accompanied by an auspicious shower of flowers from the heavens. Family priests predicted he would be either a world ruler or a great spiritual teacher, and his father the king, desiring the first, confined him to the palace and surrounded him with every imaginable pleasure.

It proved impossible to hide the harsh realities of life from the young Siddhartha. On successive journeys into town he witnessed a cripple, a sick man, a body being carried to cremation and a monk who appeared to be beyond the extremes of both pleasure and pain. Finally aware of the existence of pain, old age, sickness and death, he renounced his kingdom and became a wandering mendicant searching for the ultimate truth which lay beyond these. He lived as a hermit, practising self-mortification and yoga to no avail, before finally achieving enlightenment through simple meditation at the age of 34. He spent the rest of his long life wandering through middle India, teaching what he had realized: life, or conventional ego-consciousness, is suffering, and this suffering can be transcended by realizing one's essential nature.

Around 249 BC the great Indian emperor Ashoka made a pilgrimage to Lumbini, erecting a stone column to commemorate his visit. Lumbini developed into a major pilgrimage site, marked by temples, monasteries and stupas. A fifth-century Chinese pilgrim described what essentially remains

At the Court of Narendra Dev

The kingdom of Ni-po-lo is due west of Tou-fan (Tibet). Their king Na-ling-ti-po (Narendra Devi) wears pearls, rock crystal, mother-of-pearl, coral and amber; he has golden earrings and jade pendants, and trinkets on his waistbelt adorned with a Foutou (Buddha). He sits on a seat supported by lions, in the interior of the hall where flowers and perfume are scattered. The eminent people, the officers and the whole court, are sitting to the right and to the left on the ground; beyond them are drawn up hundreds of armed soldiers.

In the centre of the palace there is a tower of seven storeys, covered with copper tiles. Balustrades, railings, columns, and beams are all encrusted with stones and jewels. At each of the four corners of the tower water is poured into the troughs; from the dragon's mouth it gushes out as it would from a fountain.

The merchants, whether itinerant dealers or established ones, are numerous. They have copper coins which bear on one side a man's face and on the reverse a horse. The cultivators are few and they do not know how to plough the earth with bulls. They do not perforate the nostrils of their bulls. The inhabitants are accustomed to shave their hair to the very edge of their eyebrows. They pierce their ears and introduce into the perforations little bamboo tubes. They eat with their hands without using spoons or sticks. All their utensils are made of copper. They dress themelves with one piece of cloth which covers the body. They bathe several times daily.

Their houses are built of wood; the walls are sculptured and painted. They are very fond of scenic spots, and are pleased to blow the horn and beat the drum. They are fairly conversant with the reckoning of fate and in the researches of physical philosophy. They are equally skilled in the arts of the calendar. They venerate five celestial beings and carve their images on stone; each day they wash themselves with purifying water. They cook a sheep and offer it as a sacrifice.

Wang Hiuen Tse (AD 643–690)
Chinese ambassador to the Licchavi court in the seventh
century (trans. by Sylvain Levi, 1905)

today: a bathing pool, a tree, an Ashokan pillar, a Maya Devi Temple. The site declined with the waning of Indian Buddhism, and slowly vanished into the jungle. It was not rediscovered until 1895, when a German archaeologist cleared the site and unearthed the Ashokan pillar.

Lumbini remained neglected until the late 1960s, when UN Secretary General U Thant, a devout Buddhist, visited and was reportedly moved to tears by the neglect he saw. Inspired by him, an international development committee, the Lumbini Development Trust, was formed. It sponsored a grandiose master plan for the development of Lumbini, designed by a Japanese architect and involving 45 square kilometres (17 square miles) of gardens, canals, monuments and monasteries. Considerable funding has been raised by the Lumbini Development Trust (and much of it allegedly embezzled), but progress, beyond evicting a few local villages, has been slow. The largely empty compound is dotted with forlorn reminders, such as a library from Japan and an Indian-funded museum, still empty and unused. The neglect is not all bad, however, for it guarantees that Lumbini's quiet peace will continue.

Worshipping at Lumbini

Sights

The few sights remaining today are clustered together and easily viewed in
half an hour. The boxy whitewashed Mayadevi **Mandir**, once shaded by a
huge pipal tree, has been dismantled to free it from the grasp of the
snakelike roots, and is to be reconstructed on the original site. Inside is a
second-century **relief** depicting the Buddha's birth: the infant Buddha
stepping away from Mayadevi to be greeted by a retinue of Hindu gods. The
faces of the principal figures were gouged out by Muslim invaders long ago,
and a marble copy made in the 1950s has become the chief focus of
worship—ironically, by local Hindu women who revere Mayadevi as the
fertility goddess Rupadevi.

On the western side of the temple is the **Ashokan pillar**, the oldest
monument in Nepal. The inscription, dated the equivalent of 249 BC, reads:

*The king, friend of the gods, he of the kindly countenance, came here in
person twenty years after his coronation and rendered homage, because
this was the birthplace of the Buddha, the saint of the Sakya.*

A large and placid pool where Mayadevi is said to have bathed before
the birth is shaded by a spreading pipal tree. A few foundations of ruined
stupas and monastic buildings have been excavated and restored. The
hummocky ground indicates much more lies below the surface, but no full-
scale research has been carried out. The only other points of interest are two
modern monasteries, a typical **Tibetan** *gompa* built by a Sakya lama based
in Boudhanath, and a **Theravada Monastery** decorated with an odd
assembly of objects and adornments from Burma, Thailand, Tibet and
Nepal. Both are slated for relocation if the Master Plan is ever executed.

The small village of **Lumbini** is a 10-minute walk south of the
compound and hosts a lively Monday market. Twenty-seven kilometres
west of the site, down the road to Tilaurikot, the **ruined palace** of the
Buddha's father, King Suddhodhana, is being excavated.

TREKKING AND THE MOUNTAINS

An Introduction to Trekking

Nepal's northern border is lined by an unbroken 50-kilometre-wide strip of soaring snow peaks, both a barrier and an inspiration. Ancient Hindus revered these shining summits as the abode of the gods, and for centuries have journeyed on pilgrimage to sacred sites in their shadow.

The **Himalaya**, the 'Abode of Snow' in Sanskrit, are the world's highest mountains, with peaks rising to twice the height of the Alps. Nepal gets the lion's share of this splendour, with eight of the world's ten highest peaks. The Himalaya were born some 40 million years ago when the free-floating continent of India slammed into the main Asian continent, squeezing up the Himalayas at the point of impact. They are the world's youngest mountains, still growing at a rate of 10–12 centimetres a year. Behind them rises the Tibetan plateau, a giant anomaly with an average altitude of five kilometres above sea level. From here flow ancient rivers, old enough to predate even the Himalaya. Not even the eruption of the mountains could stop these from running: they simply carved out incredibly deep transverse gorges through the rock. Traditionally these river valleys were used as trade routes; today some have become popular trekking trails.

Mountain dwellers constitute less than eight percent of Nepal's total population. Virtually all are Buddhists, members of a diffused Tibetan culture which spreads across the Himalaya, far beyond the bounds of the present Chinese-controlled Tibet Autonomous Region. From Amdo to Ladakh, these mountain people share similar languages, beliefs, diets, clothing and Buddhist-influenced values. They are unbelievably hardy, adapting their lives to fit the unrelenting high-altitude land. Firewood is scarce, so they burn dried yak dung; fields are poor and stony, so they grow potatoes and barley, the latter consumed as *tsampa*, a flour that needs little or no cooking. Farmland is insufficient, so they rely heavily on high-altitude cattle, yak and crossbreeds for milk, meat, butter and dried cheese. The people of this region are also skilled traders, accustomed to working both in Tibet and lowland Nepal.

No roads penetrate this rugged region, though a few narrow airstrips for Short Takeoff and Landing craft (STOL) have been carved out of the mountainous terrain. It can be visited only on foot, a process for some reason known by the old Boer term 'trekking'. While the most popular seasons are October–November and March–April, trekking can be done year-round. Passes above 4,100 metres (14,000 feet) may be snowbound from December through March, but lowland routes come into their own at this time. The summer months are admittedly soggy, but rainshadow regions like Mustang and Manang remain relatively dry. The trick lies in tailoring the route to the weather.

Why Trek?

To begin with, there is the physical purification of pushing your body, really using it. It is a delight to walk, simply walk, through some of the most bewitching countryside in the world. You become acquainted with your body in a way few modern people experience. Trekking doesn't take tremendous exertion, just basic fitness and a certain stamina which is as much a matter of attitude as it is of physical ability. You must be willing to walk in the mountains six to ten hours a day; there is no getting around that.

'Over the first few days of any march,' noted the veteran explorer Bill Tilman, 'it is wise to draw a veil'. Especially, say, the third and fourth day, when sore muscles may be screaming. This is the darkest hour. Persevere and your body will tone, till even the steepest ascents are, if not absolute joy, nothing to worry about.

Nepal's terrain is relentless. A level stretch of a kilometre is cause for rejoicing; the status quo is up up up and down down down, ad infinitum. Tough ascents are originally the most dreaded, but many trekkers find the downhill stretches harder on the knees. Try to cushion the impact with your thigh muscles, and make sure your boots fit well. Pace yourself, and eat more rice than you believe you can possibly ingest—energy comes from food, a relationship which becomes clear out on the trail.

Cleaning out the body seems to clean out the mind as well, as you begin to delight more in the simple present rather than dwelling in the past or future. Trekking involves walking over long periods of time…that rarest of commodities in the modern world—and with time to do nothing but walk, perspective starts to take hold. All this is to say nothing of the country you're walking through; some of the most spectacular vistas in the world, inhabited by a tremendous range of fascinating peoples. Many trekkers find the reality of traditional life to be more memorable than the mountain views.

Eco–Trekking

'Eco-trekking' has become a catch phrase, in danger of sliding into the realm of pious thinking rather than action. It should be more than a slogan, however. Everyone bears responsibility for ecologically and culturally-conscious trekking, from the government down through trekking companies, lodgekeepers and, most of all, individual trekkers. Here are some suggestions for minimizing your impact on the trail:

—**Reconsider the extravagant style of organized treks.** Staff members are trained to produce large multi-course meals three times a day, and to provide boiled drinking water, hot washing water and endless cups of tea. They want to please you, and may even truly believe you can't function without these things, but if groups could agree to reduce some of this ridiculous excess everyone would be better off. This requires discussion with other members, of course, but consider these options, especially at high altitudes where wood is scarce: cutting down or eliminating the heated morning and evening washing water; doing away with the sahib custom of 'bed tea'; iodizing drinking water instead of boiling it; having less elaborate meals. The *sirdar* must understand that the group is in unanimous agreement, and the reason for it.

—**Make sure your group's food is cooked on kerosene** (discuss this with the company in advance). In an ideal world, porters would cook on kerosene too, but as long as they continue to be underequipped and unsheltered it's hard to grudge them a night-time wood fire.

Independent trekkers have no reason to feel smug. It's been estimated that a single trekking lodge burns enough wood daily to supply a Nepali family for 10-14 days. The reduction of excess also applies here.

—Eating at a lodge, **consolidate food orders with others,** ordering the same meals at the same time. Dal bhat is often cooked and on hand already. Don't keep the cooking fire burning for hours with orders for another jam pancake, another lemon tea: order everything at once.

Ama Dablam from Pangboche, Khumbu

—**Reduce hot showers** (or skip them altogether), and take them in lodges which heat water with either a backboiler system or hydro or solar power.

—**Making sure your porters have warm clothes and sleeping gear** will cut down on their use of firewood. Their welfare is your responsibility, especially when crossing potentially dangerous high passes.

—**Burn or bury trash**, and encourage trekking staff to do the same. Local people are usually happy to acquire clean, empty bottles, jars and other containers. Carry back your non-biodegradable items to Kathmandu. Don't think of litter as the biggest problem, though: litter is a Western concept, as is revulsion to it. Most Nepalis don't even perceive it as a problem, and in truth there are more serious aspects of pollution, for instance the horribly unsanitary water that kills 43,000 Nepali children each year from water-borne diarrhoeal disease.

—**Use established toilet facilities**, making sure they are at least 30 metres away from any water sources.

—Be modest when bathing. **Don't rinse soap or shampoo into streams**, not even biodegradable brands.

—**Don't give anything to begging children**; donate funds to schools or monasteries instead.

Trekking Styles

There are two principal options: through a company, which generally involves trekking with a group, or on your own. The latter is popular with budget travellers in Nepal—perhaps half of all trekkers are independent—and is easily arranged on major routes, where every village has lodges and restaurants catering to foreign tourists. Facilities are simple, but there are unexpected comforts like foam mattresses, apple pie (or 'pai'), and hot showers. And there is plenty of company, mainly young world travellers sandwiching a trek somewhere in between Bangkok, Delhi and a job. It's a sociable, interesting community, and it's easy to make friends on the trail. Guides are unnecessary on the main routes, which are virtual highways. You can hire a porter or porter-guide to carry your gear and provide some contact with local communities along the way. This type of trekking suits independent-minded people willing to put up with the inconveniences and ambiguities of organizing a trek on their own.

Group trekking through a registered trekking company raises the luxury quotient another notch. Ingenious cooks produce surprisingly gourmet multi-course meals over wood fires. Trekkers sleep on foam mattresses in tents and dine on folding stools in a dining tent. Gear is carried by a long line of porters; trekkers are assisted by assistant guides (called 'sherpas', with a small 's'), and the entire retinue is organized by a sirdar, usually an ethnic Sherpa, who's in charge of the whole operation. Occasionally a Western guide is on hand to provide commentary and bridge the cultural gaps.

Trekkers find the relationship they strike up with staff members to be among the highlights of an organized trek. Other advantages are security and minimal problems. Organized trekking is especially good for people who have a tight schedule to maintain and no time to learn the ropes in Kathmandu. Equipped with a mobile infrastructure, groups can visit remote areas devoid of lodges or other accommodation. Indeed, most of the formerly restricted areas recently opened up to trekking may only be visited through a trekking company. The disadvantages of group treks include lack of privacy, the need to observe a fixed schedule and the occasional twinge, unavoidable with a retinue of 10-20 people, of feeling part of a walking zoo.

Organized trekking subdivides into further options: signing up for a prearranged trek with a company based in your country, or booking with a Kathmandu-based company. The former usually involves several thousand dollars, as advertising and administrative costs are added onto the bill. But since foreign companies simply contract their groups out to the best local companies, the standard of on-the-trail service varies little.

Organizing a trip with a local agency takes some time and trouble, but can save a lot of money. Local companies can also provide a custom trip: just you and friends or family; an itinerary tailored to special interests like birdwatching, Buddhist monasteries or photography; or a trip to an unusual destination.

Organizing Your Trek

What to Take

Not too much, to begin with. A few changes of comfortable, durable clothes which are easy to wash and dry, as you'll probably be doing laundry by hand at the local *dhara*. Modesty counts: rural Nepalis are more conservative than in Kathmandu. Women will find that mid-calf-length skirts blend well into the culture and facilitate discrete bathroom stops where there are no bathrooms. Bring a few pairs of slacks (lots of pockets helps) and a few layers of tops, from T-shirt through shirt, sweatshirt or sweater, and light jacket. Don't underestimate the chill potential at altitude, especially during the autumn and winter. Daytime walking is usually balmy, but temperatures plummet after dark. A good down coat provides enough warmth for the coldest nights, crushes down nicely in the rucksack, and doubles as a pillow.

Expensive high-tech windproof or waterproof gear is unnecessary unless you already own it. So are gadgets like crampons and ice axes, unless you're crossing an exceptionally high pass. The most essential item is a pair of well-fitting boots, broken in before the trek starts. Most people choose lightweight hiking boots; heavy mountaineering boots are out of fashion nowadays. A pair of lightweight shoes is nice for the evenings and as emergency backup. Take lots of socks.

Other items:

—Warm hat and gloves, plus a brimmed hat, sunscreen and good sunglasses (serious sunburn is common at altitude, especially on snow).

—Durable water bottle and water treatment method (*see* **Health**). Plastic bottles of mineral water cost Rs275 apiece in high-altitude regions, and the leftover bottles create a serious litter problem.

—A daypack for short hikes.

—Toiletries, small towel, soap.

—Flashlight, extra batteries, candles for night-time reading.
—Rope for a clothes-line and laundry soap.
—Pocket knife.
—Small sewing kit (dental floss makes handy tough thread for emergency repairs).
—Medical kit (see **Health** for a rundown of frequently encountered problems, and remember that you'll be treating yourself).
—Raingear, depending on season: a poncho is sufficient for mid-autumn and winter. Big black Chinese umbrellas protect from both sun and rain.
—Entertainment: a good thick paperback, a Walkman, portable games, a deck of cards, a journal.
—Snacks and emergency pick-me-ups for long stretches of trail without teahouses.

Everyone needs a good sleeping bag (available for rent in Kathmandu). Main-trail lodges and group treks both provide mattresses. Trekkers with porters should pack gear in a duffel bag. Those carrying their own need a good, sturdy, well-fitting rucksack with either an internal or external frame. Rucksacks and duffel bags are both available in Kathmandu, though not of the highest quality.

Paperwork

Trekking permits are necessary for virtually all off-road travel in Nepal. They are issued by the Central Immigration Office in Thamel and are usually available the same day. The charge for major areas is US$5 per week for the first month, US$10 per week after that. Expensive exceptions are Mustang and Upper Dolpo, currently US$700 per week, Manaslu, US$75 per week and Lower Dolpo, US$20 per week. Permits for the Annapurna region and Western Nepal are also available at the Pokhara Immigration Office.

Two organizations near the Central Immigration Office are well worth a visit. The **Himalayan Rescue Association** (HRA) is virtually next door, on the second floor of the Hotel Tilicho building. It offers information and informative briefings on altitude sickness, essential if you're going to Khumbu or crossing a high pass like the Thorung La. Logbooks of comments from returned trekkers offer up-to-date advice on lodges, prices and trail conditions. The nearby office of the **Kathmandu Environmental Education Project** (KEEP) provides information on ecologically responsible trekking, and operates a small library, a coffeeshop, and a noticeboard for trekking partners.

Organizing Porters and Guides

With portering the major non-farming occupation in the country, it's no problem to arrange for someone to carry your rucksack. Probably he (or more rarely she) will prefer to load it in a wicker *doko* suspended from a rope slung over the forehead. This method may look uncomfortable, but it distributes the weight equally along the spine, giving the leg muscles maximum leverage up steep slopes.

Trekking with a porter has advantages beyond the sheer physical relief of walking without a load: it can open up new avenues of communication with Nepalis you meet along the way and give you insights into things you would otherwise miss. Local porters are easily hired at airstrips and road-heads across the country. Ask a shopkeeper or lodgekeeper for assistance in arranging one. They are generally reliable, but few speak English. For that, and maximum reliability, you'll have to hire a porter through a Kathmandu trekking agency. A porter–guide, while slightly more expensive, is the best combination, as he'll carry your load and translate for you along the way. A guide *per se* is, however, unnecessary on the major trails, which are virtual highways.

Lowland Nepalis are usually woefully unprepared when it comes to highland trekking. Make sure your porter is properly outfitted for high passes, especially if snow is a possibility. Either loan out warm clothes, decent shoes and sunglasses (to prevent snow blindness), or arrange for him to bring them from Kathmandu. Each year a few porters die from exposure or altitude sickness because their employers imagined they knew what they were doing and ignored them. Most of these tragedies occur on the Thorung La, the high pass on the Annapurna Circuit.

Newar man

The Routes

Which trek you choose depends on your inclination, experience, the amount of time at your disposal and the season. While trails lace the entire country, only a handful of areas are popular with trekkers. Number One is the Annapurna region, followed by the Solu–Khumbu area around Everest and, a distant third, the Langtang–Gosainkund–Helambu region north of Kathmandu. Independent trekkers on their first journey to Nepal should probably pick one of these standard routes, which are justifiably popular. Transport and trails are highly developed and accustomed to catering to Westerners; there's plenty of company along the trails, and it's virtually impossible to get lost for long. Groups, with their portable infrastructure, have the option of going to more remote areas. Experienced trekkers may choose to do these solo; inexperienced ones will probably want to hire porters and guides through a local company.

The Everest Region

This classic walk has a clear-cut goal: to see Mt Everest. Many people find the sights along the way rival the climactic views of the world's highest mountains. **Solu–Khumbu**, the homeland of the hardy Sherpa people, has been described by Sir Edmund Hillary as 'the most surveyed, examined, blood-taken, anthropologically dissected area in the world'. The Sherpas have fascinated Westerners since the earliest contacts on expeditions in the Indian Himalaya in the 1920s, when European mountaineers were impressed with their sturdiness, reliability and cheerful disposition.

The **Sherpas**' unique character is bred in the rugged mountain environment of Khumbu, where they migrated from eastern Tibet about 450 years ago (the name Shar–pa means 'Easterner'). Traditionally they combined farming, herding and trade with nearby Tibet. The system collapsed in the late 1950s with the Chinese occupation of Tibet, but in a stroke of fortune, Khumbu was opened to foreign mountaineers at precisely the same time. The Sherpas were quick to profit from new opportunities in portering, expedition work and guiding. Today, trekking and tourism has replaced the old Tibet trade as the linchpin of the Sherpa economy. The influx of wealth is apparent in the prosperous stone houses and multi-storey lodges springing up along trails.

The full–on route starts from the roadhead at Jiri and heads through Solu, crossing several monster ridges before joining the Dudh Kosi and heading up to Namche Bazaar. The relentless up–down guarantees you get in shape, and the Solu region, with its rolling hills, forests and interesting small *gompas*, is worth a visit in itself. A shorter, easier trek can be done by flying to the STOL airstrip of Lukla and joining the main trail a day below Namche, though trekkers who do this must pay special attention to acclimatization.

Above Namche, the scenery is truly spectacular. More than any other major Nepal trek, Khumbu puts you *in* the mountains. Many find slightly smaller peaks, like Lhotse or bewitching Ama Dablam, more beautiful than Everest. There are four major river valleys to explore in the region, but most trekkers head straight to Everest Base Camp.

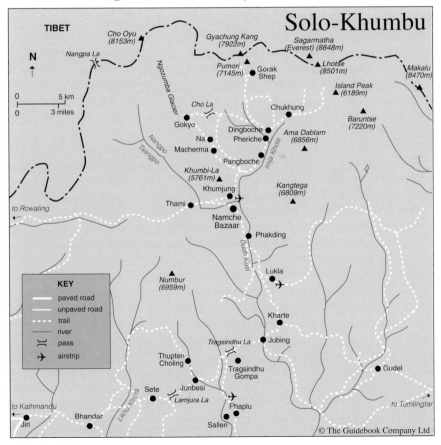

Sin Among the Sherpas

Most of the actions considered 'sins', however, concern the relations between individuals and result, in particular, from any infringement of the rights or dignity of another person. The way in which Sherpas view such infringements is demonstrated by the following list of sins enumerated spontaneously by one of my lay informants:

1. *All quarrelling is sin.*
2. *To steal is sin.*
3. *To cheat in trade is sin.*
4. *To talk ill of someone behind his back is sin, particularly if what one tells about him is not true.*
5. *To kill any living creature is sin. If someone kills a cat he commits so great a sin that he cannot make up for it even by burning as many butter lamps as the cat had hairs on its body. To kill yak and sheep is sin, even for the butchers, but not for those who buy the meat.*
6. *To have sexual relations with another person's spouse is sin.*
7. *To have sexual relations with a nun is sin, because the man involved contributes to the sin committed by the nun.*
8. *To threaten children or make them cry is sin, whatever the reason.*
9. *To marry a girl who is unwilling is sin both for the husband and for her parents, who arranged for the marriage.*
10. *To hit any animal is sin.*
11. *To fell trees is sin, though on occasion it is inevitable; even to pluck flowers is sin, and it is sinful to set fire to the forest.*
12. *For a monk it is a sin to drink too much and get intoxicated.*
13. *To cause a spirit long associated with a locality to be driven out is sin for the person who commissions the excorcizing, but not for the lamas who execute it.*

Collected by Christoph von Fürer-Haimendorf
The Sherpas of Nepal, 1964

Altitude is a constant consideration here, as Khumbu is the highest of all popular regions. Rather than crossing a high pass and dropping down, you go high and stay high. The walk above Namche is relatively level and straightforward, but you must plan periodic rest days at strategic altitudes.

Through Solu

The Solu trail begins at the roadhead of Jiri, a Wild West town consisting of a single long and dusty street lined with shops and lodges. The bus ride here is a hellish ten hours; hire a taxi if possible. The trek starts off with a nice stiff climb up to **Deorali**, a 2,713-metre (8900-foot) pass filled with new lodges. The pretty village of **Bhandar**, nestled in a green tableland below, is more interesting, but difficult to reach in a single day.

The trail drops down to cross the Likhu Khola, meanders along it, then climbs fiercely up a seemingly endless ridge to the **Lamjura Pass**, where rhododendron forests are often covered in snow. Dropping down from here, you enter Solu proper and after a while, the idyllic little Sherpa village of **Junbesi**. This small town with its excellent lodges is a great place to spend an extra day. The local *gompa* is quite elaborate for such a little place, and a 90-minute walk up-valley is the active monastery of **Thupten Choling**, the reincarnation of the Tibetan monastery of Rongbuk, which was razed during the Cultural Revolution. The inhabitants, including the present abbot, Trulshik Rinpoche, transferred here to start anew. Thupten Choling is an extraordinarily vibrant and active centre for both organized monasticism and individual retreat.

The trail continues around the Sallung ridge, revealing an early glimpse of Mount Everest. Passing through the apple-oriented little town of **Ringmo**, you climb the **Tragsindhu La**. There's a small *gompa* at the pass with beautiful murals in the main temple. Tragsindhu is better known among trekkers for its nearby **Cheese Factory**, a tidy little complex run by a Jirel family. What to order here (raclette? pie? a grilled cheese sandwich?) is the subject of much anticipatory debate among trekkers.

Drop down through **Nuntala** all the way to the Dudh Kosi, Khumbu's principal river. Cross through the charming little Rai village of **Jubing** and the bazaar town of **Karikhola** to enter the region called **Pharak**. It's neither as prosperous nor as idyllic as Solu or Khumbu. About a day from here, the Lukla trail joins at **Chaumrikharka**, and from here it's a day and a half to **Namche Bazaar**, the capital of the Sherpas.

Namche Bazaar

Built in a horseshoe-shaped natural amphitheatre facing the spectacular
Lumding Himal, Namche is the commercial centre of modern Khumbu. Its
shops are stocked with leftover goods from mountaineering expeditions:
paperback novels, crampons and down jackets for rent. It is highly
commercial and not very typical of Khumbu, but most trekkers enjoy an
extra day of acclimatization here, generally spent lounging in deluxe lodges
consuming cinnamon rolls. A more active option is to walk over to the
Sagarmatha National Park Visitor's Centre, perched on a hillock east of
town, which has informative displays on local life and geology. Namche's
big event is the Saturday *hat bazar*, a weekly outdoor trading post. Lowland
porters haul up grain, meat and oranges for sale, while Tibetan traders
bring down brick tea, salt and butter.

If time permits, head over the hill, an hour's walk north to **Khumjung**,
a large and highly traditional village that is everything Namche is not. Rows
of stone houses nestle below the sacred mountain of **Khumbi-la**, far more
highly regarded by the Sherpas than Everest. The trail to Khumjung passes
the Syangboche airstrip; near it is the **Everest View Hotel**, purportedly the
highest hotel (as opposed to lodge) in the world. Built by a Japanese
consortium, it caters to clients flown in from Kathmandu especially for a
glimpse of Everest.

To Thami

Above Namche, four main valleys branch out to the north. The shortest and
least-travelled is the westernmost valley of the Nangpo Tsangpo river, which
leads to the small village of Thami. It's a relatively easy four-hour walk.
Thami has some small lodges and a *gompa* built above the village where
masked Mani Rimdu dances are performed on the May full moon. Several
days' walk further up-valley is the broad Nangpa La pass into Tibet,
unfortunately off-limits for foreigners.

To Kala Pattar

Most trekkers opt for the trail to **Kala Pattar** and **Everest Base Camp**. A
day's walk from Namche, it passes renowned **Tengboche Gompa**, the
cultural and religious centre of Khumbu. The monastery's spectacular
location, perched on a ridgetop with stunning views of peaks all around,
has made it a popular tourist destination, though it was founded in 1912 as
a secluded retreat. Tengboche's split personality leads to some bemusing
juxtapositions: a stupa stands next to a helicopter landing pad, monks cook

up yak steaks for trekkers in the monastery-run lodge, and a sign above a wall of engraved prayer stones reads 'Please do not stand on the *mani* wall'.

The *gompa*'s recent history could be taken as a lesson in the perils of rapid modernization. Electricity was provided by foreign donors with much fanfare in 1988. Nine months later the monastery burned to the ground, in a fire probably started by an unattended heater. A large new *gompa* constructed with local and international funding was inaugurated in September 1993, but the old scriptures, costumes, images and frescoes destroyed in the blaze were irreplacable.

Tengboche's annual highlight is the annual festival of **Mani Rimdu**, the dance-drama retelling the saga of Buddhism's victory over Tibet's ancient Bon religion. Popular with both tourists and Sherpas, it is usually held in late October.

The trail continues through the old village of Pangboche to **Pheriche**, a nondescript collection of stone-walled houses that is the last permanent settlement in the valley. It's advisable to spend an extra day here acclimatizing. Go on a day hike up the valley of the **Imja Khola**, which provides marvellous mountain views of Ama Dablam, the Lhotse-Nuptse wall and Island Peak. Stay overnight at the small lodges and climb **Chukung Ri** to see the sheer, breathtaking wall of Lhotse up close.

The next stop is usually **Lobuche**, though people who stop at the small settlement of **Tukla** in between have reported better acclimatization. It is also possible to stay further up at the tiny lake of **Gorak Shep**, but sanitation is poor here. From either Gorak Shep or Lobuche, it's a day's hike up to **Kala Pattar** (5,623 metres/18,450 feet), the climax of the trek. This spur running off the peak of Pumori provides an incredible overview of the Khumbu Glacier ringed by the highest mountains in the world. Everest is clearly visible, but it's a stumpy broad snout, unimpressive compared to Nuptse's swirling fantasy of snow and ice.

The end of the line is **Everest Base Camp**, a long day from Lobuche or four hours from Gorak Shep. The mountain is blocked from view here and there's not much to see besides expedition camps and their accompanying litter, but walking on the Khumbu Glacier is an experience in itself.

To Gokyo

An equally good choice is the trek up the Dudh Kosi Valley to **Gokyo**, another superb viewing point beneath 8,153-metre (26,155-foot) Cho Oyu. It is difficult to decide whether Kala Pattar or Gokyo offers better views, but those who have visited both tend to rate Gokyo slightly higher.

From Namche, the trail heads straight north via Khumjung. Trekkers should pace themselves and include rest and acclimatization days to avoid ascending too quickly. Allow at least four days to walk up the valley, passing through various small settlements equipped with lodges. The upper trail skirts the edges of giant **Ngozumba Glacier**, the largest in Nepal. A series of tiny turquoise-blue lakes, really little more than ponds, marks your arrival at **Gokyo** (4,791 metres/15,720 feet), a small herding settlement turned tourist resort. The local version of Kala Pattar is **Gokyo Ri**, a 5,483-metre (17,989-foot) peak to the northwest providing marvellous views of Everest, Lhotse and Makalu. **Cho Oyu Base Camp** lies further north up the glacier past several more tiny lakelets.

Experienced and fit trekkers can combine Kala Pattar and Gokyo by crossing a high pass, the 5,420-metre (17,782-foot) **Cho La** connecting the two valleys. This requires a good map or guide and good weather conditions; don't try it in snow.

The Annapurna Region

This is the most popular trekking region in Nepal, visited by 70 percent of all trekkers, and for good reason. The deep valleys and high mountains encircling the giant Annapurna Himal embrace a wide range of peoples and terrains, from subtropical jungle to a geographic extension of the high, dry Tibetan Plateau. The scenery is a superb mix of lush vegetation, mountain peaks and an endlessly changing procession of peoples. Accommodation is relatively plush: lodges on the Kali Gandaki side offer enchiladas, foam mattresses, even videos.

The principal routes are up the Kali Gandaki river valley to Jomosom and the ancient pilgrimage site of Muktinath, and up the Marsyangdi river valley to Manang, with its Buddhist *gompas* and superb mountain views. By crossing a high but straightforward pass, the Thorung La, these trails can be combined into the classic Annapurna Circuit, which takes a minimum of three weeks. The other option is the Annapurna Sanctuary, a hidden pocket of meadow, moraine and glacier ringed by magnificent sheer-walled peaks.

This region also offers a range of short low-altitude treks out of Pokhara, ideal when trekking with children, with limited time, or when higher trails are snowed over. One option is starting at Phedi and climbing up through Dhampus, then Lhandruk, and up the Modi Khola to the idyllic little village of Chomrong, worth an extra day's stay. Return via Ghandruk and Birethanti, which is near the Baglung-Pokhara road, or extend your trip by a few days to go from Ghandruk to Ghodepani for views from Poon Hill, then drop down to Birethanti and the road. A combination pieced together from these parts can take as little as five days, yet provide an unforgettable taste of Nepal.

Pokhara to Muktinath

This trek requires ten days to two weeks, though the lower portion up to Ghodepani and Poon Hill is probably the most popular short trek in Nepal. It's also possible to fly in and out of Jomosom and spend a few days exploring this region, with due respect to altitude, of course.

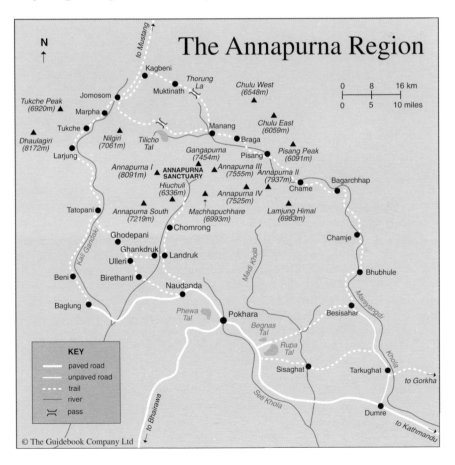

A Night in Biratnagar

Hotel Bardon, a large concrete building near the roundabout, came with back-handed recommendations which said more about its competitors than itself. 'Only hotel which isn't a knocking shop', a Nepalese technician at Pakhribas had explained. 'It's where the Royal Nepal pilots stay', another had said, as though that in itself was a seal of approval. It was a dismal place, though in retrospect I'm glad I spent a night there as it encapsulated the flavour of the industrial Terai.

I walked into the foyer and found a youngish man, an Indian, sitting reading a newspaper behind a large metal desk of the sort once found in dole offices in England in the days before there were many people on the dole. He greeted me by spitting into a metal wastepaper basket. He said they had two types of room: 'cheap room and not cheap room'. I said I'd take a not cheap room and he led me up a row of stairs to a long, wide corridor. On the way along it I caught glimpses through open doors of large numbers of people—they all appeared to be Indians–sprawled on vast beds, panting wearily like overheated dogs.

The walls of my room were a cold duck-egg blue and scarred by a mass of electric wires, some of them bare, which served an extraordinary array of appliances: two fluorescent lights, three ordinary bulbs, an air-conditioning machine, and a large fan which dangled from the ceiling. There was a plywood panel by the door with eight switches, one of which operated a light in a shower-room. The main room was as over-furnished as it was over-electrified, and most of it was taken up by two double beds which were wedged together as though awaiting occupation by a very large family. They were made up with blue nylon sheets and pink quilts. There was also a newish settee with draylon covers, a small table with vinyl topping and a cabinet whose shiny blue surface was covered with cheap bits of god-wotery. Thankfully, there were no posters of actors or pop stars; instead there was one of Krishna as a young boy, and another of Laxmi, the goddess of wealth. The latter had two pairs of arms, which presumably meant she could collect debts and count money twice as fast as mortal men (or women). The former sported an exceptionally soppy smile, much as Christ did in the paintings of my children's Bible, and he was decked out in a gold head-dress and an orange, braided jacket. His skin was blue and his lips purple. The poster reminded me of the cover for the Beatles' Sergeant Pepper album.

I sat on the bed, smoked a cigarette, fooled around with the switches, then joined a platoon of cockroaches in the shower-room. As soon as I turned on the water they marched smartly towards the WC, behind which they took refuge while I washed away the day's grime. They were the largest and most precocious cockroaches I'd come across: as soon as I turned off the water one landed on my shoulder and another crawled over my feet. Back in the bedroom I discovered an insect under the quilt the likes of which I had never seen before. It was about half an inch long and thin like a centipede, although with many fewer legs. When I poked it, it leapt into the air, bent itself double and made a loud noise like the crack of a whip. Once I'd spruced myself up I went for a wander in town.

Charlie Pye-Smith, Travels in Nepal, 1988

Long before it assumed cult status as a popular trekking trail, the Kali Gandaki River Valley was an important trade and pilgrimage route. Jingling mule trains carrying loads of wool and salt down from Tibet bear witness to this old tradition, as do barefoot Hindu *sadhus en route* to the ancient power centre of Muktinath.

Technically speaking, the Kali Gandaki gorge is the deepest in the world, flanked by Dhaulagiri (8,167 metres/26,795 feet) and Annapurna I (8,091 metres/26,545 feet). The peaks are 20 kilometres apart, however, giving one room to breathe, and it's hard to believe the summits are that high, so great is the visual foreshortening.

The trek now begins from the Pokhara-Baglung road across from **Birethanti**, a charming riverside village. As usual it starts off with a good stiff head-clearing ascent, from 1,097 metres (3,600 feet) and up an apparently endless stone staircase through **Ulleri**, then up some more to Ghodepani (2,819 metres/9,250 feet), set in a rhododendron-forested pass. **Ghodepani** (the name means 'Horse Water', referring to its former incarnation as a watering hole for trade caravans) is not a village, but a collection of several dozen lodges catering to the trekkers who flock here for the views from nearby **Poon Hill**. This viewing point scarcely deserves its cult status, as the Annapurnas and Dhaulagiri seem quite distant when compared to the views from Everest, Langtang, or even upper Manang.

The trail drops down to **Tatopani**, famed for its excellent lodges and hot springs. The village is a tourist haven, complete with VCRs in the biggest lodges—not that you walked over all those hills just to watch the latest movie. From here on the walking gets easier, following the swirling Kali Gandaki up through increasingly Tibetanized villages, their flat roofs a sure sign of the decreasing rainfall.

This region is called the **Thak Khola**, and its inhabitants are called Thakalis. Ethnically Tibetan and formerly Buddhist, they have engineered a mass conversion to Hinduism in their quest for improved social status. Historically the Thakalis served as prosperous middlemen in the Tibet-Nepal trade. Their capital is the town of **Tukche**, where Tibetan wool, salt and turquoise were once swapped for Nepali rice, cloth and cigarettes. As the old trade dwindled with increasing modernization and the Chinese takeover of Tibet, the shrewd Thakalis switched over to more ambitious trading enterprises.

Two hours up the trail is **Marpha**, a fascinating collection of stone houses, prayer flags and flagstoned streets, a good place to spend an extra day. Sample the locally produced apple or peach 'brandy' (a particularly fine *raksi*). Across the river is **Chaira**, with a Tibetan settlement and an 18th-century *gompa*.

The next town is **Jomosom**, which serves as district headquarters and base for an STOL airstrip. The new town, with its offices, banks and hotels, is dull and dusty, but the old town across the river has several lodges. If you've extra time here explore **Thinigaon**, a thoroughly Tibetan-type village two kilometers to the east.

The trail continues upriver and forks at **Eklai Bhatti**, with the right-hand branch leading directly to Muktinath. Take a half-hour detour and you can spend a night at **Kagbeni**, an old medieval fortress town set on the riverside that is as Tibetan-feeling as you can get without crossing the border. North from here and upriver lies the formerly forbidden Kingdom of Mustang, now open to trekking groups with an expensive permit.

You can proceed directly to Muktinath from here without backtracking. Climb up the slope to a magical high valley dominated by the ruined fortress of **Jharkot. Muktinath** (3,802 metres/12,475 feet) lies less than an hour beyond. This ancient holy site is a typically confusing blend of animistic, Buddhist and Hindu beliefs. It began as a natural power place, was adopted by Buddhists, and more recently was taken on by Hindus. This mix is visible in the assemblage of religious sites: a gilt-roofed pagoda to Vishnu, a Jwala Mai temple enshrining miraculous flames of natural methane gas, and a sacred spring in which devout pilgrims bathe to earn *mukti*, spiritual liberation. The entire valley is lovely, dotted with a half-dozen prosperous villages. It's possible to cross the Thorung La pass from here and continue on the Annapurna Circuit trek, though it's usually done from the other direction.

Manang and the Annapurna Circuit

This three-week epic joins the Manang and Muktinath treks by crossing the 5,380-metre (17,651-foot) Thorung La pass. While with proper preparation it can be travelled in either direction, most trekkers head counterclockwise, starting at Manang. This saves an extra 600 metres (1,969 feet) of climbing over the pass, which may not sound like much but is heartily welcomed at the time of ascent.

The Manang region is frequently ignored in the rush to the pass, but it's a worthy destination in itself, and less crowded than the Kali Gandaki side. The trek starts at the dusty little roadside town of **Dumre**, on the Kathmandu–Pokhara road. Local jeeps and trucks run from here up to **Besisahar**, a bone-rattling and crowded four-hour ride which almost everyone takes, though many wish afterwards they had walked the day and a half along the trail to Besisahar.

Besisahar is a bustling little roadhead town. The first days of the trek lead through typical middle Hills territory inhabited by Gurungs and Hindu castes. The real climbing begins at **Bhubhule**, but the water buffaloes and rice paddies continue up to **Chamje**. Then the valley narrows and forest thickens as the trail climbs through cooler zones, entering increasingly Buddhist territory. **Chame** is the district headquarters and the largest town in the entire valley.

Past Chame, spectacular views of the Annapurnas begin. **Pisang** is the first town in Manang proper, and is split into two divisions: the lower town, with the majority of lodges, and the older upper village across the river, with stone houses surrounding an old *gompa*. The landscape changes markedly from here on, into the dry terrain typical of the rainshadow area of Manang.

From Pisang there's a choice of trails, the higher, longer one offering more views. Both lead to **Braga**, a spectacular collection of flat-roofed houses stacked up against steep cliffs. Be sure to visit the 500-year-old *gompa* here, the largest and most impressive in Manang.

Most trekkers prefer to stay half an hour beyond Braga, in **Manang**, which serves as the unofficial capital of the region. There are plenty of shops and lodges, a *gompa*, and marvellous views of Annapurna and Gangapurna looming over the town. It is wise to stay an extra day here to acclimatize: there are plenty of good day hikes in the area.

The next stop is **Phedi**, which can be reached in one day, but from the point of view of acclimatization is perhaps better done in two. Its name means 'foot of the hill', an accurate enough description: Phedi is a crowded little dump of a place at the foot of the Thorung La. Everyone crowds into the few small lodges in order to get a head start on the dreaded pass, but the little enclave of **Lattar** before it is more private and pleasanter, though it adds another 90 minutes onto the next day's ascent.

The **Thorung La** (5,416 metres/17,700 feet) is not necessarily difficult or dangerous, but as the highest commonly trekked pass in Nepal it deserves a healthy dose of respect. You should be well-acclimatized and briefed on mountain sickness by the time you make it up to Phedi. Warm clothing is essential, for both your porter and yourself. The pass is generally closed from January through March or even into April, though local people may send their yaks up to plough a trail through the snow. Sudden snowstorms can quickly obscure the trail. Don't cross if the weather looks threatening, or at least follow a group or a guide who knows the route. The passage from Phedi to Muktinath takes anywhere between seven to twelve hours, depending on your acclimatization and fitness. In the main trekking season temporary lodges and teashops operate above **Muktinath**, allowing a shorter journey if necessary. See the Pokhara-Muktinath trek description for a summary of the rest of the route.

The Annapurna Sanctuary

This relatively short trek touches on some of the best of Nepal's diversity, blending attractive countryside and interesting villages, and culminating with spectacular mountain views. The drawback is overcrowding: more than 10,000 visitors a year tramp up and down the single narrow trail leading into the Sanctuary, and because the upper region is subject to heavy snowfall and avalanches, the limited season compresses most of them into the autumn and spring.

The romantically named Sanctuary is a secluded high hollow ringed by towering peaks. Traditionally it was sacred territory for the local Gurung people, who considered it the dwelling place of local gods. Most of the Sanctuary's visitors were herders bringing their sheep up for summer pasture.

The trek begins at **Birethanti**, easily accessible from the new Pokhara-Baglung Road. Climb up to **Ghankdruk**, an interesting large Gurung town of slate-roofed houses worth an extra day's stay. The trail continues to **Chomrong**, its tidy chalet-style lodges ablaze with flowers in the autumn season. This is the last permanent settlement, and accommodation gets more basic beyond. Check trail conditions with local people before setting out, as avalanches often block passage into the Sanctuary

What follows is only two days' walking, but the trail rises 2,000 metres (6,096 feet) in the last eight kilometres, requiring a slower pace for acclimatization. The unofficial entrance to the sanctuary is past the lodges of **Dhovan**, where a small *chorten* and prayer flags honour guardian spirit Pujinam Bharahar. A few hours further is the so-called **Machhapuchhare Base Camp**, and two hours beyond that, **Annapurna Base Camp** (4,130 metres/13,550 feet). Both offer incredible and slightly different views of the peaks ringing the Sanctuary: Hiuchuli, Annapurna South, Fang, Annapurna I and II, and Machhapuchhare. Returning, you'll have to backtrack to Chomrong. From there an alternative route to Pokhara crosses the river and heads up through the Gurung village of **Landruk**, then to **Dhampus**, dropping down to **Phedi** on the Pokhara road.

North of Kathmandu

The region north–northeast of Kathmandu offers at least three different major routes, all with accommodation for independent trekkers. Langtang fits nicely into 10 days, counting transportation time, and offers truly spectacular high-mountain scenery. The sacred lake of Gosainkund and the Sherpa region of Helambu to the east are admittedly more minor treks, but they can be done in as little as four or five days. A distinct advantage of all three is their proximity to Kathmandu. Helambu or Gosainkund-bound trekkers can actually start walking from the Valley. The regions can also be combined in a 16-day circuit as long as high passes are not blocked by snow.

Langtang

Langtang National Park protects a high Himalayan valley that stretches north from Helambu all the way to the Tibetan border. The trek begins with a bus ride to **Dhunche**, about ten hours. A few buses run up to Syabrubensi; otherwise the trek begins with an easy two-to three-hour walk down the traffic-free road. The first night is usually spent at the moderately interesting ridgetop village of **Syabru**, inhabited by Tamang people. The trail drops to the Langtang Khola, then ascends rather steeply along the bank through country similar to the Western United States: pine forests and rushing streams backed by vistas of snow peaks.

The standard next stop is the clearing of the **Lama Hotel**, which now boasts six different trekking lodges. Recent visitors have been disgusted with the filth, however, and recommend staying at **Rimche**, which comes about 15 minutes earlier. The narrow valley begins to open up at the meadow of **Gorhe Tabela**, as the landscape rapidly changes into a drier, colder realm inhabited by Bhotia people. They are more or less pure Tibetan, many of them refugees who fled south in 1959. Most families rely heavily on herding yaks, as the surrounding countryside is good pastureland. In the small village of **Langtang**, you can see people churning butter and sewing the finished product into skins for easy transport.

Two hours above is **Kyangjin** (3,749 metres/12,300 feet), the last permanent settlement, with a small *gompa*, a cheese factory and a fancy National Park Lodge. Use it as a base for day hikes, exploring the upper valley: try climbing the small hill north of Kyangjin, or **Tsergo Ri** (4,984 metres/16,353 feet), which lies three hours upvalley from Kyangjin. The upper valley is ringed by spectacular snow peaks, including Fluted Peak, Langtang Lirung, and the Tibetan-named Dorje Lakpa and Phurbi Chyachu.

The usual option is to backtrack down to the road, though if snow conditions allow, trekkers equipped with tent, food and a local guide can cross the steep 5,122-metre (16,805-foot) **Ganja La** pass into Helambu.

Gosainkund

Returnees from Langtang can also combine the trek with a visit to the sacred pilgrimage site of Gosainkund, adding three or four days to the trek. Or you can access it from the Kathmandu side (the Helambu route). Do not, however, expect a spectacular shimmering lake: it's really no more than a mountain pond.

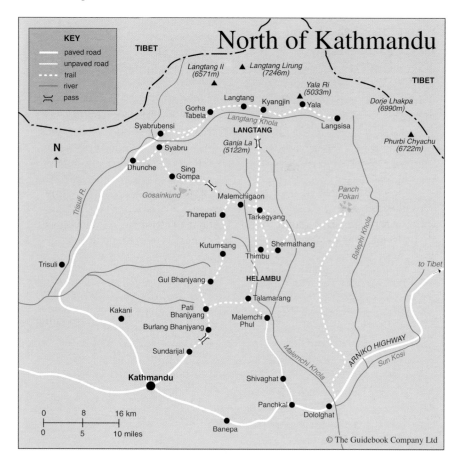

© The Guidebook Company Ltd

From Syabrubensi or Dhunche, trails climb up through pretty rhododendron forests to **Sing Gompa**, a cheese factory and lodges perched on the hillside. A few hours beyond is **Cholungpati**, a few lodges set in a saddle of the ridge. Climb the hill ten minutes to the west for spectacular views of Dhaulagiri, Annapurna and Langtang Lirung right in front of you...the best views of the entire trek. The little settlement of **Laurebina** is another popular stop, also offering good mountain views.

Crossing over the ridge, **Saraswati Kund** appears, the first of several lakes dedicated to different divinities. **Gosainkund** (4,381 metres/14,374 feet) is the third lake, sacred to Shiva. According to Hindu mythology, the gods once banded together to churn the ocean to find treasure. The first thing that emerged was a burning poison that threatened to destroy everything it came into contact with. They begged Shiva to drink and contain it, and he did, burning his throat in the process. Fleeing into the high Himalaya, he thrust his trident into the rock to create the lake and take refuge in its cold waters.

By far the most interesting time to visit here is during the festival of Janai Purnima (usually the full moon of August) when hundreds of pilgrims converge for a *mela*, led by drum-banging, whirling shamans. There is no village at Gosainkund, but several lodges are scattered about the shore of the lake, and there's a tiny Shiva temple with a Nandi about the size of a puppy in front. Climb the hills above to discern a giant underwater rock which devotees insist resembles Shiva. There are no real views from the lake, but an hour beyond, from the pass, you can see Helambu and all the lakes spread out behind. From here it's a three-day walk via **Kutumsang** (*see* Helambu trek) into the Kathmandu Valley, versus a two-day descent and a day's bus ride via Dhunche.

Helambu

This is the most easily accessible of all areas from Kathmandu. Take a taxi or bus to **Sundarijal** and simply walk up over the lower shoulder of the Shivapuri ridge, cresting the Valley at **Burlang Bhanjyang**. A day's walk brings you a world away from Kathmandu, into genuine rural Nepal. The next day's stop is at the little village of **Kutumsang**, followed by a day's hike through superbly empty herder's country—just forests and mountain views. It's possible to continue along this ridge all the way to Gosainkund, but to enter Helambu take the trail dropping steeply down to **Malemchigaon**, an idyllic little village inhabited by Sherpas who are only remotely related to their more famous Khumbu cousins.

Malemchigaon (2,560 metres/8,400 feet) is worth lingering in; a collection of neat houses with prayer flags in front and surrounded by orchards and fields. The trail drops down to cross the Malemchi Khola, then climbs all the way back up the opposite ridge to **Tarkegyang** which is at exactly the same altitude. This village is slightly larger and more commercial, and its inhabitants are famous for selling *thangkas* to tourists from a seemingly limitless supply of 'old' artifacts.

From here you can head three days north to cross the high **Ganja La** into Langtang (*see* above), or with proper provisioning and a guide visit the five sacred lakelets of **Panch Pokhari** to the east. The shortest option is to head down-valley and return to Kathmandu, a two-day trip. The trail drops through increasingly warm countryside inhabited by Hindu castes, reaching the roadhead at **Malemchi Bazaar**. From here minibuses run to Banepa on the Arniko Highway, and on to Kathmandu.

Other Treks

The following routes are best undertaken as organized treks, with porters, guides and provisioning. Some of the regions (Mustang, Manaslu, Kangchenjunga and Dolpo) are only opened to trekkers going through a company.

Mustang

This remote and isolated former kingdom north of the Annapurna massif possesses an unrivalled mystique. Mustang (Moo–stahng) is a geographic extension of the Tibetan Plateau, and the bleak beauty of its wild, bare terrain evokes the Tibetan highlands. It was founded in the 15th century by a Tibetan monarch who consolidated various small local fiefdoms into the Kingdom of Lo. Though it was eventually incorporated into Nepal, Mustang has remained isolated. Its reputation as wild country was reinforced by the Tibetan guerilla fighters who sheltered here in the 1960s to make daring raids on the Chinese across the border. Following their expulsion by Nepalese Army troops in the early 1970s, Mustang remained off-limits for trekkers. It was opened in April 1992, partly due to the requests of local people, who envy the prosperity trekkers have brought to the lower Kali Gandaki region.

The people of southern Mustang call themselves Gurung, but they are obviously related to Tibetans. They grow wheat, barley and buckwheat, grazing their herds in high pastures in the summer. In winter, many head south to trade. The people are devout Buddhists. A lama of the Sakya sect initiated a religious revival here in the 15th century, establishing monasteries which exist to this day, their mud walls striped in typical Sakya fashion.

Trekkers to this fascinating region generally start from the airstrip at Jomosom, heading slowly up the Kali Gandaki gorge. The route rises gently up with little variation, but altitude must be taken into consideration. The trail meanders through small villages, the most impressive **Tsarang**, with a crumbling *gompa* and an old royal palace. The trek climaxes at the walled city of **Lo Manthang**, the region's capital. Here are several impressive old temples and the four-storey mud-walled palace of King Jigme Paldor Bista, the last surviving traditional monarch in Nepal. With the right connections, it is even possible to meet the king: bring a white prayer scarf (*khatak*) and a gift of some sort. From all accounts he is a sort of Himalayan Renaissance man, more practical than regal.

Mustang's opening has so far been carefully controlled. The government has established a limit of 1,000 trekkers to the region per year (though this appears to be flexible), and currently charges US$700 for the minimum 10-day permit, of which 60 percent is supposed to go back to the region. Trekkers are only allowed to enter through a registered agency. Groups must be accompanied by a government liaison officer, who is supposed to ensure proper compliance with environmentally-oriented regulations, such as the requirement that cooking be only on kerosene. Despite these precautions, the pressures imposed by the tide of visitors are becoming obvious: fissures are developing over who gets what, and the average Loba (the local term for the inhabitants) is reaping little benefit from the influx, as the group–only policy means everything is imported from the lowlands. For insights into the undercurrents, read Manjushree Thapa's *Mustang Bhot in Fragments*.

Around Manaslu

This 22-day trek reportedly rivals the Annapurna Circuit for diversity and views, but it's much less crowded, resembling in that sense the Annapurna Circuit of the early 1970s. The route encircles the eighth-highest mountain in the world, 8,162-metre (26,778-foot) Manaslu. The trail starts at Gorkha, heading up the gorge of the Burhi Gandaki River thorough wild Gurung country. As the land rises the people change to more Tibetan-influenced Bhotia, and the first of many extensive *mani* walls appears. The large village of **Samagaon** is notable for its *gompa*. From here it's a long climb up to the 5,198-metre (17,100-foot) **Larkya La** pass, and an equally long way down, past an intensely blue glacial lake set below snow peaks. It is a steep, icy, spectacular descent into the lower Manang region where the trail joins the main route at the Gurung village of Tilje. From here it's a few days south to the roadhead at Besisahar.

Dolpo

David Snellgrove's *Himalayan Pilgrimage* (1961) was the first to unveil this mysterious land, where vestiges of Tibet's ancient Bon religion still linger. He termed the dazzling turquoise-blue of Phoksumdo Lake, 'one of the most blissful things I have known'. The lower reaches of this once-restricted region were opened to group trekkers in 1988.

The trek is rather difficult, full of steep, stony ascents. The usual access point is the airstrip at **Juphal** (accessible from either Nepalganj or Bhairawa). The trail leads over three days to park headquarters at **Dunahi**, then up the Suli Gad gorge through forests of spruce and Thakuri villages to **Phoksumdo Lake**. Veteran trekkers concur with Snellgrove's enthusiasm for Phoksumdo, an intensely blue pool set beneath high cliffs. The little town of **Ringmo** (3,639 metres/11,940 feet) boasts a painted entrance *chorten*; two kilometres further is a Bonpo *gompa* perched above the lake, with another at Pungmo, two hours up a side valley to the west. The Upper Dolpo region described by Peter Matthiessen in *The Snow Leopard* (1978) lies beyond here, down a difficult trail over a high pass. Shey Gompa, named after the nearby Crystal Mountain, is several hard days' walk north of the lake.

Birethanti, the Annapurna Region

Development Comes to Mustang

This is when Bikas, development worker, came along with the objective of electrifying Lo Manthang. Why? To provide alternative sources of fuel that would ease the pressure on the land; this would be especially crucial when tourists began to come in. And to improve conditions in rural Nepal so that people would not flock to the cities in search of a better life. And on the personal front, to pay back the debt he felt he owed to Nepal for having had the opportunity to study in the United States; Bikas was motivated by such sentiment.

He went to Mustang the second time on behalf of a foundation in the United States with a proposal to revive the almost-forgotten electrical scheme of Lo Manthang. He could have proposed a fresh one, but he knew about the equipment being stored in the godown in Jomosom. There was also that loan the villagers owed to the Agricultural Development Bank. He decided it was more expedient to revive the old project than to start a new one.

Instead of following the conventional procedure, which entailed discussion with only the Raja, Bikas decided to speak directly to villagers. The Raja encouraged him to do so; now that there was democracy, the Raja said, it was imperative to involve the public. So on the day of a village meeting, Bikas stood in front of a crowd in the courtyard of the Jamba Lhakhang and explained the American organization's offer in his thorough, reasonable way.

An American donor wanted to help electrify Lo Manthang. The donor was willing to pay for the entire cost except the amount already raised by the village, which amounted to Rs320 per house. The villagers were required to supply voluntary labour, though, to do away with the cost of bringing labourers from the south. The amount of time each family volunteered would depend on the amount of electricity it planned to use.

Although the project proposed by Bikas appeared to have some continuity with the previous one, it was in fact close to a full subsidy of the plant. To avoid discouraging the villages that had started electric schemes on their own, Bikas had also asked the American foundation to help pay back their debt to the ADB/N.

As Bikas spoke he sensed a strangely unreceptive reaction in the crowd; people murmured, coughed, shuffled and sighed. He knew

the chequered history of the scheme, so he decided to slow down.
He produced documents from his file to support his statements—the
ADB/N accounts of Lo Manthang's debts, the NEA policy papers,
the report by the NEA engineer regarding the decision not to build
Lo Manthang's plant, as well as the accounts of the Butwal-based
company that proved the villagers' contributions, had, contrary to
rumour, been spent on electrical equipment.

'Some of you will remember I came here to do the initial survey,'
Bikas said. 'I've known about this project right from its beginning.
Even if you decide to drop the project once and for all, you have
to pay back the loan from the ADB/N. The debt won't just go away.'

He reiterated the American organization's offer, and said it was
a good way to continue the project.

'Many promises have been made,' he said. 'But no matter what
anyone—politicians or even the King—has said, the Nepal Electricity
Authority has a policy of not building schemes smaller than a hundred
kilowatts.'

'That's not an unreasonable policy. There are forty thousand
villages in Nepal and all want to be electrified. The government
prefers to be involved in projects that small communities can't afford
to undertake. If you decide to wait for the government, Lo Manthang's
electricity could take a while coming.'

He went on to counter false campaign promises about the large
scheme in Ghemi. 'A kilometre of transmission costs about three
hundred thousand rupees, and the river is eight kilometres away
from Charang—let alone Lo Manthang and all the other villages.
It's far cheaper to build separate plants in each village. When I
return to Kathmandu I will certainly speak to Om Bikas Gauchan
to coordinate our plans.'

But after Bikas spoke, and after the Raja's secretary translated
his message into Tibetan, the villagers responded with all the force
of their pent-up fury.

'We don't want your electricity,' one old man yelled, his face
purple with anger. 'We've lived our whole lives without it and we
don't need it now.'

While others murmured in assent, some younger men scoffed.
'You don't know what you're saying,' said one. 'The problem,'—he
turned to us—'is that the elders think it's all nonsense. Don't listen
to them. They don't know how far the world has gone these days.'

'This is our chance to get electricity,' declared a man who held a sleeping baby in his hands. 'Did the other villages have it so easy? Did they have an American donor? We're lucky.'

'Let the government make it just like in Kathmandu,' the old man spat out. 'Isn't it our government too? Aren't we citizens too?'

The young man smirked. 'What? You think your candidate is going to deliver, eh Kunga? You think your politician is different from all the others?'

'Isn't it our government too?'

'First they should return the money we've put into the project,' another man proposed. 'Then start all over again. We don't want to have anything to do with the previous project.'

'Stop dreaming! How can he do that?'

'We've been cheated and swindled and I won't put up for it anymore.'

'Don't talk nonsense,' said the man with the baby. He pointed to Bikas. 'This man's brought proof.'

'Besides, that was then. This is another project,' said another young man.

The old man snorted. How do we know what connections link who to whom? 'How do we know who's scheming behind our backs? How do we know? Hunh?'

'Please, please,' Bikas said, breaking in. 'These papers verify everything I said.'

But the feisty old man just stared at him with wide eyes and tight lips. The only ones who could read were the Bistas, who were all suspect.

The discussion then switched to Tibetan. The crowd broke into small groups of men and women, young and old, Bistas and Gurungs, their hands and arms flailing, their faces reddening and their voices getting louder and louder.

Then a group of 20 or so men shouted thunderous final words and separated from the rest. They stomped theatrically to the edge of the courtyard, followed by others. Soon half the village was in one group, and the other half in scattered groups all over the courtyard.

The leader of the dissident faction, a sturdy old man in a chuba, stood on top of a wall to express his opposition to the offer. His followers climbed over the wall and walked away, turning back every two or three steps to glare at the others. Bikas looked on dejectedly.

'The problem with the previous project,' said one man, in an effort to comfort him, 'is that we didn't even want it. And we didn't know we were taking a loan.'

'That's a lie,' a Bista hissed beside us. 'We were all there when the decisions were made.'

'We couldn't say anything at that time,' the other retorted. 'That was before democracy. You tell me if it was open to discussion.'

'You liar!' the Bista shrieked. 'Who taught you to say that!'

The man just grinned menacingly.

'Okay', said one old man, coming up and holding Bikas' hand. 'We agree. You do it for us. Build the whole thing, wire all the houses, keep an operator from outside to maintain it. Whatever you do, don't involve us. We don't trust each other. We can't work together.'

Manjushree Thapa, Mustang Bhot in Fragments, 1992

Chortens, Khumjung

Eastern Nepal

This region has much to offer trekkers looking for less-crowded options to the main trails. It is greener, more prosperous and markedly friendlier than Western Nepal. People still wear traditional clothes rather than Western imports, and greet you with the full palms-together *namaste*, a nicety that's disappeared along the most popular trekking trails. This is the homeland of the **Rai** and **Limbu** tribes, independent and handsome people who are, proud of their unique culture and history. The higher regions are inhabited by Tibetan-influenced Bhotia and Sherpas, the latter only distantly related to their celebrated Khumbu cousins. Eastern Nepal's horizons are dominated by towering peaks like Makalu and **Kangchenjunga**, and Everest makes its customary intermittent appearances.

The region is still seldom visited by trekkers and is relatively undeveloped in terms of the availability of pancakes and lemon tea. The lower regions are dotted with local teahouses which will put trekkers up, though English is likely to be minimal. The higher ridges are usually uninhabited, and tents and provisions are necessary. Going with a guide is recommended, unless you're comfortable speaking Nepali.

The classic route in this area is the trek to **Kangchenjunga**, which takes about three weeks. The usual route starts from the airstrip of **Taplejung** and heads up the valley of the Tamur Khola, past Tibetan-type villages. Higher up, the terrain becomes mountain pasture and glacier. **Kangchenjunga Base Camp** lies beneath the immense Kangchenjunga massif, which at 8,598 metres (28,209 feet) ranks as the world's third-highest peak.

Other possibilities are trekking from Basantapur up the long ridge of the **Milke Danda**, through the world's most extensive pure rhododendron forest (glorious in the springtime), and possibly up onto **Jaljale Himal**, a rocky ridge with a few small lakes. The trek to **Makalu Base Camp** is more difficult, crossing a high double pass into the isolated upper Barun Valley.

The eastern route to **Everest via Tumlingtar** in the Arun River Valley is becoming popular as a less crowded alternative to Solu or the Lukla airstrip. It takes about six days to walk from the Tumlingtar airstrip to Kharte on the main Everest trail, crossing the 3,350-metre (10,991-foot) Salpa Bhanjyang *en route*.

Central Nepal

The old **Pokhara–Gorkha–Trisuli** trail is ideal for a winter trek as it's relatively low altitude; indeed, it's steaming hot by spring. The countryside is typical middle Hills, with Newar and Hindu villages, huge spreading pipal trees and good views of the Central Nepal Himalaya. Once a major trade route, it is still lined with local teahouses, though they cater mainly to local people. The route starts at Begnas Tal in the Pokhara valley and winds east through Gurung country. The old fortress town of Gorkha is only an hour's detour from the trail. From here the route continues east, dropping down to Arughat on the Burhi Gandaki and continuing two more days through small bazaar towns to end at the roadhead of Trisuli.

More remote options requiring provisioning, guides and porters are the wild **Ganesh Himal** trek, running from Gorkha to Trisuli but further north than the route cited above, and the **Jugal Himal** region northeast of Kathmandu and Helambu.

Western Nepal

This immense region, half as large again as Central Nepal, is remote, dry, poor and seldom visited by trekkers. Its inhabitants are predominately Hindu, and caste restrictions make them less than hospitable to foreigners. Supplies can be scarce and local people have little to spare, so it's best to pack everything in.

The nerve centre of Western Nepal is **Jumla**, its largest town, but not all that large, and served by regular RNAC flights. From here it's a few days' walk to **Rara**, Nepal's largest lake, surrounded by forests of pine and silver birch. This trek is unusual for the solitude it offers—a very un-Nepali characteristic. The few existing villages were evicted in the formation of Rara National Park. Flying in and out of Jumla, which can be a touchy proposition, would make the trek do–able in under two weeks.

River Rafting

As if trekking amidst the world's highest mountains were not
enough of a thrill, Nepal's adventure travel companies have
diversified into river rafting. Over 10,000 rafting permits were
issued in 1990. Rafting provides a counterpoint to trekking: it's
less strenuous (at least for the lower body), and the riverside
scenery glides smoothly by, the tranquillity occasionally broken
by whitewater rapids.

The daily schedule is similar to a trek: five or six hours a day on
the river, broken by a long lunch stop, with camping on a soft
sandbank at night. Cooks produce surprisingly good meals from
scanty resources. In warmer weather there's the opportunity to swim:
guides will alert you to 'swimming rapids' over which you can float
in a life jacket.

Autumn is the best season for a river trip. The rivers are
excitingly high in October following the monsoon, slightly slower
and cooler in November. Winter trips are chilly, spring ones
slower and warmer. Monsoon floats are possible, but they are not
always safe. Sometimes they go by so fast you don't even know
they've happened.

The most popular river by far is the **Trisuli** in Central Nepal,
which draws 90 percent of rafters. It features exciting but not-*too*-
thrilling rapids and is cheaply and easily done from either
Pokhara or Kathmandu. The usual version is three days, from
Baireni down to Narayanghat, which is an easy drive to Chitwan
National Park. Combined rafting/safari packages are popular, or
you could travel on to Sauruha on your own and find a lodge that
suits your fancy.

For a very casual trip out of Pokhara, try the easy one-or two-day
float down the **Seti Gandaki** from Damauli to the Trisuli. This
lowland area is relatively warm even in the winter, and combines
lush vegetation with some stunning mountain views.

The **Sun Kosi** ('River of Gold') offers a far more intense
experience. The eight- to ten-day float starts at Dholaghat, off the
Arniko Rajmarg and ends 272 kilometres later at Chatra in the
Terai. The area is remote and unspoiled: there are no roads or
large towns along the way, only traditional villages, lush
vegetation, and beautiful beaches to camp on. Despite its
reputation as one of the world's ten best river trips, the Sun Kosi
gets less than 1,000 rafters a year.

River fishing, Birethanti

Out in remote western Nepal, the **Karnali** is another world-class river, winding through virtually untouched territory teeming with wildlife. A trip here involves a two-day trek to the put-in point and five to seven days on the river; the rapids are fairly serious, so choose a reputable company. The trip usually ends at Chisapani, providing an opportunity to visit nearby Royal Bardiya National Park. An easier choice, equaly remote and unspoiled, is the 4≈8 day trip down the **Bheri**, also ending at Chispani.

Shop carefully when looking for a rafting company in Kathmandu. As rafting is a relatively new enterprise, regulation is nonexistent and many companies haven't the faintest idea about safety requirements. Cheaper companies may cut corners with poor or missing equipment and inexperienced guides. Establish what's included in the package (tents, sleeping bags, mattresses, food), and check the company's equipment (life vests, helmets and rafts in good condition), and the extent of the guide's experience and training. Costs range from US$20–80 per day, averaging US$30–40, and depend on the number of people in the group (the usual minimum is four).

Practical Information

Accommodation

There is a plethora of accommodation in Kathmandu, from rambling old Rana palaces to sleek modern buildings. Prices listed here are for a double room in main season, October–November (there's a smaller surge in March≈April). Some of the top hotels may be fully booked at this time, but there is never a lack of rooms. In off-season, especially during the monsoon, rates can drop by as much as 50 percent. Room rates are bargainable in all but luxury hotels: here you simply request a 'business discount'.

All but the cheapest hotels require payment in foreign currency, and state their rates in US dollars. Government tax added to hotel bills ranges from 10 to 16 percent, according to the hotel's category. The hotels listed here are rated according to the following categories:

Expensive: All the modern conveniences—shopping arcade, air-conditioned rooms (welcome in the summer months), top-class restaurants and often a swimming pool and/or tennis courts. Prices run from US$100-145 for a double room.

Moderate: Hotels in this category are smaller and have fewer facilities but often have a more creative ambience. Prices range from US$40–80 for a double room.

Budget: Dozens of budget hotels and lodges are clustered in Thamel, with the cheapest around Freak Street. Quoted prices are around US$20 for a simple but clean double room with carpet, phone and bath, though room rates are almost always negotiable. Rock-bottom budget lodges charge as little as US$2 per day.

Things to look for in a hotel are character, quiet and location (you should take full advantage of Kathmandu's walkability, and there's nothing worse than a hotel you have to beg taxi drivers to take you to late at night). The big difficulty is finding a room with character: even luxury hotels tend to have small, unimaginatively decorated rooms, often redolent of monsoon mildew. Some of the more out-of-the-way places reward their guests with extra charm. Only the most expensive hotels have heating and air-conditioning, which is all the more reason to find a hotel with a large garden or rooftop terrace to soak up the sun or relax in the shade.

Accommodation outside Kathmandu is generally much simpler. Tourist destinations like Pokhara and Chitwan National Park have a range of lodges, resorts and hotels, but even these seldom reach Kathmandu standards. Virtually all towns of note have local 'hotels', though the signboard may be only in Nepali. Usually the noise level is high, and cleanliness (and prices) low.

The Kathmandu Valley

Kathmandu and Patan
Expensive
Hotel Yak & Yeti, Durbar Marg (tel 413 999). The best luxury hotel in Kathmandu: centrally located, it combines all the amenities with a touch of class—one wing is housed in an old Rana palace.

Hotel de l'Annapurna, Durbar Marg (tel 221 711). Good location but slightly dingy rooms; fine swimming pool.

Soaltee Holiday Inn Crowne Plaza, Tahachal (tel 272 555). Kathmandu's largest hotel. Notable restaurants and mountain views compensate somewhat for the remote location.

Everest Hotel, New Baneswor (tel 220 567). Formerly the Sheraton. Good rooms, some with mountain views, but inconveniently located.

Hotel Himalaya, Kopundol, Lalitpur (tel 523 900). On the road to Patan, with superb mountain views on clear days; ask for a room facing the garden.

Hotel Malla, Lainchaur (tel 410 620). Well-situated just north of Thamel, this quiet hotel features a pleasant lobby and gardens.

Hotel Shangri-la, Lazimpat (tel 412 999). Rooms are simple but ambience and service superb. Built around a wonderful garden with a swimming pool modelled after the traditional sunken fountains. Good restaurants, reasonably well-located.

Hotel Shanker, Lazimpat (tel 410 151). The white stucco exterior of this old Rana palace is a baroque fantasy. Rooms are less than palatial, but at least they have character. Sweeping gardens, good location.

Hotel Sherpa, Durbar Marg (tel 227 102). Fine location, rooms a bit cramped, but all the amenities at a reasonable price.

A Meeting with Boris

Through the portal, the jeep turned into the expansive grounds of what I concluded must be some gigantic royal palace or centre of administration, on the other side of which I assumed we would emerge and continue our ride. It was a shock when my driver, with a wave of his hand toward the vast palace that loomed up in the lush oasis of green lawns, announced, 'Royal Hotel'.

The grounds, shaded by gigantic pine and cedar trees, recalled a British park without the rain. A pink, brick-paved driveway swooped in a wide curve across a lawn to the pillared portico, the main entrance of the hotel. The building itself was most impressive, a huge rectangular structure of white stucco, the façade composed of two superimposed galleries running for three hundred feet between two baldachin-like oriental turrents that sat lightly above the two lateral wings of the building. Crouched all around the grounds and on the steps by the entrance were dozens of Nepalese servants dressed in the same manner as the men I had seen on the streets, with thin white jodhpurs partly covered by long white shirts with straight buttoned collars like those of surgeons. Some were smoking, others taking in the sun with characteristic oriental nonchalance. Three rickshaws were lined up at the foot of a wall. The jingle of a few bicycle bells could be heard above the cawing of flocks of crows that flapped from tree to tree above my head. From all this arose a sense of peaceful luxury; only the servants added a mysterious note of exoticism.

The jeep came to a dusty halt, and immediately a rush of servants laid hands on my luggage. Hauling myself down from the front seat, I turned toward the entrance, a vast door leading to the foot of a staircase.

Standing a few steps above me on that staircase, framed by the enormous stuffed heads of two rhinoceroses, who were gaping at each other with sympathetic small beady eyes, was a sturdy, handsome man. Around him on the steps hustled four servants, carrying envelopes or bowing with timidity in an effort to attract his attention. As I entered the hall the man stepped down to greet me. It was Boris.

We spoke in French and after a few words I realized that the Royal Hotel is not so much a hotel as a decor for Boris's sense of elegance, and I felt as if I were being greeted by some exiled European lord rather than a hotel manager. When I nervously dared inquire about rates and the possibilities of staying, Boris put me at ease.

'Of course, stay here. Don't worry about the rates. Those are for tourists.' I immediately became an object of Boris's g enerosity—generosity that has kept in the Royal Hotel many of the extravagant characters, whether rich or poor, who have strayed into the Himalaya.

Boris then showed me to my room. 'It's an unusual place, you'll soon see,' he explained, as we made our way down a wide corridor into which opened large green doors. By each door squatted a servant who quickly rose to attention as Boris passed by.

'It's not the Carleton in Cannes,' Boris said, 'but remember there are no other hotels from here to Calcutta, 450 miles away.'

Climbing up a staircase, we emerged onto an open gallery. I could now look down into a vast square courtyard in the rear of the hotel, enclosed on all sides by the three-storey palace.

'This,' Boris explained, 'is the end the hotel is in.' Then, pointing beyond the massive quadrangle, he showed me the extent of the palace. Beyond it were two more such quadrangles; the palace contained perhaps seven hundred rooms in all. With a twinkle in his eye, Boris explained that this style was known as 'Kathmandu baroque', and there were nearly fifty such great palaces in the valley. 'The Ranas wanted the best from Europe', he said. 'This is what they got.'

Looking over a balustrade I could see, rising above green clumps of trees, more white turrets and the great roofs and long galleries of white palaces all around the hotel.

Boris then pushed open a door, saying, 'Will this be all right?'

I peered into what seemed a gigantic cement garage with windows. I decided Boris's question must have been a joke. Then I noticed at the far corner of this vast room a large marble trough. I understood that this great empty room was the bathroom. Through another green door, we entered an adjoining room. I say 'room,' but I felt more as if I were entering an exhibit hall of some Victorian museum. The proportions of the place were truly immense. A cool, dim light coming through great shuttered windows filtered through the air; a streak of sunlight picked out the large mass of a tiger-skin rug with a wide open, pink and jeering mouth. Two out-sized, ornate Victorian chairs, no doubt from one of London's nineteenth-century clubs, opened their vast embrace to other pieces of furniture, all equally tortured and dated. 'All carried in on coolie back', I reflected.

Michel Peissel, Tiger for Breakfast, 1966

Moderate

Hotel Vajra, Bijeswori (tel 272 719). A unique compendium of local culture, starting with the red-brick buildings set with woodcarvings and tiled roofs. Other attractions include gardens, a Finnish sauna and an active cultural scene, including traditional dance performances, an art gallery and a well-stocked library run by a genuine swami. The biggest drawback is location: it's not close to anything but Swayambhunath, and a 15-minute walk from Thamel. Rooms range from US$15–80.

Hotel Marsyangdi, Paknajol, Thamel (tel 414 105). This new, six-storey hotel even boasts an elevator, a distinct step up from the usual Thamel lodgings. Very nicely decorated rooms, some with air-conditioning and TV, and increasingly good views the higher you go.

Hotel Thamel, Thamel (tel 417 643). Another new high-rise building with decent rooms, most with balconies, and a rooftop garden.

Summit Hotel, Kopundol Heights (tel 521 894). Set on a bluff overlooking the city, this hotel features traditional architecture in a lush garden setting, complete with small pool. Rooms are simple and traditionally decorated. Location is the drawback: it isn't really walking distance to anywhere.

Hotel Mountain, Kanti Path (tel 224 086). New, centrally located, nice rooms. At the high end of moderate.

Hotel Sunset View, Baneshwar (tel 229 172). Down a side road across from the Everest Hotel, with a wonderful garden and views.

Dwarika's Kathmandu Village Hotel, Battisputali (tel 470 770). Definitely something special. The buildings are in traditional Newari style and incorporate old woodcarvings; rooms are furnished with similar attention to traditional detail. A bit out of the way, near Pashupatinath.

Budget

Kathmandu Guest House, Thamel (tel 413 632). The place that started the Thamel boom back in the early 1970s, the 'Kathouse' has become a legend in its own time, supported by an interesting world-traveller clientele. Nice lobby and garden, located in the heart of Thamel. Room rates vary according to wing, from US$3–25 for a double room, with discounts for long-term occupancy.

Mustang Holiday Inn, Jyatha, Thamel (tel 226 794). Clean and exceptionally pleasant rooms in a range of prices, secluded from the Thamel scene. Recommended.

Hotel Garuda, Paknajol, Thamel (tel 416 776). Pleasant atmosphere, scrupulously clean rooms, some with small balconies, a rooftop terrace and friendly staff make this small place exceptionally good value.

Hotel Ambassador, Lainchaur (tel 410 432). Rats occasionally scurry across the lobby, but this run-down inn with hotel aspirations has low prices and a good location.

Tibet Guesthouse, Thamel (tel 214 383). A favourite with mountaineers and return visitors; friendly and clean, with a rooftop garden.

Potala Guesthouse, Thamel (tel 220 467). Popular old stand-by run by Tibetans.

Hotel Shakti, Thamel (tel 410 121). On the outskirts of Thamel, with one wing in an old Rana palace, the Shakti is a quiet refuge with some exceptionally inexpensive rooms.

Stupa Hotel, Boudhanath (tel 470 385). Five kilometres east of Kathmandu, Boudhanath is a world in itself. Friendly staff at this reasonably priced hotel.

For rock-bottom prices as low as US$2 for a room with bath, try Hotel Star, Lodge Pheasant, or Johnny Gurkha Guesthouse in Thamel; Thahiti Guesthouse in Thahiti, the Sayami Lodge near Freak Street, or the EPeace Guesthouse in Tahachal.

Bhaktapur

Accommodation is strictly budget. Try the upstairs room at the Golden Gate Guest House (tel 610 534), which is decorated Tibetan-style, with big windows overlooking Durbar Square, or the Shiva Guest House (tel 610 740) on Durbar Square.

Dhulikhel

Dhulikhel Lodge Resort (tel 011 61494). Across the road from the town, this new resort overlooks dramatic views of the Himalaya floating above the Indrawati Valley. There's a garden terrace, a rooftop restaurant, and a fireplace for the winter months, and it's within walking distance of town. Moderate.

Himalayan Horizon Sun–N–Snow (tel 01 161 296, Kathmandu office tel 225 092). Again, located a bit outside town to take advantage of mountain views. Traditional-style buildings feature old woodcarvings and simple but adequate rooms. Outdoor dining on converted rice terraces, facing more unbelievable mountain panoramas. Moderate.

Dhulikhel Lodge (tel 01 161 114). A big traditional house in the middle of town with small simple rooms, run by a friendly family. Budget.

Nagarkot

The Farmhouse (tel 228 087 or through Hotel Vajra, 272 719). Run by the Hotel Vajra, this converted old farmhouse features tiled floors, brick-and-wood decor, and a pretty garden with prayer flags and stupa. There are four rooms with shared bath in the main building, four with separate bath in a new wing. By far the classiest place to stay in Nagarkot. Moderate rates include meals.

The Fort (tel 290 869, in Kathmandu tel 216 913). This tall, narrow brick building is a bit of an eyesore on the outside, but the interior is nicely decorated in traditional style; there's even a sauna. Moderate.

Hotel View Point (tel 290 870, in Kathmandu tel 417 424). The best of the inexpensive lodges, with friendly staff and a passable restaurant. Try for a room with a balcony. Budget.

Cottage Green Peace Horizon. Very simple and quiet: five bamboo huts perched on the edge of a dizzying view. Budget.

The Hills

Pokhara

Everything in Pokhara is lower-key than Kathmandu, and hotel prices are no exception. Listings are keyed to the following categories:

Expensive: US$40–60
Moderate: US$15–30
Budget: US$5–10

Prices plummet in the off-season, and even in-season rates are bargainable. Request a good rate and see what the lodge-keeper offers.

Fish Tail Lodge, Lakeside (tel 061 20071, in Kathmandu 221 711), run by the Hotel de l'Annapurna. Uniquely sited on a promontory at the southern end of Phewa Tal, reached by a tiny ferry. Marvellous mountain views from an enchanting garden, but rooms are disappointingly cramped and dim. Expensive.

New Hotel Crystal, Nagdhunga (tel 061 20035). Across from the airport, convenient for early-morning flights, though removed from the lake. The deluxe rooms in the new wing even have central heating. Moderate–Expensive.

Hotel Monal (tel 061 21459). Centrally located on Lakeside's main strip, with bright and airy rooms. Moderate.

Hotel Dragon, Pardi (tel 061 20391). Air-conditioned rooms, some attractively decorated with woodcarvings and Tibetan carpets; some with mountain views. Moderate.

Hotel Mountain Top, Lakeside (tel 061 20779). You can't miss this giant shiplike structure in the centre of town; like many of Pokhara's lodges, it is run by an ex-Gurkha soldier. Panoramic views of the lake from the nicely appointed corner rooms; large balconies and a rooftop restaurant. Budget≈Moderate.

Temple Villa, Lakeside (tel 061 21203). This small, very private hotel is down an unmetalled lane: actually it's a modern upper-class house doing duty for a few years. The rooms with balcony and marble-walled bath are best. Moderate.

Hotel Meera, Lakeside (tel 061 21031). Friendly, clean, cheerful service (it's run by an ex-Gurkha). Some rooms with balconies and views. Moderate.

Sarowar, Lakeside (tel 061 21934). As advertised, 'homely setting, tranquil atmosphere'. Budget.

Hotel Monalisa (tel 061 20863). The balconied back rooms feature fantastic lake and mountain views, and are kept scrupulously clean. Budget≈Moderate.

Gurkha Lodge, Lakeside. This tiny, rustic lodge tucked way down a side lane features a few thatch-roofed stone cottages in an overgrown garden. Budget.

Green Peace Guesthouse, Sedi Danda (around the ridge past Khahare). Complete peace and tranquillity in this very simple lodge with rooms with balconies right over the lake. Very Budget.

Gorkha

Gorkha Hill Resort, (Kathmandu office on Durbar Marg, tel 227 929). Located a few kilometres before Gorkha down a side road, this new, modern resort is best for groups or those with a vehicle, though a private car is available. Twelve rooms with picture windows facing the Himalaya. Moderate.

Hotel Gorkha Bisauni (tel 064 20107). The only faintly tourist-standard place *in* town, though it's not really. Large dingy rooms with bath, small garden and a sluggish restaurant which at least makes decent *dal bhat*. Ask for Room 15, which has a view. Budget.

Tansen

Hotel Srinagar, Batase Danda (tel 075 20045). Perched on a ridge above town, with one wing facing the Himalaya, the other overlooking the Madi Khola Valley. The standard is surprisingly high. Budget–Moderate.

Daman

Everest Panorama Resort (Kathmandu office in Lazimpat, tel 415 372; Daman tel 057 21346). New resort with small guest bungalows three kilometres past Daman, just below Sim Bhanjyang pass. Moderate rates include meals.

Everest View Tower and Lodge. Ugly, cold, but unique: a circular viewing tower built and run (though not maintained) by the government. Four beds in the glassed-in circular room on top showcase Daman's sweeping Himalayan views, with a telescope and a fascinating guest log for entertainment. Flaws include no electricity, outdoor toilets and broken windowpanes. Definitely Budget.

The Terai

Chitwan National Park

Book in advance for the in-park lodges, as they are otherwise inaccessible. Sauruha lodges take walk-ins and give them a much better price. Bargain hard if booking in Kathmandu: substantial discounts can often be achieved.

Deluxe Lodges

Most places follow the standard model: a collection of rustic huts in local Tharu style (more comfortable than this sounds), a circular thatch-roofed dining hall in the middle of the compound serving Nepali and possibly Continental food, and a small bar. Electricity is rare, but lamps are provided and bath water is heated by solar panels or over a wood fire. Many lodges have a slightly cheaper separate tented camp, usually located deeper in the jungle. What makes a place special is, first its location inside the park...which provides a secluded experience unavailable in crowded Sauruha...and second, its naturalists (and its elephants, if any). Most have enthusiastic and knowledgeable staff, but high turnover makes it difficult to recommend one lodge over another.

The average price for a standard package of two nights, three days, including all meals and activities, is around US$250. Transport is extra, and ranges from tourist bus to private car (around US$120) or by air to Bharatpur (US$100 for a round trip).

Tiger Tops Jungle Lodge, Durbar Marg, Kathmandu (tel 222 706). The original operation has expanded into three phases, all expensive: the **Jungle Lodge**, with bamboo-walled cottages on stilts (US$500); a **Tented Camp** on an island in the Narayani River, and a nicely decorated **Tharu Village** based on the traditional longhouse (both US$300). High prices are based on prestigious reputation, but the service and ambience is definitely special. Extremely popular; book up to six months in advance for the main season.

Machan Wildlife Resort, Durbar Marg (tel 225 001). A newish resort, slightly fancier than most, in Parsa Wildlife Reserve, with a small swimming pool and duplex huts with bath.

Chitwan Jungle Lodge, Durbar Marg (tel 222 679).

Gaida Wildlife Camp, Durbar Marg (tel 220 940). Near Sauruha, overlooking the Dungre River, with a tented camp further inside the park.

Island Jungle Resort, Durbar Marg (tel 220 162). On an island on the Narayani River at the western end of the park, with a quoted package cheaper than the norm.

Temple Tiger Wildlife Camp, Kanti Path (tel 221 585). Tented camp perched above the Narayani River at the western end of the park.

In Sauruha

The following lodges provide the same amenities and activities on a slightly less grand scale. Bungalows are smaller, chefs less skilled, and the surroundings crowded with other tourists, but you'll still get nature walks, elephant rides and everything taken care of in a prepaid package. Prices run around US$100–180 for two nights and three days.

Jungle Adventure World, Tridevi Marg, Thamel (tel 225 393). Attractive compound with bungalows and tents; the riverside setting provides nice sunset views. Good staff, too.

Royal Park Hotel, Maharajgunj (tel 414 939). The newest and classiest place in Sauruha, with spacious landscaped grounds and traditionally decorated cottages.

Rhino Lodge, Thamel (tel 417 146). A budget version of the above, with a package programme of US$70 per person, including meals and transport.

Several dozen budget lodges clustered around Sauruha cater to do-it-yourself travellers who show up on their own. All have more or less the same rates, charging Rs400–600 for a brick bungalow with bath, as little as Rs150 for a simple mud-walled hut with separate bath. Activities and meals are arranged separately. Check out **River View Hotel and Lodge**, **Tiger Camp**, and the very simple **Rain Forest Guesthouse**.

Bardia National Park

Tiger Tops Karnali Lodge, Tiger Tops, Durbar Marg (tel 226 706). Run by the same operation as Chitwan Tiger Tops, but for serious naturalists rather than jungle socialites. Lodge and tented camp on the bank of the Churia River. Expensive.

Suklaphanta Wildlife Reserve

Silent Safari Jungle Adventure Camp, Kumaripati, Patan. (tel 523 055) A tented camp which moves according to season. US$125 per night, US$88 per person for parties of three or more. Access from Dhangadhi or Mahendranagar airstrips.

Bhairawa

Hotel Yeti (tel 071 20551). Located just off the bus stop, fairly modern and clean. Budget.

    Hotel Himalaya (tel 071 20347). The only other 'tourist-class' alternative in town, which isn't saying much. Budget.

Lumbini

Lumbini Hokke Hotel (tel 071 20236; Kathmandu office tel 521 348). One of the best hotels in Nepal, marooned on the Lumbini plain. Air-conditioned Japanese and Western rooms with exquisite food and a Japanese spa. Moderate–Expensive.

    Sri Lankan Pilgrim's Rest House. Clean new brick building with dorm rooms and private beds, all with fans, and a moderately priced restaurant. Budget.

Trekking and The Mountains

The main trekking trails are lined with tourist lodges, which in the Annapurna and Everest regions verge on deluxe, with foam mattresses, private rooms and wood-heated showers. It's easy to determine the season's favourites from conversations with fellow trekkers. A few easily accessible lodges are noted below for those seeking the trekking experience without much walking.

    Nepali-style *bhatti* or trailside inns cater mainly to local travellers, offering a wooden bed, a simple evening meal and an outdoor water tap. Wherever there are people, there is lodging; if no officially designated lodge appears, you can arrange to stay in someone's home, often a more interesting experience.

Everest View, Syangboche (Kathmandu office in Trans-Himalayan Tours, Durbar Marg, tel 224 271). For those with no time to trek but plenty of money, this Japanese-built hotel situated near the airstrip above Namche Bazaar offers spectacular views of Everest. Considering the remote setting it is downright luxurious, charging US$135 per person, plus US$35 per day for meals. Air service to Syangboche airstrip by helicopter or single-engine plane costs around US$300 for a round trip from Kathmandu.

Sanctuary Lodge, Birethanti. Ideal for a very, very short trek now that the road goes near Birethanti. The lodge is only 30 minutes' walk from Birethanti, up the trail to Ghandruk. Located on the bank of a river, with a small garden, solar-heated hot water and simple rooms with private bath. Budget.

Hostellerie de Sherpa, Phaplu. This classy lodge with Tibetan-style furnishings makes a good base for exploring Solu's rolling hills and Buddhist monasteries. Idyllic villages like Junbesi are an easy day's walk away, and RNAC flies to the Phaplu airstrip four times a week in season. Double rooms are US$30.

Recommended Restaurants

For an isolated Himalayan country, Kathmandu's tourist restaurants offer an amazing variety of cuisines. Cost, in even the most expensive hotel restaurants is low: it's difficult for a fancy dinner to exceed Rs800 unless you indulge in expensive imported liquor.

The best-prepared food is Indian cuisine, featuring highly spiced meat and vegetable dishes served with rice or flat bread and an array of condiments. Go with a group of friends and order together to maximize choice: try tandoori chicken (roasted in a clay oven), chewy warm *nan* (flat bread), curried vegetables, rice, *dal*, and a cooling *raita* (yoghurt). For an intensely sweet finish, sample almond-flavoured *gulab jamun* or cardamon-spiked *rasmalai*. The bravest should conclude with *pan*, a mixture of spices and crushed betel-nut wrapped in a leaf and chewed as an enjoyable digestive, and for its mildly intoxicating effect. Sold in tiny street stalls, it stains the teeth a gory red.

Budget tourist restaurants in Thamel and Freak Street have wholeheartedly embraced foreign cuisine, with the mixed results to be expected from menus offering Mexican, Italian, French, American and Chinese food all in the same breath. Dishes are palatable, but too often everything tastes the same. Still, Rs90 will buy a large and nourishing meal.

Set breakfasts are an especially good bargain: eggs, toast, potatoes and coffee/tea for Rs40. Cakes and pies are another specialty left over from the days of Asian overland travellers; some are excellent, others rely on quantity rather than quality.

The local people generally eat at home, or at *bhojnalaya* or small hole-in-the-wall eateries dishing up snacks, simple food and home-made *rakshi*. Chinese and Indian restaurants are good choices if you're entertaining Nepali guests, and plenty of restaurants have combination Chinese–Indian–Continental menus to please everyone in a large group.

Kathmandu
Indian
Ghar-e-Kabab, Durbar Marg. Acclaimed as Kathmandu's best restaurant, though there are many others just as good. Certainly it serves excellent food at a reasonable price, with the added entertainment of watching the chefs skewer kebabs and flatten *nan* behind a glass window. The *ghazal* singing is good but obtrusive enough to ruin dinnertime conversations.

Naachghar, Hotel Yak & Yeti, Durbar Marg. Rich food served in a spectacular palatial setting: crystal chandeliers, marble floors, fluted pillars and music nightly.

Moti Mahal or **The Amber**, Durbar Marg. Local versions of the Ghar-e-Kabab, complete with lower-volume *ghazal* music and glassed-in kitchens. Food is quite good and much cheaper.

Bangalore Coffee House, Jamal. For the adventurous, a local eatery featuring inexpensive South Indian vegetarian food. Try the *dosa*, a crisp pancake of rice flour stuffed with spicy vegetables.

Nepali
Bhanchha Ghar, Kamaladi. Delicious Nepali *haute cuisine*, far different from that kind you find on the trail: spiced boar, mushroom curry and tiny clay cups of the incendiary house *raksi*. Located in a renovated old farmhouse, with an interesting bar on the top floor.

Sun Kosi, Kamaladi. Specializing in gourmet Nepali and Tibetan food, with set menus to facilitate ordering.

Nepali Kitchen, Thamel. A budget version of the above, serving reasonably priced Nepali food (a Continental menu too) in a pleasant garden courtyard.

Thyabhu, Lazimpat. For something different, an elegant restaurant specializing in Newari food.

Mixed Cuisine

Nanglo, Durbar Marg. This conveniently located rooftop terrace serving Continental food and tasty *dal bhat* is popular with both tourists and local people.

Saino, Durbar Marg. Pleasant outdoor and indoor dining with the usual multicultural menu (Indian, Chinese, Tibetan, Continental). A good place for drinks and snacks.

Western

Chimney Room, Hotel Yak and Yeti, Durbar Marg. The menu includes Chicken Kiev, steaks, lobster, and bortsch; but you should come mainly for the ambience and history of this restaurant started by legendary hotelier *Boris Lissanevitch*. The red-brick room built around a copper-chimneyed fireplace is cosiest in winter.

Al Fresco, Hotel Soaltee Oberoi, Tahachal. The best Italian food in town, in an airy trattoria-type setting.

Gurkha Grill, Hotel Soaltee Oberoi, Tahachal. Excellent continental restaurant; some vegetarian dishes too, plus music and dancing.

Shambhala Garden Cafe, Shangri-La Hotel, Lazimpat. The only 24-hour restaurant in town, with a daily breakfast buffet and dining on the portico overlooking the lovely garden. **Bhaktapur Night**, held here on Fridays during the tourist season, features costumed dancers and an elaborate buffet in the torchlit garden (reservations tel 412 999).

Mike's Breakfast, Naxal (take the road curving north from Nag Pokhari). Relocated from its former charming setting, but still *the* place for breakfast and lunch. Brewed coffee, fresh baked items, sandwiches, soups, salads and daily specials. Dinner served some evenings in tourist season.

Northfield Cafe, Thamel. Mike's place in Thamel, with Mexican food too.

K.C.'s Consequence, Balajutar. An old Newari farmhouse transformed into an unusual and elegant retreat. Dine indoors in a traditionally decorated setting or out on the peaceful garden terrace. Dishes are not always up to scratch, but at least they're imaginative. Great for kids, as there's a playground and staff to supervise.

Boris' Restaurant, Thamel. A bit more expensive than most Thamel restaurants. Pleasant indoor and outdoor dining and a decent menu featuring Russian-inspired dishes. Run by Boris' son Misha.

K.C.'s, Thamel. A cut above the usual Thamel standard, good for pizza, fettucine, sizzling steaks and baked potatoes.

Le Bistro, Thamel. Old stand-by with budget travellers enamoured of its generously portioned meat and vegetarian dishes and marvellous chocolate cake.

Pumpernickel German Bakery, Thamel. Inexpensive, simple fare—sandwiches, eggs, pastries, coffee—in a garden that is a favourite with young world travellers. Also rolls, bagels and croissants as take-aways.

Gourmet Deli/Old Vienna, Thamel. Order breakfast and sandwiches at the deli counter, or dine in the restaurant on stolid Austrian food. An excellent source for picnic fare.

Shangri-La Bakery, Lazimpat. The best French pastries in town, plus bread, cakes and coffee.

Hot Breads, Durbar Marg. All kinds of fresh breads and pastries—tasty, but all more or less the same.

Nirula's, Durbar Marg. Awful fast food, but 21 flavours of ice-cream.

Stupa View, Boudhanath. The 'Austrian vegetarian food' is only tolerable, but order cappuccino and apple strudel and enjoy the views from the rooftop terrace.

Japanese

Tamura, Thapatali Heights (tel 246 534). Hard to find—there's not even a sign—but this exquisitely decorated authentic Japanese restaurant is worth the effort. Call for directions.

Kushi Fuji, Durbar Marg. The best deal is the set menu *bento: miso* soup to green tea and everything in between.

Fuji, Kanti Path. Food is so so, but a fine setting: an old Rana concubine's cottage surrounded by a moat.

Chinese

Mountain City, Hotel Malla, Lainchaur. The mainland Chinese chef makes this restaurant a favourite with local Chinese. Sichuan and Shanghai food are the specialties.

Mei Hua, Kanti Path. A roomy, old-fashioned local restaurant serving good cheap Chinese food, including *baozi*, hot-and-sour soup, and *jiaotze*.

Patan

Summit Hotel, Kopundol Heights. All the ordinary fare, plus good Friday night barbecues. Sundays and Wednesdays feature an organic produce market followed by a multi-course vegetarian lunch.

Base Camp Cafe, Hotel Himalaya, Kopundol. Standard hotel coffee-shop with splendid mountain views on clear days.

Cafe Pagode, Patan Durbar Square. Rooftop views of ancient temples, and decent basic fare (fried noodles, fried rice, Nepali meals).

German Bakery, Jawalakhel (near the zoo). Sandwiches, cakes, coffee and tea.

Bhaktapur

Cafe Nyatapola, Taumadhi Tol. Food is unremarkable, but who can resist sitting in a real old pagoda complete with woodcarvings, overlooking the temples of Taumadhi Square.

Marco Polo, Tamaudhi Tol. Marginally better food, and a balcony with views.

Peacock Restaurant, Dattatreya Square. Situated in an elaborately carved old *math* overlooking another splendid square.

Dhulikhel

Dhulikhel Mountain Resort. Set on a steep terraced hillside facing the Himalaya. Decent if dull Continental food and a well-stocked bar.

Himalayan Horizon. Dine indoors in a room decorated with elegant old woodcarvings, or outdoors on a series of gardened terraces running down the hillside—splendid views in either case. Indian—Chinese—Continental menu.

Nagarkot

The Teahouse. Nicely decorated building with indoor and outdoor dining, and a menu featuring Indian and Nepali food.

Pokhara

The Hungry Eye, Lakeside. This popular, centrally located restaurant serves the typical international mish-mash but does it well. Good desserts too.

Once upon a Time, Lakeside. Charming ochre-walled house; a great place for tea.

Boomerang, Lakeside. Outdoor dining with lake views, especially good for breakfast.

Beam-Beam, Lakeside. Very popular restaurant with bar, fireplace and a lively night scene.

Little Tibetan Tea Garden, Lakeside. Friendly Tibetan family, good for breakfast and snacks in the outdoor garden.

The Nest, Hotel Tragopan. Good Indian food.

Rodee Lakeview Restaurant, Pardi. Idyllic lakeside setting and sunset views. The usual extensive menu, including Indian food, plus ice-cream and cakes.

Useful Addresses

Foreign Embassies and Consulates in Nepal

Australia, Bansbari, tel 411 578
Bangladesh, Naxal, tel 414 265
Belgium, Lazimpat, tel 413 129
Britain, Lainchaur, tel 411 590
Canada, Lazimpat, tel 415 193
China, Baluwatar, tel 411 740
Denmark, Baluwatar, tel 413 010
Finland, Lazimpat, tel 417 221
France, Lazimpat, tel 412 332
Germany, Gyaneswar, tel 416 832
India, Lainchaur, tel 410 900
Israel, Lazimpat, tel 411 811
Italy, Baluwatar, tel 412 280
Japan, Pani Pokhari, tel 410 397
Myanmar, Chakupat (Patan), tel 524 788
Netherlands, Kumaripati (Patan), tel 522 915
Norway, Jawalakhel, tel 521 646
Pakistan, Pani Pokhari, tel 411 421
South Korea, Tahachal, tel 270 172
Switzerland, Jawalakhel, tel 523 468
Thailand, Thapathali, tel 213 910
United States, Pani Pokhari, tel 411 179

Nepalese Embassies and Consulates Abroad

Australia: Suite 1, Strand Centre, 870 Military Rd., Mosman, Sydney, NSW 2088 (tel 2/960 3565)
Bangladesh: No 2 Lake Rd, Baridhara Diplomatic Enclave, Dhaka (tel 2/601 1790)
Belgium: Nepal House, 149 Lamorinierstraat, B 4118, Antwerp (tel 03/230 8800)
Denmark: 36 Kroinsessagrade, DK 1006, Copenhagen (tel 01/143175)
France: 7 Rue de Washington, Paris 75008 (tel 43/592 861)
Germany: 15 Im Haag, D 5300 Bonn, Bad Godesberg 2 (tel 0228/343 097)

Great Britain: 12a Kensington Palace Gardens, London W8 4QU (tel 071/ 229 1594)
India: Barakhamba Rd., New Delhi 110001 (tel 11/383 484)
19 Woodlands, Sterndale Rd., Calcutta 700027 (tel 33/452 024)
Italy: Piazza Medaglie d'Oro 20, 00136 Rome (tel 06/345 1642)
Japan: 14–9 Todoroki, 7-Chome, Setagaya-ku, Tokyo
Netherlands: 687 Gelderland Bldg., NL 1017 JV, Amsterdam (tel 020/25 0388)
Pakistan: 506 84th St., Attaturk Avenue, Ramna G 6/4 Islamabad (tel 5/ 823 642)
Thailand: 189 Sukhumvit Soi 71, Bangkok 10110 (tel 2/391 7204)
United States: 2131 Leroy Place NW, Washington DC (tel 202/667 4550)

Trekking Agents

England
Classic Nepal, 33 Metro Ave., Newton, Derbyshire DE55 5UF (tel 0773/ 873 497)
Exodus Expeditions, 9 Weir Rd., London SW12 OLT (tel 081/673 0859)
Sherpa Expeditions, 131a Heston Rd., Hounslow, Middlesex TW5 ORD (tel 081/577 2717)

United States
InnerAsia Expeditions, 2627 Lombard St., San Francisco, CA 94123 (tel 1–800/777 8183)
Mountain Travel/Sobek, 6420 Fairmount Avenue, El Cerrito, CA 94530 (tel 1–800/227 2384)
Wilderness Travel, 801 Allston Way, Berkeley, CA 94710 (tel 1-800/ 368 2794)

Nepal
Asian Trekking (Tridevi Marg), Box 3022, tel 412 821
Cho Oyu Trekking (Ghairedhara), Box 4515, tel 418 890
Nepal Himal Treks (Tridevi Marg), Box 452, tel 411 949

Useful Addresses In Kathmandu

Airlines
Royal Nepal Airlines, Kanti Path at New Road, tel 220 757
Everest Air, Durbar Marg, tel 229 412
Nepal Airways, Kamal Pokhari, tel 412 388
Necon Air, Kamal Pokhari, tel 419 145
Dynasty Aviation (helicopter service), Naya Baneshwar, tel 225 602

Rafting Companies
Ultimate Descents Nepal, Namche Bazaar, Thamel, tel 226 277
White Magic, Jyatha, Thamel, tel 226 885
Himalayan River Exploration, Naxal, tel 418 491

Mountain Biking.
Himalayan Mountain Bikes, Gaidhidhara, PO Box 2247, tel 411 724

Bhutan Travel
Shambhala Travels and Tours, Kamaladi, PO Box 4794, tel 227 229
Marco Polo Travels, Kamal Pokhari, PO Box 2769, tel 414 192
Tibet Travels, Tridevi Marg, Thamel, PO Box 1397, tel 410 303

Tibet Travel
Arniko Travels, Baluwatar, PO Box 4695, tel 414 594
Tibet Travels, Tridevi Marg, Thamel, PO Box 1397, tel 410 303

Health
CIWEC Clinic, Yak & Yeti Road (off Durbar Marg), tel 228 531
Nepal International Clinic, Hitti Durbar, tel 419 713
Patan Hospital, Lagankhel, tel 522 266

Will You Come?

'Who are you? Where are you coming from? Where will you stop today? What country are you from? What is your destination? What is your good name, sir? How far is it from here to America? How many days does it take to get there? How much does a ticket cost? What work do you do? Do you know my friend Mr Bob? He taught us English. Where is your family? What does your father do? You have older and younger brothers and sisters? What do they do? What are your qualifications? How much money do you make? How much land do you have? What crops do you raise? Do you have a cow or buffalo? Do you eat beef? What pujas do you celebrate in your village? What is your religion? Don't you believe in god? Don't you celebrate Durga Puja? Do you play Holi? Do you have a temple in your village? You have free sex in America? How old are you? Are you married? Why aren't you married? When will you get married? Do you go to the cinema? You will work in our village? Will you teach in our school? Will you teach me English? Do you play football? Do you play cards? Do you gamble? Do yo drink raksi? Do you have cultural programmes at schools in America? Do you have village dramas? Do you have a picture of your family? Is it true that it is day in America when it is night in Nepal? I want to see America. I am very poor but someday I will visit your country. Will you take me with you? Do you drink tea? Let us go to the teashop to have some tea.'

'Two glasses of especial tea. No, I will pay. This is my friend, Mr Esteben. He is from America. He is going to teach in our school. Where will you stay? You must meet the Pradhan Panch. He will, with the Headmaster, find you a place to stay. What do you eat? Do you eat rice? Can you eat hot food? Do you like yoghurt? Can you eat with your hand? Today, will you take food in my house? We are very poor, we can't offer you good food. Will you come?'

> The kind of conversation a Peace Corps volunteer can
> expect, from the Peace Corps Nepal journal

Hints on Language

Nepali is more difficult to pronounce than the basic transliteration used here would lead you to believe. There are four different ways of enunciating the sound indicated by 'D'—retroflex, aspirated, aspirated retroflex, and the 'normal' English version. The same goes for 'T'; then there are the aspirated consonants, and long and short vowels. To avoid confusion, the simplest possible transliteration is used here.

Hello	*Namaste* (*Namaskar* to indicate great respect)
Goodbye	*Namaste* or
	bistari januhos (to someone departing)
	ramro sangha basnuhos (to someone staying)
See you again	*feri betaunla*
Yes/no	*ho/hoina, cha/chaina*
There is (are)/isn't (aren't)	*cha/chaina*
Do you speak English?	*Tapai Inglis bolnu huncha?*
I don't understand	*Ma bujdaina.*
Pardon?	*Hajur?*
Excuse me.	*Maph garnuhos.*

'Please' is built into verb forms; only the polite forms are shown here. 'Thank you' is translated as *dhanyabad*, but it's not applied as indiscriminately as in English. Routine thanks for all but the most exceptional transactions is best conveyed by a smile and a nod, or even '*tenk you*'.

Shopping

Where can I get (bananas)?	*(Kera) kaha paincha?*
How much is this?	*Yesko kati?*
How much altogether?	*Jama kati bhayo?*
That's expensive.	*Derey mahango cha.*
A little cheaper, please.	*Ali sastoma dinuhos.*
good	*ramro*
no good *naramro*	
I like it	*malai man parcha*
I don't like it	*malai man pardaina*
don't need, don't want	*malai chaindaina*
money	*paisa*
change	*chanchun*

Numbers

one	*ek*
two	*dui*
three	*teen*
four	*char*
five	*panch*
six	*cha*
seven	*sat*
eight	*at*
nine	*nau*
ten	*das*
twenty	*bis*
thirty	*tis*
forty	*chalis*
fifty	*pachas*
sixty	*sathi*
seventy	*satari*
eighty	*awsi*
ninety	*nabbey*
one hundred	*ek say*
one thousand	*ek hajar*

Days of the Week

Sunday	*aitabar*
Monday	*sombar*
Tuesday	*mangalbar*
Wednesday	*budhabar*
Thursday	*bihibar*
Friday	*sukrabar*
Saturday	*sanibar*

Useful Words

here/there	*yaha/tyaha*
this/that	*yo/tyo*
yesterday/today/tomorrow	*hijo/aja/bholi*
morning/afternoon/evening/night	*bihana/diuso/beluka/rati*
day/week/month/year	*din/hapta/mahina/sal, barsa*
before/after	*aghi/pachi*
fast/slow	*chito/bistari*

a little/a lot	*ali–ali, ali kati/dherai*
the same/another (one)	*yotai/arko*
big/small	*thulo/sano*
cheap/expensive	*sasto/mahango*
clean/dirty	*safa/pohor*
hot/cold (person, weather)	*garam/jado*
hot/cold (liquid)	*tato/chiso*
difficult/easy	*gadho, aptyaro/sajilo*
near/far	*najik/tada*
new/old	*naya/purano*
open/closed	*kholeko/bhanda*
uphill/downhill	*ukalo/oralo*
cold	*jado 'lagyo*
hot	*garmi lagyo*
hungry	*bhok lagyo*
thirsty	*tirka lagyo*
tired	*takai lagyo*
lazy	*alchi lago*
pleasant, nice	*ramailo lagyo*
happy	*kushi lagyo*

Food	*khana*
rice	*bhat*
rice and lentils	*dal bhat*
cooked vegetables	*tarkari, subji*
potatoes	*alu*
greens	*sag*
spicy	*piro*
not spicy, please	*piro nabanaunuhos*
chilli	*khursani*
noodles	*chow–chow*
bread (unleavened/leavened)	*roti/pau roti*
snack	*khaja*
meat	*masu*
chicken	*khukhurako masu*
buffalo	*rungako masu*
goat	*khasiko masu*
fish	*macha*
egg	*phul, anda*

fruit	*phalphul*
orange	*suntala*
apple	*syau*
banana	*kera*
yoghurt	*dahi*
tasty	*mitho*
candy	*mithai*
milk	*dudh*
soft drink	*chiso (kok, fanta, eesprite)*
beer	*biyar*
local liquor	*raksi*
coffee	*kafi*
tea	*chiya*
milk tea	*dudh chiya*
black tea	*kalo chiya*
lemon tea	*kagati chiya*
no sugar please	*chini nahalnuhos*
drinking water	*khaney pani*
boiled water	*umaleko pani*

People

An endearing feature of Nepali is the way kinship terms are used to address strangers. When addressing someone roughly your age, say '*didi*' or '*dai/daju*' (older sister/brother). Older people are *amai* or *bajey*; younger *bahini* or *bhai*. Shopkeepers are *sahuni* (female) or *sahuji* (male)—literally, 'wealthy one'.

boy	*keta*
girl	*keti*
kids (offspring)	*bacha*
(in general)	*keta-keti*
son	*chora*
daughter	*chori*
husband	*sriman* or *logney*
wife	*srimati* or *patni* (formal), or *swasni* (informal)
(my) mother	*(mero) ama*
(your) father	*(tapaiko) ba*
(his/her) friend	*(wahako) sathi*

Useful Phrases

How are you?	*Tapailai kasto cha?*
What's the matter/what happened?	*Ke bhayo?*
What's your name?	*Tapaiko nam ke ho?*
Where do you live?	*Tapai kaha basnu huncha?*
How old are you?	*Tapaiko umer kati?*
Are you married?	*Tapaiko biha bhayo?*
What kind of work do you do?	*Tapai ke kam garnu huncha?*
I speak only a little Nepali.	*Ma Nepali ali–ali matrai bolchu.*
I don't know.	*Malai taha chaina.*
Where is this bus going?	*Yo bas kaha jancha?*
What time will we reach Kathmandu?	*Kathmanduma kati bajey pugcha?*
What time do we go?	*Kati bajey jancha?*
What time is it now?	*Ahiley kati bajyo?*
Taxi! Are you empty?	*Tyaksi! Khali ho?*
How much to go to Bhaktapur?	*Bhaktapurma janey kati parcha?*
Where is ....?	*... kaha cha?*
Which is the trail to Sankhu?	*Sankhu janey bato kun chahi ho?*

Trekking

How many hours to reach the next town?	*Pallo gau pugnalai kati ghanta lagcha?*
What's the name of this town?	*Yo gauko nam ke ho?*
Is there a place to stay?	*Basne thau cha?* or *bas paincha?*
Please show me a room.	*Kota dekaunuhos na.*
Is there anything better/cheaper/bigger than this?	*Yo bhanda ramro/sasto/thulo cha?*
One person only	*Ek jana matrai*
Two people	*dui jana*
My friend is coming	*Mero ek jana sathi auncha.*
Where can I get some food?	*Khana kaha paincha?*

Finally, the two most frequently asked questions encountered on the trail:

Where are you going?	*Kaha janu huncha?*
Where are you coming from?	*Kaha bata aunu bhaeko?*

Glossary

Nepali and Tibetan Terms

avatar incarnation or manifestation of a deity

bahal Newari Buddhist monastery complex

baksheesh a tip; often a tip given in advance to expedite service—more
bluntly, a bribe

bhajan religious hymn

Bhotia, **Bhotiya**, **Bhotey**, general term for Tibetan-influenced people of the
northern border regions

bodhisattva a buddha-to-be who has renounced individual enlightenment
to help other beings

chaitya a Buddhist monument, a miniature version of a stupa

chang (Tib.) home-made beer, usually brewed from barley

chautara shady trailside resting place with a low wall to support porters'
loads

chorten (Tib.) a small stupa, sometimes with a passage through the middle
so that people can walk through it

chowk a square or courtyard

dal bhat The national dish of Nepal: lentils (*dal*) and cooked rice (*bhat*),
served with curried vegetables

dhara water tap

doko wicker basket used for carrying loads

dorje (Tib.) see *vajra*

dyochem (Newari) 'god's house', a special shrine

gainey a minstrel caste

ghat flight of stone steps lining river banks, used for laundry, bathing and
cremation

gompa (Tib.) Tibetan Buddhist monastery

guthi traditional Newari social association

hiti sunken fountain typical of the Kathmandu Valley

jatra festival

khukri Curved Nepali knife

kora (Tib.) circumambulation

Kumari young virgin Buddhist girl worshipped as a manifestation of the
Hindu goddess Durga

ladoo a milk-based sweet
lama (Tib.) guru; religious teacher
Licchavi a ruling dynasty of the Kathmandu Valley (AD 300–879)
linga symbol related to Shiva and the phallus
makara sea serpents of Hindu mythology
mandala mystic diagram depicting the order of the universe
mani wall prayer wall: heap of flat stones engraved with mantra and
  religious images, found in mountainous Buddhist regions
mantra mystic formula of Sanskrit syllables
math Hindu monastery
mela fair, often associated with a religious festival
momo (Tib.) meat-stuffed dumplings
naga serpent deities: guardians of wealth associated with rain
pati open rest-house providing shelter to travellers
puja ritual offering and prayer
rakshi (Tib. *arak*) potent alcoholic beverage distilled from grain
sal hardwood tree (*Shorea robusta*) famed for its fine-grained wood
samsara the cycle of delusion created by the unenlightened mind
sadhu Hindu ascetic or holy man
shikhara a tapered tower surmounting a temple
shikar the hunt
sindhur red powder used as religious offering
sirdar organizer of a trek or expedition
stupa Buddhist monument: a hemispheric mound topped by a conical spire
tantra school of mysticism developed in medieval India which has
  influenced both Hinduism and Buddhism
tempo three-wheeled motor vehicle serving as an inexpensive public taxi
thangka (Tib.) scroll painting depicting religious subjects
tika auspicious mark on the forehead, made as part of worship
tol neighbourhood or quarter of a city
tongba drink made from hot water mixed with fermented mash
torana semicircular carved tympanum mounted over temple doors and
  windows
topi Nepali men's cap, brimless and slightly lopsided
tsampa (Tib.) roasted barley flour, a highland staple
yaksha graceful nymph of Hindu mythology
vajra Buddhist ritual implement representing the absolute aspect of reality

Hindu and Buddhist Deities

Ajima Newari grandmother goddesses; indigenous deities often placated
with blood sacrifice

Annapurna goddess of the harvest, a manifestation of **Lakshmi**

Ashta Matrika 'Eight Mothers', each representing a different aspect of Durga

Avalokitesvara compassionate Bodhisattva who grew eleven heads and
1,000 arms in order to help suffering beings; *see* **Lokesvara**

Bhagwati another name for the goddess **Durga**

Bhairab fierce manifestation of **Shiva**

Bhimsen patron god of traders: a minor figure in the *Mahabharata*

Buddha an enlightened being; more particularly the historical Buddha,
Siddhartha Gautama

Bunga Dyo local name for **Machhendranath**

Chandeswari fierce goddess associated with **Durga**, slayer of the demon
Chand

Devi another name for the goddess **Durga** or **Parvati**

Durga The Great Goddess, appearing in many different manifestations,
most popularly as the defeater of the evil buffalo demon Mahisasura.

Ganesh elephant-headed god of luck, son of **Shiva** and **Parvati**

Ganga goddess associated with the sacred River Ganges, usually appearing
with Jamuna, the personification of another sacred Indian river

Garuda winged man, the mount of **Vishnu**

Goraknath 12th-century yogi deified as an aspect of **Shiva**

Guru Rinpoche *see* **Padmasambhava**

Guyheswari the Secret Goddess, a name for **Shiva**'s spouse Sati

Hanuman the Monkey King, a prominent figure in the *Ramayana*,
worshipped as a protector

Indra Vedic deity honoured as King of the Gods

Kali the 'Black One', hideous goddess personifying death

Krishna blue-complexioned god of love, an incarnation of **Vishnu**

Kumari young virgin worshipped as an incarnation of **Durga**

Lakshmi goddess of wealth and abundance, consort of **Vishnu**

Lokesvara (Lokeswar, Karunamaya) 'Lord of the World', beloved
bodhisattva and god of compassion

Machhendranath rainmaking patron deity of the Kathmandu Valley,
worshipped primarily by Buddhist Newars

Mai indigenous deities transformed into 'Mother Goddesses', usually
associated with a particular locality

Manjushri bodhisattva and embodiment of wisdom and learning

Nandi mount of Shiva, depicted as a kneeling bull

Narasimha incarnation of Vishnu, half man, half lion

Padmapani lotus-holding bodhisattva; *see* **Lokesvara**

Padmasambhava Indian tantric responsible for the introduction of Buddhism into Tibet

Pancha Buddha five Buddhas, each associated with a different element, colour, direction and aspect of enlightenment

Parvati consort of **Shiva** and a goddess in her own right

Pashupati(nath) Lord of the Beasts, benevolent form of **Shiva**

Saraswati goddess of learning and culture

Shiva important Hindu deity, the transformer and destroyer

Sitala goddess of smallpox and protector of children; Newari Buddhists worship her as Harati

Taleju tantric goddess imported from India and made patron of the Malla dynasty; related to **Durga**

Tara (Tib. **Dolma**) female bodhisattva representing mercy and compassion, appearing in 21 emenations, the most important being the White and Green Taras

Vajra Yogini Tantric Buddhist deity, a fierce protector goddess

Vishnu an important Hindu god worshipped as the Preserver and appearing in 10 principal incarnations

Ihi ceremony ('bel marriage') for young Newar girls, Bhaktapur

Recommended Reading

Travel and Description

Greenwald, Jeff. *Shopping for Buddhas* (Harper & Row, 1990). Amusing personal account of Western consumers in hot pursuit of Eastern spirituality.

Herzog, Maurice. *Annapurna* (Jonathan Cape, 1952). The story of the first successful ascent of an 8,000-metre peak (the team's first problem was *finding* the mountain). That adventure pales in comparison to the harrowing saga of the long and painful return journey (most of Herzog's fingers and toes were severely frostbitten and had to be amputated along the trail). A gripping story, told with enormous dignity.

Iyer, Pico. *Video Night in Kathmandu* (Knopf, 1988). A romp through the Eastern tourism scene. The chapter on Kathmandu is not the strongest, but the book captures the bizarre mutations that occur when East meets West.

Matthiessen, Peter. *The Snow Leopard* (Viking, 1978). A luminous modern masterpiece that has probably inspired more visits to Nepal than any other book. Matthiessen accompanied zoologist George Schaller on a trip to the remote Himalayan region of Dolpo in search of the rare snow leopard. This is at once a description of the trek, and of the author's inner journey.

Peissel, Michel. *Mustang: a Lost Tibetan Kingdom* (Collins and Harvill Press, 1968). The adventurous Tibetan-speaking author became one of the few Westerners to penetrate the restricted region of Mustang with his 1964 visit.

Pye-Smith, Charlie. *Travels in Nepal* (Aurum Press, 1988). Blending good travel writing with keen observations on various projects and issues, this book is a palatable way of diving into the complexities of development in Nepal.

Snellgrove, David L. *Himalayan Pilgrimage* (Oxford, 1961). Account of the Buddhist scholar's 1956 journey through Dolpo, the Kali Gandaki and Manang. Fascinating insights into how it was, permeated with dry humour.

Thapa, Manjushree. *Mustang Bhot in Fragments* (Himal Books, 1992). Daughter of a Nepali diplomat, Thapa grew up in America and returned to Nepal as both insider and outsider. This slim volume records her observations on two visits to the newly-opened Mustang region.

Tilman, H. W. *Nepal Himalaya* (Cambridge University Press, 1952). Reprinted in *The Seven Mountain-Travel Books*, (The Mountaineers 1983). Tilman was an old hand by the time he went on this 1949 excursion, the first reconnaissance of the Langtang, Annapurna and Everest regions, but his sense of humour is as wry and sharp as ever.

Tucci, Giuseppe. *Journey to Mustang* (Reprinted by Ratna Pustak Bhandar, 1977). Essential reading for the trek to Muktinath: the celebrated Tibetologist's 1952 journey up the Kali Gandaki—his observant eye missing nothing along the way. The book is filled with both cultural insights and compassion.

People

Avedon, John. *In Exile From the Land of Snows* (Alfred A. Knopf, 1984). The heartbreaking story of Tibetans in exile, and the single best introduction to the Tibetan issue.

Chorlton, Windsor. *Cloud-dwellers of the Himalayas: the Bhotia.* (Time-Life Books, 1982). Superb photo essays and chapters documenting life in the remote valley of Nar-Phu, north of Manang. The life and customs described here apply to many Bhotia peoples.

Coburn, Broughton. *Nepali Aama: Portrait of a Nepalese Hill Woman* (Moon Publications, 1990). Black-and-white photos and quotes create a lovely, insightful documentary of an old and very spunky Gurung woman with whom the author lived as a Peace Corps volunteer.

Downs, Hugh R. *Rhythms of a Himalayan Village* (Harper & Row, 1980). A sensitive look at life in the Sherpa region of Solu, blending black-and-white photos, narrative and quotations.

Fisher, James F. *Sherpas: Reflections on Change in Himalayan Nepal* (Oxford University Press, 1990). Thoughts on changing Sherpa culture by an observer who first visited Khumbu in the early 1960s. Notable for the extent it allows Sherpas to speak for themselves.

Fürer-Haimendorf, Christoph von. *Himalayan Traders* (John Murray, 1975). Broad examination of Tibetan-oriented trading communities across the Nepal Himalaya and how their lives have changed with the advent of modern times.

Macfarlane, Alan, and Indra Bahadur Gurung. *Gurungs of Nepal* (Ratna Pustak Bhandar, 1990). This slim volume on modern Gurung life makes good reading for trekking in the Annapurna region.

History and Culture

Anderson, Mary M. *The Festivals of Nepal* (Unwin Hyman, 1971). The standard classic, though somewhat outdated. Engagingly written descriptions of major and minor festivals of the Kathmandu Valley.

Bista, Dor Bahadur. *Fatalism and Development: Nepal's Struggle for Modernisation* (Longman, 1990). A provocative examination of how the 'culture of fatalism' embedded in the Hindu caste hierarchy has hampered Nepal's development. The author's jaundiced look at the dominant culture has been severely censured by Brahmin Chetri critics; the only way he can get away with it is being a Chetri himself, and a respected anthropologist.

Farwell, Byron. *The Gurkhas* (Allen Lane, 1984). The history of the fearless Nepalese mercenaries who are often called the world's finest infantrymen.

Goodman, Jim. *Guide to Enjoying Nepalese Festivals* (Pilgrim Book House, 1993). Excellent summary of festivals in the Kathmandu Valley, with handy notations on what occurs when and where.

Landon, Percival. *Nepal* (Constable, 1928). Detailed two-volume set examining the history of the Valley, interesting for period notes but marred by the author's obsequious attitude towards his Rana hosts.

Levy, Robert I. *Mesocosm: Hinduism and the Organization of a Traditional Newar City in Nepal* (University of California, 1990). An incredibly complex, detailed study of the traditional Newari society of Bhaktapur, with special emphasis on spatial relations.

Sever, Adrian. *Nepal Under the Ranas* (Oxford University Press, 1993). Comprehensive, balanced survey of 104 years of Rana rule, well-written and illustrated with rare historic photographs.

Slusser, Mary. *Nepal Mandala: A Cultural Study of the Kathmandu Valley* (Princeton University Press, 1982). Massive (and expensive) two-volume study of the Valley's Newari culture and its unique blending of Buddhist and Brahmanical traditions, both serious and fascinating.

Whelpton, John. *Jang Bahadur in Europe.* (Sahayogi Press, 1983). An entertaining account of the Prime Minister's 1850 visit to England and France, including a translation of a narrative written by a member of the party.

Religion

Anderson, Walt. *Open Secrets: A Western Guide to Tibetan Buddhism* (Viking, 1979). A very accessible introduction to Tibetan Buddhism, emphasizing its psychological aspects.

O'Flaherty, Wendy Doniger (editor). *Hindu Myths* (Penguin, 1975). Wide selection of the essential Hindu myths which permeate Nepalese art and religion.

Sogyal Rinpoche. *The Tibetan Book of Living and Dying* (Harper, San Francisco, 1992). A lucid and inspiring account of Tibetan Buddhism by an Oxford-educated lama.

Stutley, Margaret. *Hinduism: The Eternal Law* (The Aquarian Press, 1985). Basic introduction to Hindu literature, deities and beliefs.

Art

Aran, Lydia. *The Art of Nepal* (Sahayogi Prakashan, 1978). A remarkably relevant study of Nepalese art, focusing on the Kathmandu Valley and doubling as a study of religious iconography.

Bernier, Ronald. *The Nepalese Pagoda—Origins and Style* (S. Chand, 1979). This scholarly yet readable examination of the complex symbolism embedded in Nepalese temples adds much depth to Valley sightseeing.

Macdonald, Alexander W., and Anne Vergati Stahl. *Newar Art: Nepalese during the Malla Period* (Vikas, 1979). Architecture and paintings of the Kathmandu Valley examined in the context of classical Newari culture.

Pal, Pratapaditya. *Art of Nepal* (University of California Press, 1985). Catalogue of the Los Angeles County Museum's marvellous collection of Nepalese art.

Natural History

Cameron, Ian. *Mountains of the Gods* (Century, 1984). An illustrated survey of the Himalaya, its history, geology, ecology and peoples.

Fleming, Dr Robert L., Jr. and Lain Singh Bangdel. *Birds of Nepal* (Nature Himalayas, 1976). The standard classic, with colour illustrations of 1,000 individuals of 753 species accompanied by lucid descriptions for easy identification.

Gurung, K.K. *Heart of the Jungle: The Wildlife of Chitwan Nepal* (André Deutsch, 1983). Well-written account of the natural history of Chitwan National Park.

Hillard, Darla. *Vanishing Tracks: Four Years Among the Snow Leopards of Nepal* (William Morrow, 1989). Enjoyable story of the first study of the endangered snow leopard, focusing on the cultures as well as the environment of the Western Nepal Himalaya.

Mishra, Hemanta R., and Margaret Jeffries. *Royal Chitwan National Park: Wildife Heritage of Nepal* (The Mountaineers, 1991). A thorough guidebook to the flora, fauna and people of Chitwan.

Trekking and Rafting

Bezruchka, Stephen. *A Guide to Trekking in Nepal*. (The Mountaineers, 1985). The classic trekkers' guide: thorough, sincere and responsible, with detailed trail descriptions of 40 different routes and in-depth sections on culture, language and health.

Duff, Jim and Peter Gormley. *The Himalayan First Aid Manual* (World Expeditions, 1992). Handy pocket-sized guide to doctoring yourself and others on the trail. Available at the HRA office in Kathmandu.

Hayes, John L. *Trekking North of Pokhara* (Roger Lascelles, 1993). A brief essential guide to the most popular trekking region in Nepal.

Knowles, Peter and David Allardice. *White Water Nepal: A Rivers Guidebook for Rafting and Kayaking* (Rivers Publishing, 1992). The first guide to river rafting, written by experienced rafters. It's helpful in choosing a reliable commercial operator and in planning trips to remote areas.

McGuiness, Jamie. *Trekking in the Everest Region* (Trailblazer, 1993). Up-to-date, detailed guide to the Everest region; perfect if this is the only region you plan to visit.

Uchida, Ryohei. *Trekking Mount Everest* (Chronicle Books, 1991). A souvenir rather than a guidebook, lavishly illustrated with colour photographs.

Fiction

Han Suyin. *The Mountain is Young* (Jonathan Cape, 1958). Purple prose from the author of *A Many-Splendoured Thing*: a shy, sensitive Englishwoman, a 'wayward writer in search of herself', finds love in the Kathmandu of the early 1960s.

Robinson, Kim Stanley. *Escape from Kathmandu* (Tor, New York, 1989). An amusing romp through Everest, Yetis, trekking, lamas, Ranas, and other Nepal clichés.

Literature

Hutt, Michael James (translator and editor). *Himalayan Voices* (University of California, 1991). An eye-opening introduction to the riches of modern Nepali literature, both poetry and short stories.

Lienhard, Siegfried. *Songs of Nepal* (University of Hawaii Press, 1984). Anthology of Newari folksongs and hymns providing fascinating insights into culture and legends.

Rubin, David. *Nepali Visions, Nepali Dreams* (Columbia University Press, 1980). The translated poems of Lakshmi Prasad Devkota, considered Nepal's finest poet.

Photographic Studies

Gilman, Peter (editor). *Everest: The Best Writing and Pictures from 70 Years of Human Endeavour* (Little, Brown & Co., 1993). Magnificent photographs with a nice mix of essays excerpted from accounts of various encounters with the world's highest peak.

Kelly, Thomas L., and Patricia Roberts. *Kathmandu: City on the Edge of the World* (Abbeville Press), 1988. An in-depth look at the Valley's history, culture, festivals and people.

Valli, Eric, and Diane Summers. *Dolpo: Hidden Land of the Himalayas* (Aperture Foundation, 1987). Insightful, capturing the rhythms of life in a remote region.

—. *Honey Hunters of Nepal* (Thames & Hudson, 1988). Spectacular large-format book documenting the age-old honey extraction methods of the Gurungs of Central Nepal, who climb up sheer cliffs on rope ladders to boldly steal the honey from swarming bees.

Language

Clark, T. W. *Introduction to Nepali* (Ratna Pustak Bhandar, 1989). Formal, wide-ranging survey of grammar and vocabulary: one of the best books, and everything is in Romanized Nepali, which means you don't have to read the Devanagari script to learn the language.

Karki, Tika B., and Chij Shrestha. *Basic Course in Spoken Nepali* (Published by the authors, 1979). Peace Corps volunteers learn from this simple, situationally based book very good for hammering in the basics.

Meerdonk, M. *Basic Gurkhali Dictionary* (Straits Times Press, 1959). Handy pocket-sized volume with Nepali–English and English–Nepali.

Index